"Kostenberger gives us a here a solid, sad, scrupulously fair case study of ideology deflecting exegesis over an entire generation. She shows conclusively that the attempts of a long series of scholars to find Jesus affirming women's leadership in some way have entirely failed. Surely this is an important cautionary tale for our times."

—J. I. Packer, Board of Governor's Professor of Theology,
Regent College

"Who is Jesus? Was he a chauvinist? A feminist crusader? Or an egalitarian emancipator of women? In this significant work, Köstenberger investigates whether the portraits of Jesus painted by proponents of women's equality truly fit the gospel narrative. Her analysis of underlying hermeneutics is careful and concise. Her conclusions, balanced and well-reasoned. Is Jesus who they say he is? This is a valuable resource for all who seek to answer this all-important question."

—Mary A. Kassian, Distinguished Professor of Women's Studies,
The Southern Baptist Theological Seminary

"Köstenberger expertly surveys the scholarly work of feminists on the person of Jesus Christ. We are treated to the entire landscape of feminist scholarship on Jesus, from radical feminists to egalitarian evangelicals. Most important, Köstenberger subjects the claims of feminist scholarship to critical scrutiny, showing that they fail to measure up with the teaching of Scripture. Köstenberger's criticisms are irenic, but at the same time they show the deficiencies of the feminist paradigm."

—Thomas R. Schreiner, James Buchanan Harrison
Professor of New Testament Interpretation,
The Southern Baptist Theological Seminary

"The strength of this manuscript lies in the way it surveys the main figures of English-language theological feminism, carefully noting developments, differences, and trends. I know of no survey to compare with it. The hermeneutical analysis at each step is introductory, accessible, and sensible. Highly recommended."

—D. A. Carson, Research Professor of New Testament,
Trinity Evangelical Divinity School

"Provides an excellent case-study on just why a correct hermeneutic matters. Even more to the point: getting Jesus right matters! Köstenberger should be commended for winsome and scholarly dismantling of feminist distortions of Jesus, thus providing assistance toward this goal."

—Bruce A. Ware, Professor of Christian Theology,
The Southern Baptist Theological Seminary

"Köstenberger succeeds at bringing historical perspective to bear on feminist understanding of Scripture and Christ. Her analyses of radical, reformist, and evangelical wings of this movement are methodical, clear, thorough, and mature. Her findings are highly significant. They force the question, *Is Jesus Lord over Western culture's ideologies or their servant?* Today a new generation stands poised to replace the aging leaders who ushered feminism into our churches. Köstenberger points the way to honor their concerns while avoiding their unjustified concessions."

—Robert W. Yarbrough, Associate Professor of New Testament and
New Testament Department Chair,
Trinity Evangelical Divinity School

"Köstenberger has done a remarkable job in linking carefully documented scholarly research with very practical conclusions in such a way as to enable students and scholars to explore what interpretations feminists are peddling in the marketplace of ideas. I am grateful to have such a resource to use as textbook and supplementary reading for my classes in women's studies."

—Dorothy Kelley Patterson, Professor of Women's Studies,
Southwestern Baptist Theological Seminary

"In this insightful and winsome book, Köstenberger shows that the debate over feminism is not, first of all, about whose name has 'Reverend' in front of it. It is, first of all, and last of all, about Jesus. Those wishing to engage the feminist culture all around us will find an excellent resource in this volume."

—Russell D. Moore, Dean, School of Theology;
Associate Professor of Theology and Ethics,
The Southern Baptist Theological Seminary

"This book is an exceptionally valuable guide to feminist writings about Jesus. It summaries the entire history of feminist interpretation, summarizing each author fairly and then providing a thoughtful critique. Kostenberger's patient, clear argument shows that the multiple feminist reinterpretations of Jesus are inconsistent with the actual text of the Gospels. A very useful, readable resource for those who want to understand how feminism has continually reinterpreted the Bible to advance its own agenda."

—Wayne Grudem, Research Professor of Bible and Theology,
Phoenix Seminary

# JESUS *and the* FEMINISTS

## *Who Do They Say That He Is?*

MARGARET E. KÖSTENBERGER

CROSSWAY BOOKS

WHEATON, ILLINOIS

Cover design: Jessica Dennis
Cover illustration: Veer Images
Design and typesetting: Lakeside Design Plus
First printing 2008
Printed in the United States of America

Trade paperback ISBN:  978-1-58134-959-7
PDF ISBN:            978-1-4335-0466-2
Mobipocket ISBN:     978-1-4335-0467-9

**Library of Congress Cataloging-in-Publication Data**
Köstenberger, Margaret Elizabeth.
    Jesus and the feminists : who do they say that He is? / Margaret E. Köstenberger.
      p. cm.
    Includes bibliographical references and index.
    ISBN 978-1-58134-959-7 (tpb)
    1. Jesus Christ—Person and offices. 2. Feminist theology. 3. Bible—Feminist criticism.
  I. Title.
  BT205.K67 2008
  232.082—dc22

                                            2008011651

| VP | 16 | 15 | 14 | 13 | 12 | 11 | 10 | 09 | 08 |
|----|----|----|----|----|----|----|----|----|----|
|    | 9  | 8  | 7  | 6  | 5  | 4  | 3  | 2  | 1  |

*To those women who are most precious in my life:*
*my mother, Mary Gerrard, with gratitude*
*for everything you have done for me;*
*my daughters, Lauren and Tahlia,*
*with love, affection, and friendship.*

*May you be drawn close to the Lord Jesus*
*and serve him ever more faithfully.*

*"The wise woman builds her house,*
*but with her own hands*
*the foolish one tears hers down."*
*—Proverbs 14:1 (NIV)*

# CONTENTS

# TABLES

# Acknowledgments

*I would like* to acknowledge and express my gratitude to those who have guided and helped me in my research for this volume: Adrio König, my dissertation mentor, who represented an opposing viewpoint and sharpened my thinking; and my husband, Andreas, who supported me in this project in ways too numerous to mention. Thank you also, Lauren, Tahlia, David, and Timothy, for your patience while I worked on this book. May God bless all of you.

Over the years I have benefited spiritually from many special individuals God has provided to mentor and instruct me: pastors, seminary professors and their wives, and friends. Thanks also to my local church, Richland Creek Community Church, for providing a context for ministering with and mentoring women. I am also grateful for my students in the Women and Biblical Interpretation class at Southeastern Baptist Theological Seminary with whom I have had stimulating discussions on the subject and who encouraged me that a book on the topics of hermeneutics and women's issues would be meeting a vital need in the lives of women. Last but not least, I would like to express my gratitude to Lydia Brownback for going the extra mile in editing this book; to Allan Fisher for his encouragement and guidance in revising the manuscript; and to the dedicated staff of Crossway Books for producing this volume in such a timely and competent fashion.

May you who read this book be drawn more closely to the Lord Jesus and be encouraged to serve him ever more faithfully. Together, let us aspire to the biblical portrait of mature women in the church: "faithful to her husband . . . well known for her good deeds, such as bringing up children, showing hospitality, washing the feet of the saints, helping those in trouble and devoting herself to all kinds of good deeds" (1 Tim. 5:9–10 NIV).

# PART 1

# FOUNDATIONS

*For the wrath of God is revealed from heaven against all ungodliness and unrighteousness of men, who by their unrighteousness suppress the truth. For what can be known about God is plain to them, because God has shown it to them.*

—Romans 1:18–19

When Jesus was at a critical juncture in his ministry, he took his closest followers aside and asked them a very simple yet profound question: "Who do people say that I am?" (Mark 8:27). When they gave him a variety of answers, Jesus, even more pointedly, followed up with another question: "But who do *you* say that I am?" (v. 29). In the end, Jesus' point was that every person must come to their own decision regarding Jesus' identity, regardless of what anyone else says about him.

Over the centuries there has been no more influential or controversial figure than Jesus. At the beginning of the last century, the German theologian Albert Schweitzer chronicled the variegated portraits of Jesus in his famous *The Quest of the Historical Jesus.*[1] After several hundred pages of survey of other scholars' opinions on Jesus, Schweitzer concluded that their understanding depended considerably more on their own contexts and biases than on the actual testimony of Scripture. For many, Schweitzer concluded, looking for the historical Jesus was like looking in the mirror—what they saw was not Jesus but themselves.[2]

1. A. Schweitzer, *The Quest of the Historical Jesus: A Critical Study of Its Progress from Reimarus to Wrede* (London: A. & C. Black, 1968).
2. See also H. Osborne, ed., *Whom Do Men Say That I Am? A Collection of the Views of the Most Notable Christian and Non-Christian Modern Authors about Jesus of Nazareth*

In a sense, this book represents a kind of sequel to Schweitzer's work but with a more narrow focus: chronicling the *feminist* quest of the historical Jesus. We will see that what emerges from feminist scholarship on Jesus is not *one version* of the true Jesus but many different accounts of who feminists perceive Jesus to be. This strikingly confirms Schweitzer's diagnosis of the scholarship he surveyed. A full century after him, people still claim to reconstruct Jesus "as he really was," resulting in a large variety of portraits even among those who share a basic feminist viewpoint.

These divergent understandings of Jesus found among feminists, in turn, raise concerns regarding the viability of feminism at large. Since feminists are not able to come to an essential consensus on Jesus' true identity, the validity of feminist biblical interpretation itself comes into question. The evidence shows that the feminist quest for self-fulfillment and self-realization leads to a distortion of the message of the Bible. In an attempt to fit Jesus into their feminist mold, feminists are ultimately kept from experiencing the fulfillment they are seeking, the joy that comes only from living life in keeping with God's truth as revealed in his Word.

The message of the Bible for us as women is certainly vital, though often countercultural. Attention to its teaching is essential for us to live spiritually vibrant lives in a world that vies for compromise, accommodation, and independence from the authority structures in which God wants us to serve. In the case studies that follow, I have tried to supply you with the facts—the story of these women and their views of Jesus—so that you can form your own opinion as to whether their positions are tenable and biblical. As you read on, monitor attentively how the answer given by various feminist writers to Jesus' question, "But who do *you* say that I am?" squares with the biblical answer: "You are the Christ, the Son of the living God" (Matt. 16:16).

(London: Faber & Faber, 1932), which, among others, includes selections by A. Harnack, J. H. Newman, G. K. Chesterton, D. F. Strauss, L. Tolstoi, F. Nietzsche, B. Russell, E. Renan, R. Browning, M. Arnold, G. B. Shaw, H. G. Wells, and D. H. Lawrence.

# 1

# ALL WE'RE MEANT TO BE: FEMINISM CONFRONTS THE CHURCH

*Today we stand at the crossroads. As Christians we can no longer dodge the "woman problem."*

*To argue that women are equal in creation but subordinate in function is no more defensible than "separate but equal" schools for the races.*

—Letha Scanzoni and Nancy Hardesty,
*All We're Meant to Be* (1974)[1]

**It is** an undisputable fact that over the course of church history women have been misunderstood and undervalued. In the first few centuries of the Christian era, women were generically blamed for Eve's sin and viewed as temptresses and morally inferior. Only slowly did the Enlightenment change people's attitudes toward women, and even fairly recent American history reveals that women were denied basic human rights.

On March 31, 1776, Abigail Adams wrote in her famous letter to her husband, Congressman John Adams, "I desire you would Remember [*sic*] the Ladies, and be more generous and favourable to them than your ancestors" in the "new code of laws." John chose not to grant her request, and

1. L. Scanzoni and N. Hardesty, *All We're Meant to Be: A Biblical Approach to Women's Liberation* (Waco, TX: Word, 1974), 205.

"all men" were pronounced equal in the Declaration of Independence. It was less than a century ago that women received the privilege to vote and were given equal pay for equal work, along with many other common human freedoms in America.

While it is certainly healthy and appropriate for women to be valued and to receive these kinds of liberties, a woman who is committed to God and his purposes will want to be open and submissive to the plan God has for her in Scripture. It is true that in the midst of the conflicting voices on how a woman's identity is to be construed in this world, determining and practicing what the Bible has to say and what Jesus' own teaching and practice were with regard to women is a challenge.

Many influential feminist voices have risen to challenge the long-held conservative interpretation of Scripture regarding women, and it is my hope to honestly address and wrestle with these alternative views on Jesus in order to enable women to clarify and lay aside the misunderstandings or misrepresentations that linger. This direct confrontation should help to clear up the confusion and wavering in women who desire to serve him in committed submission. True freedom comes from obedience to God's will.

In order to set the stage for the study of Jesus' approach to women, the treatment below will begin with a survey of the rise of feminism. This will be followed by an explanation of some of the most important issues impacting the feminist interpretation of Scripture. The remainder of the book will focus on and evaluate each of the major schools of feminist thought on the topic of Jesus and women.

#### Table 1.1: The Three Waves of Feminism

| Movement | Rise of Movement | Central Concern |
| --- | --- | --- |
| The First Wave | 1830s | Racial and social justice |
| The Second Wave | 1960s | Gender equality |
| The Third Wave | 1990s | Radical pursuit of feminine self-realization |

### The First Wave of Feminism

The period of church history leading up to the Protestant Reformation is a good place to begin examining the rise of the feminist movement, a time when ecclesiastical authority was firmly vested in the hands of men. The Reformation itself, with its emphasis on the right and obligation of individual believers to study the Scriptures for themselves, embodied the seeds of a greater consciousness of the value of women. This consciousness led certain women to assert their right to preach and teach.[2]

---

2. W. Baird, *History of New Testament Research, Vol. 2: From Jonathan Edwards to Rudolf Bultmann* (Minneapolis: Augsburg Fortress, 2003), 331–32, 335–37.

Among the first was Anne Hutchinson, who was condemned for dissenting from Puritan orthodoxy in 1638.[3] Later, women rose to a prominent role in the campaign to abolish slavery in the American South, a campaign that extended also to women's rights. This quest for legal equality of women in conjunction with the appeal for the abolition of slavery is commonly known as the "first wave" of feminism.[4]

In the 1830s, Mary Stewart was the first to advance issues of gender equality and social justice in the United States.

The Grimké sisters, Angelina and Sarah, contributed the treatises "Appeal to the Christian Women in the South" (1836) and "Letters on the Equality of the Sexes and the Condition of Women" (1837), respectively, claiming that the Bible had been misunderstood and mistranslated.[5]

The Seneca Falls "Declaration on Women's Rights" issued in 1848 summed up women's concerns with regard to the male-dominated system in their day.

The Quaker Lucretia Coffin Mott argued in an 1849 sermon that Scripture was not supremely authoritative or divinely inspired. In the same year, Antoinette Brown published an article in the *Oberlin Quarterly* in which she set forth the argument that 1 Corinthians 14:34–35 and 1 Timothy 2:12 merely proscribe *inappropriate* teaching by women.[6] She was ordained in the Congregational Church, New York, in 1853—probably the first American woman to undergo ordination.

Other outspoken women in the second half of the nineteenth century included Catherine Booth, cofounder of the Salvation Army; Frances Willard, who established the Woman's Christian Temperance Union; and Katharine Bushnell, leader of women's equality Bible studies.

First-wave nineteenth-century feminists used two primary methods for interpreting Scripture. The first method sought to counter the argument of those who limited the role of women by reasoning from passages that

3. See also C. Bolt, *The Women's Movements in the United States and Britain from the 1790s to the 1920s* (Amherst, MA: University of Massachusetts Press, 1993), 19, who refers to Mary Astell, whose anonymous publications appeared primarily between 1694 and 1705, as "perhaps the best-known English feminist before Mary Wollstonecraft" a century later.

4. Bolt, in ibid., 26, also mentions that, in the 1820s, Catherine Beecher, daughter of the well-known Congregational preacher Lyman Beecher, opened a female seminary in Hartford, Connecticut. She notes that Beecher and others did not proclaim themselves feminists but maintains that these women "prepared the ground for the nineteenth-century women's movement." See also J. Cottrell, *Feminism and the Bible: An Introduction to Feminism for Christians* (Joplin, MO: College Press, 1992), chap. 1.

5. C. Gifford, "American Women and the Bible: The Nature of Woman as a Hermeneutical Issue," in *Feminist Perspectives on Biblical Scholarship,* ed. A. Y. Collins (Chico, CA: Scholars Press, 1985), 14–20; D. W. Dayton, *Discovering an Evangelical Heritage* (New York: Harper, 1976), 89–91; and Bolt, *Women's Movements,* 61–78.

6. A. Brown, "Exegesis of I Corinthians XIV, 34, 35 and I Timothy II, 11, 12," *Oberlin Quarterly* 4 (1849): 358–73; see Dayton, *Discovering,* 88–89.

spoke of the "equality"[7] of men and women in Christ. The second method made use of female characters in Scripture that could serve as role models for women in leadership, such as Deborah, Ruth, and Esther.[8] Toward the end of the nineteenth century, a more critical approach began to take hold. This approach labeled the actual biblical texts as sexist and challenged their integrity, including their view of women. All of these approaches mark the first stage of feminist hermeneutics—methods of interpretation—and form the foundation of feminist biblical interpretation.

The rising tide of women active in Christian ministry and scholarship reached a culmination point in *The Woman's Bible*, edited by Elizabeth Cady Stanton (1895, 1898).[9] The work resembles a commentary more than a translation, with twenty women contributors enlisted to comment on selected biblical passages judged significant for women.[10]

Stanton herself did not consider the Mosaic law to be inspired,[11] yet she acknowledged the powerful influence of the Bible as the bedrock of male-dominated Western law and civilization. Believing that women's emancipation would be impossible if Scripture's position continued to be accepted, Stanton applied a supposed "higher criticism" to erode its authority, particularly with regard to biblical teaching on women.[12] The historicity of biblical narratives was challenged and certain criteria of authenticity were applied to test their reliability. In so doing, Stanton attempted to correct traditional interpretations of passages related to women and sought to achieve legislative reform through a reinterpretation of the Bible.

**Table 1.2: The First Wave of Feminism**

| Major Figures | Significance and Contribution |
| --- | --- |
| Angelina Grimké | "Appeal to the Christian Women in the South" (1836) |
| Sarah Grimké | "Letters on the Equality of the Sexes and the Condition of Women" (1837) |
| Antoinette Brown | First American woman to be ordained (1853) |
| Catherine Booth | Cofounder of Salvation Army |
| Frances Willard | Founder of Woman's Christian Temperance Union |
| Katharine Bushnell | Leader of women's equality Bible studies |
| Elizabeth Cady Stanton | Editor of and contributor to *The Woman's Bible* (1895, 1898) |

7. As will be seen later in this book, the definition of *equality* is at the very heart of the controversy surrounding women's roles. Is "equal" to be understood in terms of equality in worth or does it encompass what God has called women to do in the church and in society?

8. A. Y. Collins, ed., *Feminist Perspectives on Biblical Scholarship*, 4.

9. See the summary in Cottrell, *Feminism and the Bible*, 26–37.

10. Gifford, "American Women," 27–30.

11. E. C. Stanton, *The Woman's Bible* (repr. New York: Arno, 1972 [1895]), 12.

12. Ibid.

### The Second Wave of Feminism

Through the efforts of Stanton, her friend Susan B. Anthony, and many others, women in America gained the right to vote in 1919.[13] The decades subsequent to this female milestone (1920–1960) saw little growth in the women's movement. Only when American society entered a major social upheaval in the 1960s, with an anti-establishment message and a civil rights emphasis, did modern-day feminism emerge. Initially, this second wave of feminism was a radical, secular phenomenon seeking only to extend the feminist movement to the social and economic realm.[14]

It received its major impetus from the French author Simone de Beauvoir's *The Second Sex* (1949; English translation 1952).[15] In the United States, women such as Betty Friedan, author of *The Feminist Mystique* (1964) and first president of the National Organization of Women (NOW) founded in 1966, and Gloria Steinem, who launched *Ms.* magazine in 1971, which she edited until 1987, also had a large impact on the general culture as they sought to promote women's emancipation in the larger society, the workplace, and the home.[16]

Soon, however, Christian feminists took up the task of providing an interpretation of Scripture that sought to give special consideration to women's concerns and interests, especially in the ecclesiastical realm, and this had a marked impact on Christian theology.

Table 1.3: The Second Wave of Feminism

| Major Figures and Groups | Significance and Contribution |
|---|---|
| Simone de Beauvoir | *The Second Sex* (1949; English translation 1952) |
| Betty Friedan | *The Feminist Mystique* (1964) |
| Gloria Steinem | Launched *Ms.* magazine (1971) |
| Evangelical Women's Caucus | Emphasis on social action, split over homosexuality (1973) |
| Christians for Biblical Equality | Emphasis on gender equality in all spheres of life (1986) |

13. See Bolt, *Women's Movement*, chaps. 5 and 6.
14. See Cottrell, *Feminism and the Bible*, chap. 2.
15. See M. A. Kassian, *The Feminist Mistake: The Radical Impact of Feminism on Church and Culture* (Wheaton, IL: Crossway, 1992), 18–22.
16. See Cottrell, *Feminist and the Bible*, 43–48, who lists Friedan and Steinem together with Kate Millett and Germaine Greer as the "architects of the movement" (i.e., Second Wave feminism); and Kassian, *Feminism Mistake* 23–27. Kassian discerns three stages in the development of Second Wave feminism: (1) naming self (1960–1970); (2) naming the world (1970–1980); and (3) naming God (1980–1990).

Developing feminist theologies within existing cultural and social contexts included the African-American "womanist" and the Hispanic *mujerista* theology in America, as well as emerging feminist theologies from European, Latin American, Asian, and African origins.[17] Feminist theology, in its diverse manifestations, confronted the issue of authority, challenging traditional understandings and seeking to address the patriarchal and sexist domination and marginalization of women in all sectors of society—political, social, and religious.

The term *thealogy*, coined by Canadian Naomi Goldenberg, called for reflection on the divine feminine and on coinage of feminist terms. Hence, a major task of feminist theology was the rethinking of traditional male symbols and concepts in an effort to eliminate patriarchy and legitimize female power.

It was at a conference in Chicago in 1973, "Evangelicals for Social Action," that the Evangelical Women's Caucus was started. From 1975 to 1983 the movement grew, but so did tensions regarding biblical interpretation and inerrancy. An organizational fracture took place in 1986 when divergent views on the authority of Scripture emerged surrounding the issue of homosexuality. This led to the establishment of Christians for Biblical Equality (CBE), a leading advocate of *biblical* or *evangelical feminism*, also called *egalitarianism* owing to its emphasis on women's equality to men in all spheres of life.[18]

Over time, three general groups of feminists emerged: (1) radical feminists, (2) reformist feminists, and (3) biblical evangelical feminists or egalitarians.[19] In simple terms, radical feminism rejected the Bible and Christianity as unusable because of their male patriarchal bias. Instead, it focused on feminine religious experience as a key to interpretation. Reformist feminism essentially rejected Christian tradition about women and used the Bible as a means to reconstruct a "proper" positive theology. However, the Bible itself was not seen as inerrant or authoritative. The third movement, evangelical feminism, rejected a critical stance toward

---

17. For an interesting treatment see L. A.-L. Abrahams, "A critical comparison of Elisabeth Schüssler Fiorenza's notion of Christian ministry as a 'Discipleship of Equals' and Mercy Amba Oduyoye's notion as a 'Partnership of both men and women'" (minithesis, University of Western Cape, 2005). Cf. M. A. Oduyoye, "African Women's Hermeneutics," in *Initiation into Theology: The Rich Variety of Theology and Hermeneutics*, ed. S. Maimela and A. König; (Pretoria: J L van Schaik, 1998), 359–71; and D. M. Ackermann, "Feminist and Womanist Hermeneutics," in ibid, 349–58.

18. P. D. H. Cochran, *Evangelical Feminism: A History* (New York; London: New York University Press, 2005), 77–109.

19. For the most part, "evangelical feminism" will be used in the remainder of the book to describe this movement also known as biblical feminism or egalitarianism.

Scripture. Evangelical feminists said that nothing in the Bible should be rejected, and Scripture was seen as teaching complete male-female equality.[20]

Table 1.4: The Three Types of Feminism

| Type of Feminism | Major Tenet/Stance toward Scripture |
| --- | --- |
| Radical Feminism | Rejects Bible and Christianity because of their patriarchal bias |
| Reformist Feminism | Uses Bible as means to reconstruct "positive theology" for women |
| Evangelical Feminism | The Bible, rightly interpreted, teaches complete gender equality |

The 1980s witnessed the first conservative responses to evangelical feminism, including works by Susan Foh and James Hurley.[21] In addition, further works advocating the egalitarian viewpoint, such as those by Mary Evans and Mary Hayter, appeared.[22] Two North American organizations were established during this period. One, which promoted egalitarianism, was the above-mentioned group Christians for Biblical Equality (CBE), and the other group, rooted in complementarianism, was The Council on Biblical Manhood and Womanhood (CBMW).[23] Subsequently, the hermeneutical and exegetical dimension of this debate was explored with increasing sophistication.[24] Gender wars over men's and women's roles in the home, the church, and society were raging.

20. Kassian, *Feminist Mistake*, 249–50.
21. Such as S. T. Foh, *Women and the Word of God: A Response to Biblical Feminism* (Phillipsburg, NJ: Presbyterian and Reformed, 1979); J. B. Hurley, *Man and Woman in Biblical Perspective* (Grand Rapids, MI: Zondervan, 1981).
22. E.g., M. J. Evans, *Woman in the Bible* (Downers Grove, IL: InterVarsity, 1983); M. Hayter, *The New Eve in Christ: The Use and Abuse of the Bible in the Debate about Women in the Church* (Grand Rapids, MI: Eerdmans, 1987).
23. Representative works from these two camps are *Women, Authority and the Bible,* ed. A. Mickelsen (Downers Grove, IL: InterVarsity, 1986), as well as now *Discovering Biblical Equality,* ed. R. W. Pierce and R. M. Groothuis (Downers Grove, IL: InterVarsity, 2004), and *Recovering Biblical Manhood and Womanhood,* ed. J. Piper and W. Grudem (Wheaton, IL: Crossway, 1991). The work by Mickelsen includes essays on biblical authority and feminism; the meaning of *kephalē* in the New Testament; and exegetical chapters on 1 Corinthians, Gal. 3:28, and 1 Tim. 2:12, plus thoughts on contemporary implications. Piper and Grudem's work covers much of the same territory from a complementarian perspective yet is even more comprehensive. *Discovering Biblical Equality* follows the exact same format as the work by Piper and Grudem and provides a chapter-by-chapter egalitarian response. For a survey of biblical feminism see chap. 19 in Kassian, *Feminist Mistake.*
24. See A. J. Köstenberger and T. R. Schreiner, eds., *Women in the Church: An Analysis and Application of 1 Timothy 2:9–15,* 2nd ed. (Grand Rapids, MI: Baker, 2005); A. J. Köstenberger, "Gender Passages in the NT: Exegetical Fallacies Critiqued," *Westminster Theological Journal* 56 (1994): 259–83; S. J. Grenz with D. M. Kjesbo, *Women in the Church* (Downers Grove, IL: InterVarsity, 1995); and W. J. Webb, *Slaves, Women, and Homosexuals* (Downers Grove, IL: InterVarsity, 2001).

## The Third Wave of Feminism

The most recent development of feminism is often referred to as Third Wave feminism. Its beginnings can be traced to the early 1990s. Third Wave feminism is characterized by an even more radical pursuit of feminine self-realization completely removed from any guiding Christian principles. For this reason it is not addressed in this book where the focus is on the feminist use of Scripture with regard to Jesus and his approach to women.

We will now look at some of the major interpretive issues affecting the feminist understanding of Jesus and then start our study with radical feminists.[25]

---

25. The major features and proponents of Third Wave feminism can be gleaned from L. L. Heywood, ed., *The Women's Movement Today: An Encyclopedia of Third-Wave Feminism*, 2 vols. (Westport, CT: Greenwood Press, 2005). See also J. Baumgardner and A. Richards, *Manifesta: Young Women, Feminism, and the Future* (New York: Farrar, Straus and Giroux, 2000); and L. Heywood and J. Drake, eds., *Third Wave Agenda: Being Feminist, Doing Feminism* (Minneapolis; London: University of Minnesota Press, 1997).

# 2

# WHAT'S AT STAKE: "IT'S HERMENEUTICS!"

*Hermeneutics is the unfinished item on our agenda of theological prolegomena. It must be seriously and comprehensively addressed by all evangelical theologians and biblical scholars in the immediate future. Without a hermeneutical consensus, any hope for a consensus in theology and ethics is mere wishful thinking. We evangelicals rightly make a great deal of the normative nature of the biblical text. Our views must be judged in the light of Scripture. But our agreement on this point has real significance only to the extent that we "correctly handle the word of truth."*

—Stanley N. Gundry, "Evangelical Theology:
Where *Should* We Be Going?" (1978)[1]

***During the*** 1992 United States presidential campaign, Bill Clinton's advisers kept hammering home one simple truth: "It's the economy!" They were convinced that the state of the American economy was the number-one issue

1. S. N. Gundry, "Evangelical Theology: Where *Should* We Be Going?" *Journal of the Evangelical Theological Society* 22/1 (1979): 13; repr. in A. J. Köstenberger, ed., *Quo Vadis, Evangelicalism? Perspectives on the Past, Direction for the Future. Presidential Addresses from the First Fifty Years of the* Journal of the Evangelical Theological Society (Wheaton, IL: Crossway, 2007), 90. This was Gundry's presidential address delivered at the 1978 annual meeting of the Evangelical Theological Society. The quote reproduces the conclusion of Gundry's address.

in that election, and in part owing to their dogged insistence and determination their candidate triumphed. As our study of feminist scholarship on Jesus will demonstrate, something similar is the case in biblical studies: "It's hermeneutics!" In other words, people's understanding of individual passages of Scripture largely depends on their overall view of the nature of Scripture and on the interpretive methodology they bring to the table in the first place.

As we will see, in the case of radical feminists, their approach to Scripture is, in a word, rejection, owing to what they perceive to be the Bible's irredeemably "patriarchal" nature; i.e., it springs from and provides for a disproportionate amount of male power.

The same is true to a lesser extent with reformist feminists, except that they do not reject Scripture in its totality but selectively use or discard what does or does not conform to their feminist presuppositions. In keeping with the Enlightenment spirit, reformist feminists start out with the "enlightened notion" that all men—and women—are equal, and then they critique and supplement Scripture as they see fit, whether by rejecting the authority of Scripture where it does not conform to their feminist outlook or by adding additional writings to their "canon" that reflect more closely their own beliefs.

As for evangelical feminists or egalitarians, Scripture is accepted as inerrant and authoritative, and a hermeneutic aimed at discerning the authorial intention is supported. For egalitarians, Scripture is treated with more respect than it is with radical or reformist feminists. Unlike the latter, who already start out with the presupposition that feminism is right and the Bible wrong where it stands in conflict with feminism, evangelical feminists claim to show inductively that the Bible, rightly interpreted, teaches male-female equality, including women's eligibility to all church offices and roles of leadership in the church.

There is a wide range of interpretations among feminists with regard to Jesus and women. How do we account for this diversity of views, even among those who all hold to a form of feminism? And how do we know which interpretation is right? Since a proper approach to the study of Scripture is foundational to its interpretation and also essential for the construction of sound theology, it is important to unearth the theological method, including the hermeneutical method, of various schools of interpretation with regard to Jesus' approach to women. For that reason, before delving into a study of feminist interpretations of Jesus, you might find it helpful to review Appendix 2 to see how Scripture ought to be interpreted.[2]

2. For a helpful summary see D. J. Smit, "Biblical Hermeneutics: the first 19 centuries," in *Initiation into Theology: The Rich Variety of Theology and Hermeneutics*, ed. S. Maimela and A. König (Pretoria: J L van Schaik, 1998), 275–96.

## Special Issues in the Feminist Debate

In our efforts to understand feminist hermeneutics, it will be helpful to take a quick look at a few hermeneutical issues with particular relevance for the feminist interpretation of Jesus.

### Reconstructing History

Reconstructing biblical history is the first such issue, an endeavor that has had a major impact on the discussion of the feminist interpretation of Jesus' stance toward women. In the prevailing climate of postmodernism in much of American culture, including academia, the question of the nature of history and of historical research naturally arises. How do we really know what happened in history? Since history is forever past, how can one properly investigate it? Since all historical research is conducted by historians with various views and agendas of their own, is not the entire enterprise of historical research hopelessly subjective? Recent scholarship, including the feminist variety, has increasingly questioned whether history "as it actually happened"[3] can be recovered with any degree of confidence from the available sources.[4] Postmodern theorists believe that history is written by the winners; those victorious in a given struggle are the ones who recount the story from their point of view. According to them, history is a function of power rather than truth. History is but a fable agreed upon.[5]

There is, of course, some truth to these claims. As mentioned, sources must still be evaluated, and they will often—some would say *always*—reflect the bias of a particular historian. At the same time, few would go to the extreme of denying that it is possible to reconstruct history "as it actually happened" to at least some extent. For example, few would question that Jesus Christ lived as a historical person or that he was crucified under Pontius Pilate, because a variety of sources, biblical and extrabiblical, attest to his existence and the facts of his life. The same can be said with many other historical persons and events both ancient and modern. As P. W. Felix notes:

> It must be granted that twentieth-century exegetes are outsiders to the culture in which the Bible was written, and for this reason can never achieve a complete understanding of the original meaning of the Bible in its historical

---

3. The phrase is that of the German historian von Ranke: *wie es eigentlich gewesen ist.*
4. See further on this point the interaction with E. S. Fiorenza elsewhere in this volume.
5. For conservative evangelical evaluations of postmodernism see D. A. Carson, *The Gagging of God: Christianity Confronts Pluralism* (Grand Rapids, MI: Zondervan, 1996); and M. J. Erickson, *Truth or Consequences: The Promise and Perils of Postmodernism* (Downers Grove, IL: InterVarsity, 2001).

setting. An undue emphasis upon this limitation, however, loses sight of the fact that all historical study is a weighing of probabilities. The more evidence we have, the higher degree of probability we can attain. The practice of exegesis, therefore, is a continued search for greater probability and a more refined understanding.[6]

Once doubt is cast on the interpreter's ability to determine history with a reasonable degree of confidence, we can no longer be sure of the very foundations of our Christian faith, which is of necessity grounded in historical events such as Christ's incarnation, crucifixion, burial, and resurrection (1 Cor. 15:3–4).

Most feminists, however, still seek to reconstruct the historical circumstances surrounding Jesus' ministry to determine his approach to women in order to critique or commend it, though different feminists do not necessarily agree on a particular reconstruction. In this quest, of course, evangelical interpreters will trust the testimony preserved in Scripture as their primary historical source.

### Epistemology

A foundational issue related to hermeneutics is the question of how we know anything to be true, the study of which is called *epistemology*. Is knowing truth strictly subjective, varying from person to person as postmodernism claims, or is truth absolute and applicable to all individuals regardless of their cultural context? The postmodernism view is that truth is but the linguistic expression of a socially constructed notion of customs and values characterizing a particular community. Yet noted philosopher J. P. Moreland, among others, has recently raised some serious questions about its validity.[7]

Moreland's critique of postmodernism implies that truth is not merely subjective, as if there were the possibility of many different Jesuses roaming first-century Palestine. Nor is truth based merely on the perspective of the interpreter so that the first-century Jesus is hopelessly irrecoverable. The "real Jesus" is attested by eyewitness testimony in our primary sources, the Gospels, and these sources essentially cohere. For this reason we can approach Scripture with confidence, hoping to discover who Jesus really was, as long as we are aware, and properly suspicious, of our own presuppositions.

6. P. W. Felix Sr., "The Hermeneutics of Evangelical Feminism," in *Evangelical Hermeneutics: The New Versus the Old*, ed. R. L. Thomas (Grand Rapids, MI: Kregel, 2002), 386, citing R. Thomas.
7. J. P. Moreland, "Truth, Contemporary Philosophy, and the Postmodern Turn," in *Whatever Happened to Truth?* ed. A. J. Köstenberger (Wheaton, IL: Crossway, 2005), 75–92.

Table 2.1: Special Issues in the Feminist Debate

| Issue | Pertinent Question |
|---|---|
| The difficulty of reconstructing history | Can we determine "what really happened"? |
| Epistemology | How do we know? |
| The role of the reader vs. authorial intent | Where does textual meaning reside? |
| Issues related to canonicity | What is the extent of the canon? |
| The alleged patriarchal nature of Scripture | Does Scripture have a "patriarchal bias"? |
| Evangelicalism vs. fundamentalism | Are evangelicals "fundamentalists"? |

### The Role of the Reader vs. Authorial Intent

The question must be raised not only about *what* we are interpreting but also about *who* is doing the interpreting.[8] Evangelicals endeavor to operate within the Bible's own frame of reference, accepting the reality of a transcendent God and of the supernatural. But many who approach the Bible from a postmodern perspective allow their personal situation and experience not only to influence but even to determine the outcome of the interpretation.

This premise is paramount in feminist interpretation of Scripture; it is approached self-consciously by women with predetermined outcomes. Yet, arguably, if we desire to interpret Scripture, we must attempt to allow its authors to have weight in the interpretive outcome. This procedure should be applied in as fair and unbiased a fashion as possible, whether or not we believe that Scripture is the inspired, authoritative, and true Word of God.

It is a realistic danger for any interpreter from whatever point of view to read her own agenda into the Bible rather than to let the Bible speak for itself. She must recognize that she has presuppositions but not allow these to be determinative in her interpretive outcome. Using proper exegetical methods will help interpreters overcome their own lack of knowledge or deficiency and will enable them to come as close as possible to the author's intended meaning of Scripture and to determine its significance for their own lives.

The quest for the intention of the author is heavily criticized in many circles and is not without its challenges and in some cases proves inconclusive, but it must be maintained that, in principle, determining authorial intent is an academically defensible and legitimate strategy for discerning textual meaning.[9] An author-oriented approach to interpretation also cor-

8. Klein, "Evangelical Hermeneutics," 324–25; chap. 5 in Klein, Blomberg, and Hubbard, *Introduction to Biblical Interpretation*, 2nd ed. (Dallas: Word, 2004).
9. E. D. Hirsch Jr., *Validity in Interpretation* (New Haven; London: Yale University Press, 1967); G. R. Osborne, *The Hermeneutical Spiral: A Comprehensive Introduction to Biblical Interpretation*, 2nd ed. (Downers Grove, IL: InterVarsity, 2006); K. J. Vanhoozer, *Is There a*

responds best to reality and common sense, since every text has an author and is willed by that author to express a particular message. Texts do not simply come into being, nor do they, properly understood, mean anything apart from authorial intention.

In recent years, certain approaches to interpretation have completely turned away from authorial intention and put the interpretive emphasis in discerning meaning squarely on the reader. According to some, a text means what it means to a given reader. This renders interpretation very difficult since a given text will mean different things to different readers; there are no criteria for determining what constitutes a valid interpretation.[10]

What various postmodern hermeneutical approaches have in common and what they share with much of recent feminist approaches is an emphasis on the reader rather than on the author of a given piece of writing. No longer do interpreters seek to discern authorial intention in attempting to understand the meaning of a given passage. Instead, they deny that a passage has the same meaning for all who interpret it; a passage has only a multiplicity of readings, and these readings, in turn, are a function of the subjectivity and experience of the reader, whether feminist, Hispanic, white Anglo-Saxon male, or African-American. The end result is that the meaning of a given text will be different for different readers, and there are no clear standards by which to evaluate the validity of different readings. All are equally valid.

Now, there surely is an element of truth in these postmodern approaches. It is true that the focus on authorial meaning can be misguided if not properly conceived.[11] Nevertheless, the radical shift from authorial intent to reader-created meaning is too reactionary. In the end, there is no adequate substitute to make up for the loss of the author in determining the meaning of a given text. Moreover, it is important to remember that there is no way to know the author's intention other than by what is expressed in a given text.

The conclusion must be that *authorial meaning is textual meaning*, and the meaning of a given text is the meaning intended by its author. The reader's role is largely passive, seeking as much as possible to discern the various textual clues for the original author's intended meaning. Only after this approach has been followed is it appropriate for the reader to apply the text to her personal life.

---

*Meaning in This Text? The Bible, the Reader, and the Morality of Literary Knowledge* (Grand Rapids, MI: Zondervan, 1998).

10. Anticipated by Hirsch, *Validity*.

11. See W. K. Wimsatt and M. C. Beardsley, "The Intentional Fallacy," in *On Literary Intention*, ed. D. Newton-deMolina (Edinburgh: Edinburgh University Press, 1976), 1–13.

While objectivity in interpretation is clearly impossible in light of a reader's presuppositions, this does not mean that sound interpretation is doomed to failure. Interpreters who approach the text with an openness to be engaged by its message and by its ultimate author—God himself—will find their understanding of its meaning increasing.

### Issues Related to Canonicity

Given the perceived patriarchal bias that both radical and reformist feminism bring to Scripture, whole portions have been excluded by them and its authority is rejected. Other books have been co-opted or materials have been created and put in their place.[12]

Historically, the Scripture that we are interpreting has come down to us in church history as a canon of biblical books.[13] The canon of Old Testament books was possibly set as early as the end of the first century A.D. The New Testament canon took shape in the first few centuries of the early church. Paul's letters were given recognition before the end of the first century (2 Pet. 3:16). At the Reformation, the church removed several Old Testament apocryphal books from its canon while continuing to affirm the canonicity of all twenty-seven New Testament books that had been included at least since Athanasius's famous Easter letter of A.D. 367. Therefore, the church through the ages, both Roman Catholic and Protestant, has held that the twenty-seven books of the New Testament, and they alone, are the inspired and authoritative New Testament books.

Regarding the canon, the church has historically affirmed, first, that the canon is *closed*; that is, the early church's determination of canonicity was definitive and binding on the church ever since.

Second, the canon of Scripture is characterized by what has been termed "progressive revelation," which means that later revelation builds on earlier divine self-disclosure. This is important for interpretation, since it means that earlier material must be interpreted in the light of later revelation.

Third, the canon of Scripture is characterized by both an underlying theological *unity* and *diversity* in expression on the part of the different biblical authors.[14] For example, with regard to unity, all of Scripture is the story of God's dealings with humankind. This theme runs through

---

12. See, e.g., R. R. Ruether, *Womanguides: Readings toward a Feminist Theology* (Boston: Beacon, 1985) and various works by E. S. Fiorenza.

13. B. F. Westcott, *A General Survey of the History of the Canon of the New Testament*, 7th ed. (London: Macmillan, 1896); B. M. Metzger, *The Canon of the New Testament: Its Origin, Development, and Significance* (Oxford: Clarendon, 1987); F. F. Bruce, *The Canon of Scripture* (Downers Grove, IL: InterVarsity, 1988); Klein, "Evangelical Hermeneutics," 324; chap. 4 in Klein, Blomberg, and Hubbard, *Introduction*; R. L. Harris, *Inspiration and Canonicity of the Scriptures* (Greenville, SC: A Press, 1995).

14. Klein, "Evangelical Hermeneutics," 324.

Scripture as a common thread and lends unity and coherence to the various biblical books. At the same time, different writers of Scripture may express themselves in diverse ways. A classic example is the way in which Paul and James address the issue of justification by faith. The implication of this for our topic is that evangelicals will expect the biblical teaching on the role of women, such as that of Jesus and Paul, to be coherent and consistent.

Fourth, though there is a diversity of perspectives represented in the biblical books, there is no justification for a "canon within a canon" as many feminists have postulated. Feminists regularly seek to determine a "canon within a canon." They seek to determine the "central message of Scripture" and to interpret portions of Scripture that seem to be at variance with that central message in light of it.[15] The problem with this procedure, however, is that only what is considered to be the central message is important while less central passages may be neglected. Also, there is danger in an interpreter arbitrarily selecting a "central theme" of Scripture in keeping with her preference while neglecting teachings that are countercultural or otherwise offensive.

In keeping with the church's historic affirmation, then, it is affirmed here that the canon is closed and consists of the sixty-six books traditionally included in the Protestant Scriptures, and all of its teachings are relevant and true in the varied presentations and portraits presented by its different authors.

### The Alleged Patriarchal Nature of Scripture

Another issue at stake, mentioned earlier, is the question of the perceived patriarchal nature of Scripture. Those who hold to this view believe that Scripture was written and settled in a framework controlled by men, thereby affording men an inordinately large share of authority. The question is whether such male authority is to be taken as God's will for all people at all times.

It is undeniable that patriarchy as a cultural system of family relations existed in the Old Testament period. So should we consider patriarchy as a cultural institution that expresses God's will for human relationships? Or is this system culturally determined and thus relative, if not intrinsically evil, because it permanently enshrines male supremacy over women, justifying the removal of portions of the canon of Scripture? How is patriarchy to be

---

15. This is found not infrequently in the writings of biblical feminists, though they may not use the "canon within a canon" terminology. See, e.g., I. H. Marshall, "An Evangelical Approach to 'Theological Criticism,'" in *The Best in Theology*, Vol. 3, ed. J. I. Packer (Carol Stream, IL: *Christianity Today*, 1989), 45–60. The article first appeared in *Themelios*, as cited and critiqued by A. J. Köstenberger, "Gender Passages in the NT: Hermeneutical Fallacies Critiqued," *Westminster Theological Journal* 56 (1994): 278–79.

defined in the first place? If patriarchy is God's intention for us, how is this authority to be exercised? What do Jesus' teachings and practice contribute to this discussion?

All sides can agree that concerted efforts should be made to combat abuse of male authority, which is still found in many homes and cultures today. In the end, this is not merely an academic issue but one that has enormous practical consequences. This is one of the great strengths of feminism, which has always strongly rejected male domination and the abuse of women. Yet it is necessary to elaborate on the difference between patriarchy and what may be called *patricentrism*, between harsh male dominance on the one hand and loving, caring leadership on the other.

Is the Bible's teaching, then, hopelessly patriarchal and thus irrelevant for today's enlightened, egalitarian culture? How do we rightly interpret Scripture in any case? Is not all biblical interpretation irredeemably subjective? And is not historical research fraught with insurmountable difficulties? Feminism has brought all these issues to the fore. In arguing for an interpretation of Scripture, including an interpretation of Jesus, that is ideologically and experientially driven, feminists have set themselves over Scripture, critiquing it and determining what Scripture may or may not say to modern, or postmodern, men and women.[16]

What are we to say, then, regarding the charge leveled by radical feminists that Scripture is to be rejected since it enshrines patriarchy, understood as the exercise of a dominant, heavy-handed type of male authority? Without exception, patriarchy is characterized as the source of all evil in feminist literature. This, however, may be shown to reflect feminist bias rather than scriptural deficiency.

In fact, Daniel Block has made a strong case that ancient Israel practiced not the kind of patriarchy depicted by today's feminists but by what he calls "patricentrism."[17] According to Block, like the spokes of a wheel, life in ancient Israel revolved around the father in his role as the provider and protector of the extended family. It was not so much the "rule" of the father (patri-archy) but his loving care and provision for the well being of his own that were most central to the father's role.

Scripture in its entirety is pervaded by the principle of men bearing the ultimate responsibility and authority for marriage and the family as well as for the church, "the household of God" (1 Tim. 3:15). This principle

16. See the surveys in M. E. Köstenberger, "Feminist Biblical Interpretation" and "Feminist Theology," in *Encyclopedia of Christian Civilization*, ed. G. T. Kurian (Oxford: Blackwell), forthcoming.
17. D. I. Block, "Marriage and Family in Ancient Israel," in *Marriage and Family in the Biblical World*, ed. K. M. Campbell (Downers Grove, IL: InterVarsity, 2003), 33–102, esp. 40–48.

of male headship reaches from God's creation of the man first (Gen. 2:7), to his holding the first man accountable for humanity's sin (Gen. 3:9–12), to the ancient Israelite practice of "patricentrism," to the all-male Levitical priesthood in Old Testament Israel, to Jesus' choice of twelve men as his apostles, to Paul's teaching that men bear ultimate responsibility and authority for the church (1 Tim. 2:12). In fact, Paul himself believed that his teaching of male headship was rooted in the Genesis creation narrative (see 1 Cor. 11:8–9; 1 Tim. 2:13).

It is true that the historical narrative books of the Hebrew Scriptures witness to numerous abuses of this abiding principle of male headship in the Old Testament period, such as arbitrary divorce (Deut. 24:1–2), the intermittent practice of polygamy, adultery, rape, incest, and so on. Scripture does not condone these behaviors and attitudes.[18] At the same time, the New Testament does not abrogate the principle of male headship even subsequent to redemption in Christ. Thus Paul still can call Christian wives to submit to their husbands (Eph. 5:22–24), and Peter similarly enjoins wives even of unbelieving husbands to submit to them (1 Pet. 3:1–6).

Feminists regularly stress women's need for liberation. There can be no doubt that all over the world millions of women are oppressed, often just because of the traditional structures remaining intact, though by and large this is not a feature of North American society, which is very much egalitarian in practice. Christian wives should experience liberation from the dominant, unloving, abusive exercise of their husband's authority (see Gen. 3:16), a form of "rule" that in the Bible is contrasted with the loving, sacrificial exercise of the husband's servant leadership in Christ (Eph. 5:25–28). But the gospel does not entail a promise of, or call to, women's liberation from all forms of male authority over them.

The point is that true freedom in life is not found in the abolishing of any authority over oneself, especially if it is God-ordained. Scripture presents men's authority in the home and in the church not as autocratic or grounded in male superiority or merit but in the mysterious, sovereign divine will subsumed under the supreme lordship and authority of the Lord Jesus Christ. Living within God's created male and female order allows for a genuine experience of fulfillment and freedom for everyone.

### Evangelicalism vs. Fundamentalism
The diminishment of biblical authority in feminism has left a vacuum that has been filled by a vast array of feminist readings of Scripture and interpretations of Jesus. These readings make Jesus an extension of feminist

18. A. J. Köstenberger, *God, Marriage, and Family: Rebuilding the Biblical Foundation* (Wheaton, IL: Crossway, 2004), 42–51.

aspirations, domesticating him rather than allowing him to speak with his own unique voice to today's world and church.

Some are dismissing an evangelical approach to Scripture out of hand for illegitimate reasons. For example, conservative evangelical Christians may at times find themselves confronted with the label "fundamentalist," and their conservative viewpoint on gender issues gets rejected without further discussion.[19] But there is quite a difference between fundamentalism and a conservative evangelical reading of Scripture. Fundamentalism often tends toward a narrow-minded approach to Scripture. It at times may impose systematized doctrine onto the text and tend toward legalism. It is also often characterized by simplistic thinking. Some have even used the Bible in the past to justify such terrible things as slavery and racism.

Other more balanced conservative evangelical interpreters of Scripture, while attempting to interpret the Bible literally, are open to taking all the relevant factors into account to aid interpretation in order to acknowledge their own presuppositions, and they can therefore be more nuanced and open to complexity and diversity.

These foundational considerations will enable us to evaluate the various feminist proposals regarding Jesus' approach to women, and we turn now to a discussion of radical feminists. How would they answer Jesus' question, "Who do you say that I am?"

19. For a classic example of these two approaches to Scripture see the work by J. Barr, *Fundamentalism*, 2nd ed. (London: SCM, 1981), on which see the critique by M. Silva, "'Can Two Walk Together Unless They Be Agreed?' Evangelical Theology and Biblical Scholarship," in Quo Vadis, *Evangelicalism?* ed. A. J. Köstenberger, 111–20.

# PART 2

# JESUS AND RADICAL FEMINISM

*Are Christianity and feminism compatible? Is it acceptable that, as a feminist, one should have at the center of one's religion a male figure? What does it mean for the symbolism of this religion that this man alone was seen as the Son of God, in a way in which this was true of none other?*

—Daphne Hampson, "On Not Remembering Her" (1998)[1]

Who do radical feminists say Jesus is?[2] On the whole, radical feminists have abandoned biblical, historic Christianity and have embarked on a search for alternate paradigms.[3]

Owing to their negative assessment of Scripture's authoritative nature, truthfulness, and relevance for women today, radical feminists do not criti-

1. D. Hampson, "On Not Remembering Her," *Feminist Theology* 19 (1998): 72.
2. The material selected for comment pertains to Jesus' approach to women only and will not include treatments of larger Christological issues, such as Jesus' own identity in terms of male vs. female or issues related to gender language applied to God. Also not considered are pieces that speak in general terms about the need to liberate the oppressed in society but do not specifically deal with the question of how Jesus treated women according to the Gospels. The following treatment aims at selected coverage of representative works and does not attempt to be exhaustive.
3. In essence, the division into radical, reformist, and evangelical feminism in this book distinguishes between two types of feminist groups and their approach to Scripture: (1) those who see the Bible as furthering patriarchy or sexism (radical and reformist feminists); and (2) those who claim to view the Bible as an inspired witness to the grace of God in Christ (evangelical feminism or egalitarianism). This closely resembles the classification of K. Greene-McCreight, *Feminist Reconstructions of Christian Doctrine: Narrative Analysis and Appraisal* (New York; Oxford: Oxford University Press, 2000), 36–41. See also J. Cottrell, *Feminism and the Bible: An Introduction to Feminism for Christians* (Joplin, MO: College Press, 1992), who distinguishes between goddess feminism (chaps. 3–4), liberal Christian feminism (chaps. 5–6), and biblical feminism (chaps. 7–8).

cally interpret specific texts on Jesus' treatment of women. Rather, they tend to focus on broader theological or Christological issues such as the nature of God as Father or Mother and on the maleness of Jesus as an obstacle to full gender equality.

Mary Daly urges transcending the "Christian fixation on Jesus." Virginia Ramey Mollenkott pursues a vision of an "omnigender" society in which all gender distinctions are left behind. Daphne Hampson envisions a world "After Christianity." In the place of Jesus, radical feminists advocate an eclectic mix of spirituality. Whatever vestiges of Christianity remain are leftovers from a tradition that has failed to yield satisfactory answers for feminists' quest for meaning and significance.

# 3

# Mary Daly: Overcoming the Christian Fixation on Jesus

*It is not necessary to look to the past generation of theologians to see the almost universal pervasiveness of this fixation upon Jesus and the seemingly compulsive need to baptize and legitimate religious thinking, even of the most "radical" type, as "Christian." . . . I am proposing that Christian idolatry concerning the person of Jesus is not likely to be overcome except through the revolution that is going on in women's consciousness.*

—Mary Daly, *Beyond God the Father* (1983)[1]

**Mary Daly** is doubtless one of the most radical feminists of the past few decades.[2] Born on October 16, 1928, in New York and educated at Roman Catholic schools, she received doctoral degrees from St. Mary's College, Notre Dame University, in 1954 and from the University of Fribourg in Switzerland in 1963 (theology) and 1965 (philosophy). She taught at Boston College from 1967 until her forced retirement in 2001. Daly steadfastly refused to allow men

1. M. Daly, *Beyond God the Father: Toward a Philosophy of Women's Liberation* (Boston: Beacon, 1973), 70–71.
2. For a helpful summary see M. A. Kassian, *The Feminist Mistake: The Radical Impact of Feminism on Church and Culture* (Wheaton, IL: Crossway, 2005), 262–68.

into her classroom, contending that their presence would cause women to be less open to share their struggles. A lawsuit against her was settled out of court at the last minute, which included her agreement to resign her position.[3]

## Daly's First Major Work

Daly wrote her first major work, *The Church and the Second Sex*, in 1968, alluding to Simone de Beauvoir's work *The Second Sex*. Daly's hope was that women's liberation would take root in the Roman Catholic Church subsequent to the Second Vatican Council. In her book Daly documents the history of misogynism in the Roman Catholic Church from the time of the early church fathers. She calls on strong, independent women to fulfill their potential and on the church to stop discriminating against women in ministry.

Ecclesiastical reform was slow, however, and Daly became more radical, moving outside the boundaries of the church. Daly also came close to losing her position at Boston College and was granted tenure only after several months of student protest and attention in the media. Experiences such as these served to transform Daly from a reform-minded Catholic to a radical feminist.

---

**Fact Sheet 1: Mary Daly**

**Born:** October 16, 1928 in Schenectady, New York

**Education:** Ph.D. in religion, St. Mary's College/Notre Dame University (1954); Ph.D.s in theology (1963) and philosophy (1965), University of Fribourg, Switzerland

**Academic Position:** Boston College (1967–2001)

**Religious Background:** Roman Catholic

**Major Works:** *The Church and the Second Sex* (1968); *Beyond God the Father* (1973)

**Type of Feminist:** Radical

**View of Jesus:** Worship of Jesus is idolatry; women must overcome "fixation" on Jesus

---

## Mounting a Challenge

In 1973 Daly wrote the considerably more radical *Beyond God the Father*, outlining the case against the Bible and Christianity. According to Daly, Christianity is a male structure in which God is man, and thus man is God. Here Daly contends that the mere use of inclusive language is insufficient to liberate women from the bondage imposed on them by Scripture because the Bible's core symbolism remained patriarchal. So, Daly calls for a "*castrating* of language and images that reflect and perpetuate the structures of a sexist world."[4] In other words, the women's movement must mount a

---

3. Office of Public Affairs Staff, "Mary Daly Ends Suit, Agrees to Retire," *The Boston College Chronicle* 9, no. 11 (Feb. 15, 2001).

4. Daly, *Beyond God the Father*, 9 (emphasis in original).

challenge to the patriarchal religion of Christianity, a spiritual revolution in which the old order of sexism would be overthrown and a "new being" would be manifested in women.

### Further Radicalization

Daly's radical turn continues in her publications *Gyn/Ecology: The Metaethics of Radical Feminism* (1978); *Pure Lust: Elemental Feminist Philosophy* (1984); *Webster's First New Intergalactic Wickedary of the English Language* (1987); *Outercourse: The Be-Dazzling Voyage* (1993); and *Quintessence: Realizing the Archaic Future* (1999), in which she attacks both Christianity and Christian feminism.

According to Daly, only lesbian radical feminists can rise above the normal experience of male patriarchy. With this Daly completely breaks away from Christianity and represents the major proponent of this brand of feminism in North America. She is one of several who traveled through a form of Christianity and arrived at radical post-Christian feminist conclusions.

### Daly's Jesus and Her Rejection of Scripture

At the heart of Daly's hermeneutic is her complete rejection of Scripture owing to what she perceives to be its irremediable patriarchal bias. While reformist feminists seek to salvage non-patriarchal elements of Scripture and continue to use Scripture as at least one source in their theological work, Daly rejects this approach and takes strong issue with her fellow feminists. Consequently, Jesus and his treatment of women in the Gospels play little part in her model.

While Christians value Jesus as Son of God and Savior and look to him as an example and for guidance in the area of gender roles, Daly takes issue with what she perceives to be the "Christian fixation upon the person of Jesus."[5] In fact, Daly laments the fact that the "death of God" movement did not also lead to the "death of Jesus" in the twentieth century, "at least in the sense of transcending the Christian fixation upon the person of Jesus."[6] In her view, feminist theology ought not to be Christ-centered but Christ-decentered.

For this reason Daly urges feminists to overcome the "idolatry" related to the person of Jesus. She sees the problem in the exclusively masculine symbols for the idea of incarnation: "As a uniquely masculine image and language for divinity loses credibility, so also the idea of a single divine incarnation in a human being of the male sex may give way in the religious

5. Ibid., 70. Compare Fiorenza's somewhat less radical call to "decenter Jesus" from Christianity in her work *Jesus and the Politics of Interpretation* (see chap. 8 in this volume).
6. Ibid.

consciousness to an increased awareness of the power of Being in all persons."[7] It is hard to imagine a more radical rejection of Jesus and Christianity by feminists or others.

## Evaluation

Mary Daly's program of biblical interpretation reveals her unduly strong reaction against the patriarchalism she perceives in Scripture. Daly's antipathy toward males causes her to try to decenter maleness, not only from Scripture but also from Christianity and even from Jesus. In the process, she recasts religion as the human experience of the "power of Being," manifested in all persons.

This clearly contradicts Scripture's emphatic claim that God revealed himself uniquely and definitively in Jesus (e.g., John 1:18; 14:6) and that salvation is found only in him (Acts 4:12). Speaking of the "power of Being" is an inadequate substitute for the scriptural witness to the one true God, the Creator and Redeemer; and Daly's focus on human religious experience does not adequately take into account the scriptural claim that God revealed himself to humans.

Daly's work is an example of someone whose rejection of the authority of Scripture has led also to a radical recasting of morality. We see it in her progression of thought, evidenced in her later writings *Pure Lust* and *Webster's First New Intergalactic Wickedary of the English Language*. Daly first gave up her Christian faith and appears subsequently to have rejected any form of morality, promoting lust and evil as part of a radically libertarian agenda.

From the perspective of a postmodern feminist interpreter, Daly's radical stance toward biblical authority and historic Christianity may be viewed as one "legitimate" expression of an individual interpreter's right to reject traditional readings and sources of authority and to pursue alternative avenues of finding meaning and relevance. If Christianity is false, Scripture should not be awarded authority, and meaning will be found in something other than the foundational document of the Christian faith. However, it is this very radicalism of Daly's position that makes it appealing to some as a viable non-Christian alternative belief system.

As far as her approach to biblical interpretation is concerned, Mary Daly does not attempt to employ a conventional hermeneutical procedure. First and foremost, she does not make it her goal to determine authorial intent or to interpret a passage in its proper historical and literary context. Scripture is not allowed to be helpful in interpreting other Scripture. Daly's feminist ideology is presupposed and overrides the overt teaching of Scripture so that her positions cannot be said to derive from the actual interpretation of Scripture itself.

7. Ibid., 71.

# 4

# Virginia Ramey Mollenkott: Godding and Omnigender

*Prior to that "holy instant," I had inched my way from believing my-self totally depraved . . . to believing myself a basically decent human being who was having some lovely spiritual experiences. But one day while I was meditating, I experienced a reality that was even better than that: like my Elder Brother, Jesus, I am a sinless Self traveling through eternity and temporarily having human experiences in a body know[n] as Virginia Ramey Mollenkott.*

—Virginia Ramey Mollenkott, *Sensuous Spirituality: Out from Fundamentalism* (1993)[1]

***Another North*** American radical feminist of note is Virginia Ramey Mollenkott, professor of English at William Paterson University in New Jersey. Mollenkott comes from a Plymouth Brethren background, where women are not permitted to preach, pray aloud, or even ask questions at the Bible readings.[2] Mollenkott evinced considerable movement in her position with regard to her treatment of Jesus and women. Having started out with an egalitarian stance, she later on advocated a reformist feminist position and

1. V. R. Mollenkott, *Sensuous Spirituality: Out from Fundamentalism* (New York: Crossroad, 1992).
2. V. R. Mollenkott, *Speech, Silence, Action! The Cycle of Faith* (Nashville: Abingdon, 1980), 22.

finally moved to a pronounced radical feminist approach in her more recent work.

## Mollenkott's Egalitarian Moorings

In her first work, *Women, Men, and the Bible,* Mollenkott supports egalitarian tenets such as mutual submission in marriage, contending that God is not male but transcends human gender and arguing that the term "head" in Paul's writings denotes "source or origin," not a position of authority. Mollenkott notes that the church ought to follow Jesus' egalitarian example in the interpretation of Scripture and urges that the church implement "the pervasive and liberating theology of human unity in the spirit of God" evidenced in Jesus' ministry.[3]

In the revised edition of this work, Mollenkott states that she is committed to "human mutuality and equal partnership out of respect for God's image in us all."[4] She characterizes her own volume as an "easy-to-comprehend introduction to some of the most basic concerns of Christian feminism,"[5] her prime target being "Christian patriarchalism."[6] At the very outset, Mollenkott affirms the notion of "mutual submission,"[7] maintaining that "health and justice demand that submission must be mutual, not unilateral."[8] The Bible must be the central force and Jesus the major standard.[9] According to Mollenkott, extremists on either side argue for male or female superiority; the middle road is egalitarianism.

Mollenkott also takes up the question, "Is God masculine?" In doing so she contends that God is not male; the first and second persons of the Trinity are associated with both male and female. She claims that Jesus "pictured God as a woman" in the parable of the woman and the lost coin in Luke 15.[10] Consequently, Mollenkott advocates the use of inclusive language with reference to God and calls for freedom from gender-related stereotypes.

In 1978, Mollenkott cowrote a book with Letha Scanzoni titled *Is the Homosexual My Neighbor?* in order to assuage the fear that feminism might lead to the "homosexualization" of society.

In her 1980 work *Speech, Silence, Action!* Mollenkott contends forcefully that the Bible, rightly understood, teaches the liberating message of

---

3. V. R. Mollenkott, *Women, Men and the Bible* (Nashville: Abingdon, 1977), 99.
4. V. R. Mollenkott, *Women, Men and the Bible* (2nd ed.; Nashville: Abingdon, 1988 [1977]), vii; see the survey in M. A. Kassian, *The Feminist Mistake: The Radical Impact of Feminism on the Church and Culture* (Wheaton, IL: Crossway, 2005), 273–76.
5. Mollenkott, *Women, Men and the Bible* (2nd ed.), viii.
6. Ibid.
7. Ibid., 13–18.
8. Ibid., x.
9. Ibid., 1.
10. Ibid., 45.

egalitarian relationships. She explains that her esteem for the Bible derives from her Plymouth Brethren "fundamentalist" background. In this work Mollenkott seeks to make a "case for an all-inclusive, egalitarian, nondualistic, global Body of Christ—the single organism of the New Humanity," strongly opposing traditional readings of well-known gender passages: "We have had enough of that [proof-texting] in sexist plucking out of context such passages as Ephesians 5:22 (wifely submission) or 1 Timothy 2:12."[11] Mollenkott advocates a "holistic reading of the Bible" in its *whole-Bible* context which she believes teaches a prevailing liberating and nonrepressive message.

In 1983 Mollenkott published *The Divine Feminine: The Biblical Imagery of God as Female*, in which she sets forth biblical images of God, including a chapter titled "Christ as Female Pelican," or "the Mother Christ." She acknowledges that most of the biblical language about God is masculine but seeks to show that Scripture also uses a considerable amount of *female imagery* for God, which, she argues, is significant in a patriarchal culture. Mollenkott draws the implication that "if we truly believe that the Bible's intentions are all-inclusive—that redemption is intended for everyone—we will not want to continue practices that exclude certain listeners."[12]

---

**Fact Sheet 2: Virginia Ramey Mollenkott**

**Born:** 1932 in Philadelphia

**Education:** Doctorate, New York University

**Academic Position:** Professor Emeritus of English at William Paterson University in Wayne, NJ, where she taught for 44 years

**Religious Background:** Plymouth Brethren

**Major Works:** *The Divine Feminine* (1983); *Godding* (1987); *Omnigender* (2001)

**Type of Feminist:** Radical

**View of Jesus:** Jesus is our "Elder Brother"; humanity is corporately "Christed" into God-consciousness; erases gender boundaries

---

## Mollenkott's Radical Turn

In her subsequent writings Mollenkott turns increasingly radical. In her 1987 work *Godding: The Bible and Human Responsibility*, Mollenkott speaks of all people of faith being corporately "Christed" new humanity.[13] For Mollenkott, the human presence of God is located in *relationship* and

11. Mollenkott, *Speech, Silence, Action!*, 28.
12. V. R. Mollenkott, *The Divine Feminine: The Biblical Imagery of God as Female* (New York: Crossroad, 1983), 114.
13. See Kassian, *The Feminist Mistake*, chap. 16.

*caring.*[14] "Godding," then, is the making known of God's presence in mutual service, support, and caring.[15] The intention is for everyone to grow toward the recognition of God's image in everyone and everything and toward mutual respect.

In *Godding,* Mollenkott embraces monism, the metaphysical and theological view that all is one. She also embraces pantheism, the view that "God is all" and "all is God" and that God and nature are equivalent, as well as the notion of Self as God.[16] According to Mollenkott, "God is both 'other' and ourselves . . . more all-encompassing than we could image Her to be."[17] As in her previous works, Mollenkott's thought is motivated by an egalitarian agenda that seeks to do "justice to those people who were formerly excluded from the good basics of life."[18]

Mollenkott's radical turn continues with the publication of *Sensuous Spirituality: Out from Fundamentalism* in 1992, dedicated to her life partner Debra Lynn Morrison, whereby "sensuous" (in distinction from sensual) was used in the sense of "embodied" or "physical." Mollenkott writes:

> I speak and always have spoken in a lesbian voice; the feminism came much later than the lesbianism, signs of which were apparent in me by age four. . . . Although I have come to identify myself essentially as a spiritual being who is currently having embodied human experiences, those experiences have been authentically lesbian for as long as I can remember. (My heterosexual marriage was the attempt of a brainwashed fundamentalist to fit herself into the heteropatriarchal mold.)[19]

In this work Mollenkott describes how she was liberated from her fundamentalist understanding of total depravity and came to understand herself as "an innocent spiritual being," involving the study of hermeneutics, interpretation of dreams, journaling, Tarot cards, psychotherapy, and mystical experiences.[20] In the course of time, she came to understand herself, "like my Elder Brother, Jesus," as "a sinless Self traveling through eternity and temporarily having human experiences in a body know[n] as Virginia Ramey Mollenkott."[21] It was "the all-embracing Consciousness" that she calls God,

14. V. R. Mollenkott, *Godding: Human Responsibility and the Bible* (New York: Crossroad, 1987), 2–3.
15. Ibid., 4.
16. See Kassian, *Feminist Mistake,* 273–76.
17. Mollenkott, *Godding,* 4.
18. Ibid., 33.
19. Mollenkott, *Sensuous Spirituality,* 11–12.
20. Ibid., 16.
21. Ibid.

and that "consciousness is mine, and mine is Hers."[22] Mollenkott's earlier emphasis on Godding has now evolved even further to an eclectic mix aligning her with Eastern views of reincarnation and mysticism.

## Mollenkott's Claims

Mollenkott anticipates that some of her readers might think she had deserted Christianity in favor of a new metaphysic. She counters that she was "drawn back to the essence of what Jesus actually believed, lived, and taught" and that she had recovered the true meaning of Jesus' teaching in the original Aramaic, "a multivalent Middle Eastern language that does not draw sharp distinctions between inner qualities and external actions" but rather views the cosmos as "fluid and wholistic."[23] To illustrate, she quotes "one possible translation from the Aramaic" of the Lord's Prayer:

> O Birther! Father-Mother of the Cosmos,
> focus your light within us—make us useful:
> Create your reign of unity now—
> Your one desire then acts with ours,
> As in all light, so in all forms.
> Grant what we need each day in bread and insight.
> Loose the cords of mistakes binding us,
> As we release the strands we hold of others' guilt.
> Don't let surface things delude us,
> But free us from what holds us back.

"Gone," Mollenkott concludes, "are traditional Christianity's emphasis on sin, guilt, and retribution; instead, we are empowered toward co-creatorship, welcomed to continual renewal on a continuous Great Non-Judgment Day."[24]

Believing that she understands Jesus' true thinking better than traditional historical Christian interpretation and doctrine, Mollenkott substitutes her preferred view of the *world*, *God*, and *self* for the biblical view. Her self-understanding—that of an "innocent" spiritual being—likewise does not derive from scriptural exegesis but from her self-acknowledged quest to move out from fundamentalism.

Mollenkott's next major work continues her radical turn. Her 2001 book, *Omnigender: A Trans-Religious Approach*, represents an attempt to "move beyond the binary gender construct in order to set forth a new gender paradigm, which seeks to include and offer liberation to everyone

22. Ibid.
23. Ibid., 26.
24. Ibid., 27.

who has been oppressed by the old model."[25] Based on a "new literal" reading of Paul's statement that in Christ there is no male or female (Gal. 3:28), Mollenkott imagines and constructs an omnigendered society in which all gender distinctions are transcended, lesbianism is celebrated, and cross-dressing practiced.

In her advocacy of lesbianism and an omnigendered society, Mollenkott cites D. S. Herrstrom, who contends that "Jesus inhabits a shape-shifting universe, where above and below merge, the human and the natural world flow into each other, worlds without limits where any transformation is possible."[26] To cross a boundary is to erase it, Mollenkott contends. *Omnigender* thus represents Mollenkott's effort to erase gender boundaries and to imagine a society where this had been done.

## Evaluation

Like Mary Daly and other radical feminists, Mollenkott began in a more conservative vein and moved gradually to a radical viewpoint, illustrating the slippery slope of feminism that tends toward increasing radicalization. It is not uncommon for feminist thinkers to start out trying to reform the church, historic Christianity, and biblical interpretation from within. Eventually, however, it becomes obvious that a certain primacy in authority and responsibility continues to be invested in men. This proves unacceptable to the radical ideology of feminism.

In *Women, Men, and the Bible* Mollenkott espouses several doubtful egalitarian views, such as the notion of mutual submission or the understanding of "head" as "source or origin."[27] Also, while aptly noting that God is not male but transcends human gender, she claims that Jesus pictured God as a woman in the parable of the woman and the lost coin in Luke 15. However, while the woman in the parable may manifest the divine characteristic of perseverance in seeking that which was lost, it is an overstatement and theologically inaccurate to say that Jesus pictured God as a woman.

Throughout the book Mollenkott all but assumes that Jesus interpreted the Scriptures in an egalitarian manner. However, she does not adequately demonstrate the truthfulness of this assumption. She urges the church to

---

25. V. R. Mollenkott, *Omnigender: A Trans-Religious Approach* (Cleveland, OH: Pilgrim Press, 2001), vii.

26. D. S. Herrstrom, "The Book of Unknowing: Ranging the Landscape" (unpublished manuscript, 1999), 83.

27. See, e.g., with regard to mutual submission, W. Grudem, "The Myth of 'Mutual Submission,'" *CBMW News* 1, no. 4 (October 1996): 1, 3–4; and A. J. Köstenberger, *God, Marriage, and Family: Rebuilding the Biblical Foundation* (Wheaton, IL: Crossway, 2004), 362, n. 23 (with further bibliographic references). With regard to "head," see A. J. Köstenberger, "Head," in *The New Interpreter's Dictionary of the Bible*, vol. 2, *D–H* (ed. K. D. Sakenfeld; Nashville: Abingdon, 2007), 754–55.

pursue "human unity" but does consider the possibility that such unity may not be incompatible with differences in gender roles.

In *Speech, Silence, Action!* she urges a holistic reading of the Bible—by which she means an egalitarian reading—and charges those who point to passages in Scripture that appear to limit the appropriate ministry of women, such as 1 Timothy 2:12, or who do not interpret Ephesians 5:21–22 in terms of mutual submission, with proof-texting. However, it can be countered that it is actually those who recognize that these are some passages that affirm the equality of women and others that restrict women's ministry who engage in a whole-Bible reading of Scripture. Mollenkott favors only those passages that are amenable to her egalitarian viewpoint.

Her claim that a holistic reading of Scripture means uncovering its liberating and nonrepressive message, likewise, does not follow. If the Creator built an authority structure into the way in which he ordered the universe, and this is taught in the Bible, is this message necessarily repressive? Such a position assumes a negative view of authority. Yet God, at least, exercises authority in a benevolent manner, and there seems to be no reason to exclude the possibility that his vice-regents on earth are called to exemplify a similar use of authority, both in the original unfallen state and in their restored relationships in Christ.

A response should also be made to Mollenkott's claim that anyone who affirms gender role distinctions excludes certain listeners. It does not follow from the fact that redemption is offered to everyone that no gender distinctions apply to ministries and offices in the church. What is more, those who believe that the pastorate is open only to men on the basis of passages such as 1 Timothy 2:12 or 1 Timothy 3:2 do not exclude women from redemption or even from participation in the life of the church, but only from authoritative offices. Mollenkott's charge here is akin to the serpent's insinuation that God did not want the first couple to eat from *any* tree in the garden when God's prohibition, in fact, pertained to one tree only.

Mollenkott's pursuit of an omnigendered society in her more recent work likewise rests on doubtful scriptural foundations. In fact, it is surprising that Mollenkott continues to invoke Scripture to support her views in her more recent work, since she has clearly abandoned the Bible as authoritative in any meaningful sense. Certainly Mollenkott may choose to reject Scripture and construe an alternative system. Demonstrably, however, Mollenkott's approach, including her advocacy of lesbianism, does not square with a responsible reading of the author's intended meaning of Scripture and is not acceptable as an adequate description of reality.

# 5

# DAPHNE HAMPSON:
# AFTER CHRISTIANITY, WHAT?

*Indeed it was only in my late teens that I discovered that some people thought that Jesus was God! . . . I had not come across that and I was amazed and horrifed [sic]. I could not believe that. At the same time I was told . . . that Jesus had taken my sins. I could no more deal with that one! That Jesus was a very fine human being who loved God—that might be the case—but I do not see how people can think more than that.*

—Daphne Hampson, "BISFT Interview" (1998)[1]

**Daphne Hampson** is a prominent radical feminist in Britain. Hampson started her career as a historian in Oxford, England. She completed a Harvard doctorate in systematic theology and in 1977 assumed a post as lecturer in systematic theology at the University of Saint Andrews, Scotland. Hampson took a leading part in the campaign to allow women to be ordained to the priesthood in the Anglican Church. She now considers herself a "post-Christian feminist" (see, for example, her work *After Christianity*, published in 1996) and holds that Christianity and feminism are incompatible and that Christianity is a mere myth.[2]

1. "BISFT Interview with Dr. Daphne Hampson," *Feminist Theology* 17 (1998): 49–50.
2. Ibid., 39.

Convinced that feminism represents the death-knell of Christianity as a viable religious option,[3] Hampson is seeking for new ways to conceptualize God that are in continuity with the Western tradition. Only a small fraction of Hampson's writings is concerned with Jesus. This may be explained by the fact that as a post-Christian radical feminist, Hampson is looking for alternate ways to construct a worldview and religion that are in keeping with radical feminist beliefs.

---

### Fact Sheet 3: Margaret Daphne Hampson

**Born:** 1944 in Croydon, England

**Education:** D.Phil. in modern history, Oxford University (1974); Th.D. in Systematic Theology, Harvard University (1983)

**Academic Position:** Professor Emerita in Systematic Theology at the University of St. Andrews

**Religious Background:** Anglican

**Major Works:** *Theology and Feminism* (1990); *After Christianity* (1996)

**Type of Feminist:** Radical

**View of Jesus:** Jesus is not God; Jesus did not die for our sins; Christianity is a myth

---

## A Search for Alternate Paradigms

In an intriguing critique of the work of Elisabeth Schüssler Fiorenza, whose background is Roman Catholic, and Phyllis Trible, an Old Testament scholar whose roots are in the Southern Baptist movement, Hampson writes that the problem with their approaches is that both still seek to place themselves within "the trajectory of biblical religion" and "to close the gap between past and present."[4] Hampson lodges a fundamental criticism against the approaches of both of these eminent reformist feminist scholars:

> Why, unless one is a Christian, should one be wanting to undertake such a re-reading? Indeed, in Trible's case, unless one is a conservative Christian who believes the text to be the word of God? If one is a fundamentalist Christian who believes the text to be inspired, then one sees why the text is alone to be interpreted in terms of the text. But if one is not fundamentalist (and not simply working as a literary critic) then there are questions which need to be brought to the text. What authority could, for example, the text of the creation story possibly have post-Darwin?[5]

Once one accepts some form of Scripture's authority, Hampson contends, one assumes that Christianity in some sense is true. If a basically critical stance

---

3. D. Hampson, *Theology and Feminism* (Oxford: Blackwell, 1990), 1.
4. "BISFT Interview," 32–41; the quotes are from pp. 35 and 37.
5. Ibid., 39.

toward Scripture is adopted, such an assumption is no longer warranted. As a result, Hampson adopts what she calls a "post-Christian position."[6]

In her search for suitable paradigms, Hampson posits the "paradigm of mutual empowerment" as a basis for constructing her religion.[7] "Can this paradigm be found in the Judeo-Christian tradition?" Hampson asks. At the very outset, she rejects the Trinity as a possible candidate, since it contains an element of hierarchy and dependence, with the Son submitting to and depending on the Father.

Jesus' life, too, according to Hampson, did not model a paradigm of mutual empowerment. Jesus was *not* a feminist, and there is "no evidence that the equality of women was even an issue in the society in which he lived."[8] Jesus did not challenge the secondary role women played in Jewish religion, and he accepted the prevailing male and female roles in his society. He also referred to God as his Father.

To be sure, perhaps against the mores of his day, he permitted a woman to sit and learn at his feet, but we "have no picture of Jesus sitting at a woman's feet, learning from her."[9] Jesus (and Paul) may have been personally kind to women, even ahead of their time, but this did not make them feminists. For this reason God, as traditionally conceived, and Jesus, seen as God or as symbolic of God, were unusable as sources for the feminist paradigm of mutual empowerment.

## Feminism vs. Christianity

According to Hampson, women "have no use for a God who condescends to be with them in their weakness. Paternalism fits ill with feminism."[10] She claims that women want to be whole, self-directed, free, and interdependent with others. They want a God who does not override their will and who is non-dominative.[11] Hampson calls for "a model of the self as being related in its very being to God," whereby God does not stand over us as one "who could potentially dominate us, or who could suggest an action which to carry out would be for us to act heteronomously."[12] She expresses the need for a utopian world in which power is not exercised, in which the few do not coerce the many or one sex does not dominate the other—a world in which service and self-giving, which are unproductive for the one who serves and

---

6. Ibid., 41; D. Hampson, *After Christianity* (Valley Forge, PA: Trinity Press International, 1996).
7. D. Hampson, "On Power and Gender," *Modern Theology* 4/3 (1988): 234–50.
8. Ibid., 247.
9. Ibid.
10. Ibid., 248.
11. Ibid.
12. Ibid.

gives, are reduced to a minimum.[13] Feminism, she says, is the "last great hope" for our world.

Clearly, Hampson presents a stirring vision but one that, as Hampson herself states, is at variance with the biblical message regarding the nature of God, Jesus, and many other facets of scriptural teaching. In fact, the only reason Hampson still refers to Christianity is to position her vision of feminism against it. In essence, she claims that feminism is whatever Christianity is *not*.

Feminism is self-actualizing rather than self-giving. It is assertive of its independence and autonomy rather than service-oriented, since service gives up self while feminism is all about reclaiming power over self. Feminism is strong rather than weak and self-sufficient rather than dependent.

Remarkably, her radical egalitarianism extends even to God, the Creator. In order for Hampson's vision of feminism to be realized, God must be one of us. He must be like us, for any form of power is excluded. There is also no need for the cross, for Hampson denies any need for women to come to God in dependence, weakness, or need. Everything that the cross of Jesus Christ represents—service, self-sacrifice, loving self-denial—is excluded from Hampson's feminist vision.

In her book *Theology and Feminism* (1990), Hampson develops some of these ideas further. She observes that Christian feminists seek to counterbalance the male orientation of Christianity (e.g., God as Father, Jesus as Son) by locating or positing female figures or feminine motifs "within what is a deeply masculine religion."[14] Hampson states that she has never been a Christian feminist, because Christianity is not truly egalitarian at its core.[15] She also rejects efforts at compensation by some who say that while Jesus was incarnated as a male, the Spirit should be conceived as female.

Similar to Mary Daly's view of Jesus, Hampson has harsh words for what she called the recent "fixation" on Mary by some feminists. She challenges the actuality of the virgin birth and claims that there is no basis for elevating Mary along the lines of a high Mariology. Mary was in no way equivalent to the male Christ, and biblical religion is not about Mary but about Christ. What is more, Mary was not a role model feminists today could aspire to emulate, for "she conforms to the masculinist construction of femininity."[16] Mary's major role was that of a mother giving birth to a

13. Ibid., 248–49.
14. D. Hampson, *Theology and Feminism*, 71; see Mollenkott's "female pelican" example above.
15. Ibid., 71.
16. Ibid., 74.

male child, and her significance was solely construed in relation to the one to whom she gave birth, Jesus.

## To Remember Her or Not to Remember Her?

In an article published in a 1998 issue of *Feminist Theology*, provocatively titled "On Not Remembering Her," Hampson goes head-to-head with Elisabeth Schüssler Fiorenza's hermeneutical program set forth in her landmark volume *In Memory of Her*. In a fascinating piece of interaction among feminists who agree on their underlying feminism but differ with regard to methodology, Hampson, in essence, charges that Fiorenza did not go far enough in her interpretation of Jesus and Scripture.[17]

Fiorenza claimed that today's women ought to identify with past women in their struggles against male oppression and domination, foremost with female characters in Scripture. But why, Hampson challenges, should any woman today identify with these particular women? To do so would presuppose some sort of privileged status of Scripture in general and a positive assessment of the truth of Christianity in particular. Hampson contends that the truth of Christianity must not be assumed. In fact, she states, Christianity is *not* true; it is a mere myth. It follows that feminists, at least radical feminists, have no place for Scripture or Christ. Their quest for fulfillment must proceed apart from these.

Hampson's fundamental critique of Fiorenza and her reformist feminist approach is well illustrated here:

> Christianity, I pointed out, has been assumed: it is because one is a Christian that one has reason to look to this community. But for myself the question of the truth of Christianity can in no way be assumed. I would argue that one needed to go a step back behind the starting point of *In Memory of Her* to decide whether one had reason to commence on this project. Is Jesus lord, king, messiah? Jesus was, from the start, understood in terms of his uniqueness—if only through saying of this man, as was said of none other, that God raised him. . . . But is Christianity true? Can there have been a unique person, differently related to God than are all other persons? Indeed can there have been a resurrection when that would represent a breaking of the laws of nature? There are not resurrections of which we know—so that this resurrection should simply be one of the category of "resurrections" and hence unremarkable. Thus not only the question of the possibility of Christianity for feminists, but the question of the truth of Christianity, has made its entrance again through the backdoor. It too is not to be evaded. One cannot simply remain with the community.[18]

17. See also the dialogue between D. Hampson and R. R. Ruether, "Is there a place for feminists in the Christian Church?" *New Blackfriars* 68 (1987): 7–24, where Hampson argued that in feminism "Christianity has met a challenge to which it cannot accommodate itself."
18. D. Hampson, "On Not Remembering Her," *Theology* 19 (1998): 72–73.

Hampson concludes that the strategy of reinterpretation proposed by reformist feminists falls short. Rather than associate with victimized women in the past, women must live in the present:

> We need women with a new confidence, willing to build something new which has not been on the scene before. Women have the opportunity to be a new kind of person, a person who is not cowed or subordinate, but who takes her place as an equal and who refuses to have anything to do with a male ideology such as Christianity in which she must needs be secondary. I may be religious, and I may be western. But I need not be Christian, seeking my identity in a past religious community and its scriptures.[19]

## Christianity as Myth

Further insight into Hampson's thought is provided by a 1998 interview with Julie Clague[20] in which Hampson says that she is not a Christian because she believes Christianity is a mere myth, and she cannot "conform to the kind of view of 'woman' that there is within this myth."[21] According to Hampson, feminism had brought about a revolution in the way in which women were conceived, and there must be no return to a society in which women were assigned a place to which they must conform.[22]

After working for the ordination of women in the Anglican Church, Hampson takes a feminist "leap into maturity" in the conviction that one can be a religious and spiritual person without believing in Christian doctrine.[23] In her interview with Julie Clague, Hampson says that in her late teens she discovered that some people think Jesus is God. She was "amazed and horrifed [sic]," because she found this completely unbelievable.[24] At the same time, she was told that Jesus had died for her sins. She could not accept this either. At the most, Jesus "was a very fine human being who loved God"[25]—no more. As for the Bible, Hampson regards it as "just part of human literature in which people had recorded their experience and awareness of God." There is no way in which she would consider the Bible inspired in a way that other literature was not.[26]

Hampson believes that "we need to be deeply in tune with who we most truly are." We must come home to ourselves so as to find ourselves and realize who we are meant to be. Hampson defines the problem with Christianity as

19. Ibid., 83.
20. D. Hampson, "BISFT Interview," 39–57.
21. Ibid., 39.
22. Ibid., 43.
23. Ibid., 50.
24. Ibid., 49.
25. Ibid.
26. Ibid., 50.

its being a religion of revelation with a transcendent God who is other than humankind, and, by definition, it holds that there has been a revelation in a past period of human history.[27] This kind of heteronomy (subjection to the rule of another) is impossible for Hampson: "I have got to see myself, in my relation to others, as at the centre of my world . . . a law unto myself . . . and not be a slave to anything which is outside myself."[28]

### Hampson's Rejection of Christianity

"Christianity is a Father-Son religion [and as such] has no place for independent, adult women who are self-directing people."[29] Why would a woman want to see herself as "in Christ"? Why should she relate to God through someone else?[30] For her, therefore, Christianity is most profoundly at odds with the central tenets of feminism, so being a "Christian feminist" is an improper conception of one's identity. Hampson's view of God, Jesus, and the Bible places her outside the church and outside Christianity. Outside the Christian faith is a place she desires for herself, and she sees it as the only place any truly radical feminist woman can legitimately occupy.

With this, Hampson rejects Christianity as something impossible for feminists to embrace. She arrived at this conclusion not by the exegesis of specific passages of Scripture but by first examining the tenets of Christianity *in light of her feminist presuppositions* and finding Christianity wanting. Hampson in no way allowed herself to be engaged by Scripture. Nor did she permit herself any attempt at "reforming" the message of Scripture by employing something such as a "hermeneutic of suspicion." She did not accept the hermeneutical program of reformist feminists—the critique of the "patriarchal bias" of Scripture. In this Hampson represents an uncompromising, radical form of feminism.

### Evaluation

Like the other radical feminists discussed here, Hampson's hermeneutic is based on rejection of Scripture as inextricably patriarchal and of Christianity as untrue. From this rejection follows Hampson's quest for alternate approaches to theology suitable for feminists seeking to reshape a world more in keeping with their ideals. Her paradigm of mutual empowerment and her rejection of Scripture and Christianity set her apart from reformist and evangelical feminist thinkers.

27. Ibid., 51.
28. Ibid.
29. Ibid., 54.
30. Ibid., 55.

Hampson's paradigm of mutual empowerment seems to find a measure of support in Scripture. The husband, while occupying a place of authority, is called to love his wife sacrificially as Christ loved the church and to nurture her both physically and spiritually, empowering her to live out her God-ordained role (Eph. 5:25–29). Yet, at the same time, the woman is called to submit to her husband in everything as the church submits to Christ (Eph. 5:22–23) and to be his helper in the work God has called him to do, empowering him for fulfilling the role God has assigned to him as leader. This shows that sacrificial love and mutual empowerment coexist with, and are set in the larger framework of, a scriptural paradigm of authority and submission.

Hampson's aversion to hierarchy and dependence leads her to unduly discard the balance of the biblical teaching on the subject. Therefore, her alternate paradigm is reductionistic when judged in the light of the entirety of the Bible's teaching. To her credit, Hampson herself recognizes that her paradigm of mutual empowerment is found neither in the Trinity nor in the life of Jesus. Yet Scripture does present the persons of the Trinity as coexisting and as working in tandem in our world, most notably in the plan of redemption, yet not in a context of relationships that are devoid of all authority and submission.

In contrast to the vast majority of reformist feminists and virtually all evangelical feminists, Hampson acknowledges that Jesus was not a feminist. Rather than engage in a revisionist reading of the biblical evidence, she is able to discern that the biblical portrayal of Jesus, while showing him as reaching out to women, does not have him challenge the prevailing male and female roles in society. In this she is to be commended for her intellectual clarity.

Of course, the notion that Jesus affirmed male leadership is offensive only to those who hold to feminism as a foundational tenet. Hampson's reading of the biblical evidence is therefore defensible; her rejection of the biblical portrayal of Jesus is required only for those who start with a feminist viewpoint.

Another point of concern is Hampson's rejection of the biblical values of service and self-sacrifice, epitomized in Jesus' assumption of humanity in the incarnation and in his substitutionary sacrifice at the cross. For Hampson, the ideal of strong, independent individuals excludes any notion of weakness or dependence on others, and service and self-giving are perceived as unproductive. As much as this is Hampson's ideal for humanity, such a paradigm runs counter to most systems of morality, which affirm the value of one person helping another and of loving one's fellow human beings. All that can be said is that Hampson is intellectually rigorous in following her rejection of biblical Christianity to its logical conclusion; but it is questionable whether her utopian world is superior to the morality and value system taught in Scripture. Of course, it must be acknowledged here once again that Christians do not always live in accordance with the high ethical standards upheld by the biblical teaching, and this is regrettable.

Her radical aversion to any form of authority leads her beyond rejecting any form of submission and authority in the human realm to rejecting even any form of submission to God, since he might potentially dominate us or suggest actions that we should carry out. So, in Hampson's case, feminism has inexorably led not merely to a rejection of biblical theology, soteriology, and morality but ultimately to atheism, a world without God, in which strong, interdependent individuals owe allegiance or submission to no one but themselves.

Though some at first may find Hampson's radicalism attractive in its intellectual rigor and consistency, it is doubtful that her feminist utopia represents an improvement. Authority need not be construed as an inevitably negative concept. In her rejection of all forms of authority, Hampson fails to come to terms with the basic reality of her own existence as a creature. If God is the Creator of all things, it would be appropriate for him as Creator to exercise authority over his creation. And if God is good, as Scripture teaches, and if all his purposes for humanity are benevolent, including the structure he has set for us to live in, it is beneficial for us to accept his plan for male-female relationships rather than to substitute our own.

Hampson indicates that she has no place for Jesus Christ in her theological system. How can it be otherwise for Hampson, who holds the view that she is "a law unto herself"? She demonstrates that ultimately biblical Christianity and feminism cannot coexist. In stark opposition to reformist and evangelical feminist approaches to Scripture, Hampson accurately discerns that "Christian feminist" is a contradiction in terms.

Yet every one of Hampson's beliefs regarding Jesus is itself open to question. Many have pointed to Jesus' performance of numerous miracles, the fulfillment of countless scriptural prophecies in Jesus' life and ministry, the fact that the rapid rise of early Christianity is best explained by the fact that Jesus actually rose from the dead, and the presence of a plethora of eyewitnesses who could have countered the apostles' account of events surrounding Jesus in their early preaching. None of this removes the need for faith in the biblical testimony, but Christians do have a proper basis for belief in the scriptural record, and radical feminists such as Hampson ignore Jesus to their eternal peril.

While someone who adheres to historic biblical Christianity will obviously not agree with Hampson's feminist vision and her view of Christianity as a myth, she is to be commended for the consistency with which she holds and develops her approach and for her clear understanding of Christian doctrine and tenets. If Christianity were indeed a myth, there is no reason why anyone should embrace the view of women within that myth. Despite this, Hampson continues to engage Christianity in her work.

Hampson's exceptional clarity of thought also discerns that Christianity and Scripture do contain a clear emphasis on male authority. Her condemnation of any approaches that seek to diminish the androcentric bias of Scripture by uncovering feminine images for God or female role models in Scripture is also consistent from within her frame of reference. Her writings also helpfully expose the weakness of other positions, such as evangelical feminism and aspects of reformist feminism, that strenuously work to find the feminist viewpoint validated in Scripture.

# JESUS AND REFORMIST FEMINISM

*If Historical-Jesus discourses are to position themselves not in the spaces of domination but in the critical alternative spaces of emancipation, . . . they need to shift their theoretical focus and frame of reference away from the Historical-Jesus, the exceptional man and charismatic leader, to the emancipatory Divine Wisdom movement of which he was a part and whose values and visions decisively shaped him.*

—Elisabeth Schüssler Fiorenza,
*Jesus and the Politics of Interpretation* (2000)[1]

Who do reformist feminists say that Jesus is? The major difference between radical and reformist feminist scholars is that the former reject the Bible and the Judeo-Christian tradition wholesale, whereas the latter opt to stay within the Christian tradition and seek to reform it from within. Such reformist efforts include the use of gender-inclusive language, the reinterpretation of biblical texts, and various other means. Reformist feminists do *not* consider Scripture to be inerrant or authoritative, though they do use it in their theological formulation and reflection.[2]

Carolyn Osiek proposes a division of reformist feminism into two groups: *revisionists*, theorists who endeavor to remove the underlying patriarchal bias of biblical texts; and *liberationists*, political activists emphasizing women's need for justice and liberation from oppression and using the biblical text

---

1. E. S. Fiorenza, *Jesus and the Politics of Interpretation* (New York; London: Continuum, 2000), 20–21.
2. In reading the following chapters on reformist feminism in particular, it will be helpful to keep in mind the discussion on the various general and special hermeneutical issues in Appendix 2.

61

as a springboard for such teaching.[3] Osiek deals also with a third group she calls "loyalists," more commonly known as egalitarians or biblical/evangelical feminists. (In this book, evangelical feminism is discussed separately because of its claim that Scripture is inerrant and authoritative.)

Table 6.1: Types of Reformist Feminism

| Type of Reformist Feminism | Explanation |
| --- | --- |
| Revisionists | Theorists who seek to remove "patriarchal bias" of biblical texts |
| Liberationists | Political activists seeking justice and liberation for women |

Reformist feminists differ with regard to the specific methodologies they employ. As Margaret Farley states, "There is pluralism within feminism as in any other rich and comprehensive interpretation of humanity and the world."[4] She lists, however, as shared principles the notions of equality, equitable sharing, and mutuality. Also, while methods differ, feminists do share in common the conviction that the text should be read from their feminist perspective and that traditional interpretation is patriarchal and in need of revision. Dorothy Sakenfeld writes:

Recognizing the patriarchy of biblical materials, Christian feminists approach the text with at least three different emphases:

(1) Looking to texts about women to counteract famous texts used "against" women.
(2) Looking to the Bible generally (not particularly to texts about women) for a theological perspective offering a critique of patriarchy (some may call this a "liberation perspective").
(3) Looking to texts about women to learn from the intersection of history and stories of ancient and modern women living in patriarchal cultures.

. . . Feminist interpretation moves back and forth among these options.[5]

This hermeneutical program involves the "decoding" of a biblical text, i.e., removing the patriarchal bias inherent in Scripture, and a subsequent "recoding" in keeping with a feminist outlook. Often reformist feminists

3. C. Osiek, "The Feminist and the Bible: Hermeneutical Alternatives," in *Feminist Perspectives on Biblical Scholarship*, ed. A. Y. Collins (Chico, CA: Scholars Press, 1985), 93–105.
4. M. A. Farley, "Feminist Consciousness and the Interpretation of Scripture," in *Feminist Interpretation of the Bible*, ed. L. M. Russell (Philadelphia: Westminster, 1985), 44.
5. K. D. Sakenfeld, "Feminist Uses of Biblical Materials," in *Feminist Interpretation of the Bible*, ed. L. M. Russell (Philadelphia: Westminster, 1985), 56.

claim to use historical criticism, while at other times they employ a form of literary criticism of the Bible. Other methods in their hermeneutical program include form and genre criticism, text linguistics, structuralism, literary criticism, reader-response criticism, semiotics, depth psychology, and social-historical approaches.[6]

As we will see, Letty Russell believes Jesus provided a unique revelation of true personhood. According to Russell, Jesus was a feminist who considered men and women to be equal.

Rosemary Radford Ruether views Jesus as a mere man, a religious seeker and "paradigmatic liberator." At the same time, Ruether struggles with the question of how a male Savior could save women.

Elisabeth Schüssler Fiorenza suggests Jesus was Sophia's prophet who launched a renewal movement within Judaism and established a "discipleship of equals."[7] Kathleen Corley and others critiqued Fiorenza's work, showing that her notion of Jesus establishing a "discipleship of equals" is itself a feminist myth of Christian origins.

Amy-Jill Levine notes that Judaism was more diverse and the "Jesus movement" less egalitarian than Fiorenza claims. All of these feminists built on early precursors and developed more complex and sophisticated systems of feminist interpretation.

6. L. Schottrott, S. Schroer, and M.-T. Wacker, eds., *Feminist Interpretation: The Bible in Women's Perspective* (Minneapolis: Augsburg Fortress, 1998), 63–82.
7. Cf. J. Cottrell, *Feminism and the Bible: An Introduction to Feminism for Christians* (Joplin, MO: College Press, 1992), chaps. 5 and 6, who likewise focuses on Russell, Ruether, and Fiorenza in his treatment of what he calls "liberal Christian feminism."

# 6

## LETTY RUSSELL:
## LIBERATED TO BECOME HUMAN

*Christian women can see in Jesus a unique revelation of true person-hood: One who helped both men and women to understand their own total personhood. . . . In his own life he was a "feminist" in the sense that he considered men and women equal; equal in their need to be helped, and equal in their need to be pointed toward the new future of God's Kingdom.*

—Letty Russell, *Human Liberation
in a Feminist Perspective* (1974)[1]

**Contrary to** radical feminism, reformist feminist biblical interpretation uses Scripture as a sourcebook for theology and endeavors to redeem "us-able" elements from the Bible's portrayal of women for its construction of feminist thought. This characteristic can be seen clearly in the work of one early notable representative of Reformist feminism in the United States, Letty Russell.

Letty Russell was born in 1929 in Westfield, New Jersey. After studying biblical history at Wellesley College, she attended Harvard Divinity School, where she graduated in 1958. Not only was she one of the first women to

1. L. M. Russell, *Human Liberation in a Feminist Perspective: A Theology* (Philadelphia: Westminster, 1974), 138.

attend Harvard Divinity School, Russell was also one of the first women to
be ordained to the ministry of Word and sacrament in the United Presbyterian Church (USA), in 1958. Russell's ministry focused on the East Harlem
Protestant Parish where she worked mostly with an African-American and
Hispanic congregation. Her parish ministry proved to be an important
influence in shaping her feminist theology. After earning a doctoral degree
from Union Theological Seminary in New York in 1969, Russell was appointed professor of theology at Yale University, where she taught from
1974 until 2001.

---

**Fact Sheet 4: Letty Mandeville Russell**

**Born:** 1929 in Westfield, New Jersey
**Died:** July 16, 2007
**Education:** B.A. in biblical history and philosophy, Wellesley College (1951); S.T.B. in
   theology and ethics, Harvard Divinity School (1958); Th.D. in mission theology and
   ecumenics, Union Theological Seminary, New York (1969)
**Academic Position:** Professor of Theology at Yale University (1974–2001)
**Religious Background:** Presbyterian
**Major Works:** *Human Liberation in a Feminist Perspective* (1974); *Becoming Human*
   (1982); *Feminist Interpretation of the Bible* (1985)
**Type of Feminist:** Reformist
**View of Jesus:** Jesus is a unique revelation of true personhood; a "feminist" who con-
   sidered men and women to be equal

---

As a professor at Yale, Russell's was an influential voice that wrestled
with the hermeneutical challenges that reformist feminists faced, including
the issue of Jesus and women. She also served on the Faith and Order Commission of the World Council of Churches and on the National Council of
Churches of the USA. Russell wrote over one hundred articles and books.
In 1970 she married Johannes Hoekendijk, a professor at Union Seminary,
who died in 1975. After her retirement from Yale in 2001, Russell began
to identify herself openly as a lesbian. She lived in Connecticut with her
partner until her death in July 2007.

### Feminist Liberation Theology

Russell's first major work, *Human Liberation in a Feminist Perspective: A
Theology*, appeared in 1974. The purpose of this work was that of "relating
the experience of both oppression and liberation to the Tradition of Jesus
Christ."[2] She holds out a vision of a "truly androgynous world" where

---

2. Ibid., 185.

"men and women are equal and each can express his or her life style in a variety of ways."[3]

At the outset, Russell notes that women, in their search for liberation, are "rejecting oppressive and sexist religious traditions that declare that they are socially, ecclesiastically, and personally inferior because of their sex."[4] Her goal is to establish the political, economic, and social equality of the sexes. She defines liberation theology as a concern with "the liberation of all people to become full participants in human society."[5]

In her search for "usable history," she finds scriptural support for her feminist quest in Jesus' reference to preaching the gospel to the poor in Luke 4:18. According to Russell, Jesus constituted a "breakthrough"—he treated women as "full persons."[6] In her treatment of "usable language," she opposes generic "he" as "generic nonsense" and locates female images for God and Jesus in Scripture.[7]

Russell also devotes chapters to salvation and conscientization and to incarnation and humanization. Jesus *was* a feminist, she claims, in the sense that he considered men and women equal[8] and taught servanthood, not subordination.[9] Russell approvingly cites Harvey Cox, who writes, "We should not invest monogamy with the sacred significance of being the only legitimate Christian or human form of familial structure."[10] She contends that new experimental relationships may "help men and women to find alternative ways of lasting relationships of full personhood," relationships that are driven by "a deep regard for the partner as a person and subject."[11]

Russell's emphasis on feminism as a quest for attaining women's full humanity found fuller expression in her 1982 work *Becoming Human*. This was essentially a popular anthropology or doctrine of humanity from a feminist perspective.

In a chapter titled "Not Quite Human" Russell discusses Jesus' interaction with the Samaritan woman in John 4:1–42. Russell observes that Jesus related to the woman as a full human being, calling her to a "new history" as one who had a task in her community and full participation in a new future.[12] She advocates viewing life as "a rainbow of partnerships" rather

---

3. Ibid., 183.
4. Ibid., 18–19.
5. Ibid., 20.
6. Ibid., 87, citing Matt. 11:2–6; John 4:7–30; Luke 8:1–3; 24:1–11.
7. Ibid., 97–102.
8. Ibid., 138.
9. Ibid., 140–42.
10. Ibid., 152.
11. Ibid.
12. L. M. Russell, *Becoming Human* (Philadelphia: Westminster, 1982), 25.

than as a pyramid of domination.[13] God's presence in Christ as our neighbor meant that "every person has become our partner."[14]

Along the way, Russell redefines christology, soteriology (the doctrine of salvation), and hamartiology (the doctrine of sin). For her, Philippians 2 demonstrated that Jesus was willing to become less than human, so God exalted him to become more than human.[15] Salvation means freedom not so much from sin as from (male) oppression and freedom to be human, which Russell defines as wholeness, *shalom*, and divine-human and human-human partnership.

### Russell's Liberation of Scripture

Perhaps Russell's most significant hermeneutical contribution is in the edited volume *Feminist Interpretation of the Bible* (1985), a work focusing primarily on literary approaches to Scripture. Here Russell claims that Scripture has been held captive by patriarchal, sexist interpretation, or as she put it, "one-sided white, middle-class, male interpretation," and is in need of liberation,[16] Russell claims:

> [Scripture] needs liberation from abstract, doctrinal interpretations that remove the biblical narrative from its concrete social and political context in order to change it into timeless truth. . . . Feminist and liberation theologians [read] the Bible from the perspective of the oppressed, [and] they note the bias in all biblical interpretation and call for clear advocacy of those who are in the greatest need of God's mercy and help: the dominated victims of society.[17]

Rather than rejecting Scripture outright because of its patriarchal perspective, Russell continues to look to the Bible for its general message of liberation, citing the story of Israel's redemption from slavery in Egypt as well as God's liberative action in the person of Jesus Christ.[18] Russell asks, "How can feminists use the Bible, if at all? What approach to the Bible is appropriate for feminists who locate themselves within the Christian community? How does the Bible serve as a resource for Christian feminists?"[19] Liberation is Russell's interpretive key in her reading of Scripture. While she does not reject the Bible entirely as a source of her theology, she does reject many of its teachings as well as its overall patriarchal cultural context.

13. Ibid., 29.
14. Ibid., 45, citing Karl Barth.
15. Ibid., 52.
16. L. M. Russell, ed., *Feminist Interpretation of the Bible* (Philadelphia: Westminster, 1985), 12.
17. Ibid.
18. Ibid., 17.
19. Ibid., 11, citing Katharine Sakenfeld.

One important aspect of this kind of feminist interpretation is the use of inclusive language and interpretation, by which the canon is consequently changed and its authority weakened. *The Feminist Interpretation of the Bible*, therefore, is an exercise in the inclusive interpretation of the Bible for the purpose of affirming women "as fully human partners with men, sharing in the image of God."[20]

The roots of the book were found in the Liberation Theology Working Group of the American Academy of Religion (AAR) and the Society of Biblical Literature (SBL). Russell chronicles the history of feminist hermeneutical reflection over the course of several years of these meetings. At the 1980 meeting, women were reminded that Elizabeth Cady Stanton in *The Woman's Bible* identified the Bible itself as the major culprit in the oppression of women owing to its patriarchal orientation and use by others.

The major topic of discussion at the 1981 Dallas meeting was the proper role of Scripture in feminist reflection. At the 1982 New York SBL meeting, the discussion turned to the feminist understanding of biblical authority and canon with the conclusion that the Bible does not function as the Word of God if it "contributes to the continuation of racism, sexism, and classism."[21]

According to Russell, "The Word of God is not identical with the biblical text."[22] Russell contends, "The story of these texts is *experienced as God's Word* when it is heard in communities of faith and struggle as a witness to God's love for the world" by the guidance of the Holy Spirit.[23] We see here a crucial shift from authority inherent in the biblical texts themselves to authority being vested in a person's experience. This emphasis on the role of experience and community became a bedrock of feminist hermeneutics.

Russell claims that "liberation is an ongoing process expressed in the already/not yet dynamic of God's action of New Creation" and that the "word is already liberated as it witnesses to God's liberation action in the story of Israel and of Jesus Christ."[24] Here Russell looks to the Bible in general for a liberation perspective, which she seeks to salvage from the overall patriarchal orientation of the Scriptures. Thus the theme of liberation determines her "canon within a canon"; it provides the criterion for what is or is not to be experienced as the "Word of God" and, therefore, as authoritative.

20. Ibid., 13.
21. Ibid., 16.
22. Ibid., 17.
23. Ibid., emphasis added.
24. Ibid.

## Rebuilding a Feminist Approach

Russell also edited *The Liberating Word: A Guide to Nonsexist Interpretation of the Bible* in 1976 on behalf of a small task force on sexism in the Bible. This task force held the conviction that the message of the Bible needs to be liberated from sexist interpretation.

Her 1986 Annie Kinkead Warfield Lectures, named after the wife of the famous Princeton scholar B. B. Warfield, were published in the following year as *Household of Freedom: Authority in Feminist Theology*. Here Russell contends that Jesus did not use his authority to exercise dominance or to rule in an institutional sense. His authority was to forgive sins, to drive out demons, and to preach the gospel; his power was to heal.[25] In her discussion of the source of authority, Russell makes a case for the authority of experience.[26] She also refers repeatedly to the authority of the future—it is her commitment to God's new creation that controls her theological thought and praxis.

Interestingly, Russell appeals to the sociology of knowledge. She claims that our understanding of reality is socially constructed, which is a well-known feminist principle.[27] In order to eliminate the unwelcome patriarchal, male image of God as king in the concept of the kingdom of God, Russell proposes the metaphors of God's household and of good housekeeping, which bring in a more overtly female dimension. Russell also discusses the power of naming and gender-inclusive language and suggests alternative paradigms of speaking about God in female terms, such as *Sophia*. She posits the following tools for rebuilding a feminist approach to Scripture:

1) "Depatriarchalize" the Bible by adopting a stance of radical suspicion regarding the patriarchal bias of the biblical writers.
2) "Listen to the underside," i.e., the oppressed.
3) "Work from the other end," i.e., the feminist future.

Essentially, Russell takes her programmatic cue from Elisabeth Schüssler Fiorenza, whom she quotes as follows: "The common hermeneutical ground of past, present, and future is not 'sacred history' or 'sacred text' but commitment to the biblical vision of God's new creation."[28] She also cites Rosemary Radford Ruether as "appealing to the future as well as the past as her basis of authority."[29] This suggests that while Russell was more overtly political

25. L. M. Russell, *Household of Freedom: Authority in Feminist Theology* (Philadelphia: Westminster, 1987), 24.
26. Ibid., 30–33.
27. Ibid., 30.
28. Ibid., 69.
29. Ibid.

in her thought than some other feminists, she took her basic hermeneutic from seminal feminist thinkers such as Fiorenza.

Finally, in *Church in the Round* (1993) Russell proposes the metaphor of three tables—the Round Table of connection, the Kitchen Table of solidarity, and the Welcome Table of partnership, thereby setting forth her vision of a church that does not alienate women, non-whites, and laypeople. She calls for a church where all strive for justice and freedom and where church leaders make everyone feel welcome as they gather around God's table of New Creation. Russell challenges the notion that "right" administration of sacraments is limited to those ordained to a particular church office, and she calls for a spirituality that unites all people regardless of class, race, or gender.

### Evaluation

Perhaps the best place to start in an evaluation of Russell's approach to feminist liberation theology is her hermeneutical key of justice and liberation, designed to help people, especially women, attain to full humanity and personhood. As a result, she blurs gender distinctions. Her program of revisioning human relationships is deeply problematic. It redefines biblical morality, according to which God created humans male and female (Gen. 1:27–28) and instituted heterosexual, monogamous, lifelong marriage as the norm (Gen. 2:24–25). By engaging in these biblically sanctioned relationships, men and women attain to full humanity and wholeness, whereas they will not in relationships that are at variance with the revealed will of the Creator.

Another point of concern is Russell's negative view of all forms of authority. Russell's claim that Jesus was a feminist because he taught servanthood, not subordination, erects a false dichotomy. In Scripture, the husband is called the "head," i.e., one who holds a position of authority, but who is called also to serve his wife in love (Eph. 5:25–29). Jesus, likewise, came to serve (Mark 10:45) and yet has been given "all authority in heaven and on earth" (Matt. 28:18). This clearly demonstrates that, according to Scripture, the exercise of authority and servanthood are compatible.

It is only *abusive* forms of the exercise of authority that Scripture condemns (cf. Jesus' comment that "their great ones exercise authority [in a negative sense] over them" in Mark 10:42). Authority itself, both on God's and Christ's part and in the human realm, is everywhere acknowledged as not only inevitable to govern the affairs of humanity but also as inextricably built into the fabric of human existence, be it government (Rom. 13:1–7; 1 Pet. 2:13–17), the church (1 Thess. 5:12; 1 Tim. 5:17; Heb. 13:17; 1 Pet. 5:1–5), work (Eph. 6:5–9; Col. 3:22–4:1; 1 Pet. 2:18–25), marriage (Eph. 5:21–33; Col. 3:18–19; 1 Pet. 3:1–8), or the family (Eph. 6:1–4; Col. 3:20–21).

| Authority Requiring Submission | New Testament References |
|---|---|
| Government authorities (instituted by God) by citizens | Rom. 13:1, 5; Titus 3:1; 1 Pet. 2:13 |
| Authorities in workplace (even cruel ones) by workers | Eph. 6:5–9; Titus 2:9; 1 Pet. 2:18 |
| Husbands (even unbelieving ones) by wives | Eph. 5:21, 24; Col. 3:18; Titus 2:5; 1 Pet. 3:1, 5 |
| Parents by children in the home | Eph. 6:1–3; Col. 3:20 |
| Jesus Christ by the spirit world | 1 Cor. 15:27–28; Eph. 1:22; Phil. 3:21; 1 Pet. 3:22 |
| Elders in the church by younger men, others | 1 Cor. 16:16; 1 Tim. 5:17; Heb. 13:17; 1 Pet. 5:5 |

Therefore, Russell's negative stance toward all forms of authority is not only contradicted by Scripture but is also naïve. It fails to account for common human experience in which authority is a fact of life. The same can be said for her vision of life as a rainbow of partnerships rather than as a pyramid of domination. In between these two extremes of human relating—one in which biblical morality is diluted for the sake of human fulfillment and the other which is an abusive form of authority—is the middle ground. This middle ground, revealed in Scripture and experienced by many believers past and present, consists of fulfilling relationships that respect the parameters set by the Creator and that acknowledge the reality of authority, not only as a necessity, but as actually good and God-ordained for the proper functioning of loving, caring human relations.

Although Russell does not reject the Bible completely as a source for her theology, she does reject many of its teachings as well as its patriarchal context. For Russell, her own exercise of reformist feminist interpretation is profoundly paradoxical: "One must defeat the Bible as patriarchal authority by using the Bible as liberator."[30] Reading the Bible still helps Russell make sense of who she is, owing to her background and tradition, but Scripture directly contradicts her worldview. Russell, in a move that she herself calls paradoxical but that others may consider inconsistent, affirms parts of Scripture while rejecting others.

How, then, is Russell's approach biblical? She frequently cites Scripture and claims that her perspective is even more biblical than conventional theology because it exposes its patriarchal bias. However, her reading of

30. Ibid., 140, citing M. A. Tolbert, "Defining the Problem: The Bible and Feminist Herme-neutics," *Semeia* 28 (1983): 113–26.

Scripture through a feminist lens and eliminating what she deems unacceptable do not award true authority to Scripture's statements. Having started with a feminist outlook, she uses only what agrees with her basic presuppositions and enlists suitable passages in support of her alternative construal. However, such a procedure is circular and selective.

According to Russell, salvation means freedom, not so much from sin but from male oppression. The freedom is positively stated as that of being human, which she defines as wholeness and divine-human and human-human partnership. Yet contrary to her assertion, the primary oppressor of humans, according to Scripture, is not males but sin, that is, rebellion against God and his created order.

Also, not every exercise of authority is domination in a negative, coercive, abusive sense. Contrary to Russell, for God in Christ to lower himself to become human in order to secure our salvation does not mean that his being is exhausted, or that his role in relation to humanity can best be described as becoming a "partner" for humans. Rather, Jesus is himself God who preexisted eternally with God and subsequent to his earthly mission returned to his heavenly glory with God.

The primary problem with Russell's hermeneutical approach of "depatriarchalizing" the Bible is its bias, specifically against males and any form of authority. Any feminism that at the very outset pits men against women is itself divisive and fails to recognize that men and women were not created to war against each other but to co-labor in God's mandate to fill the earth and subdue it (Gen. 1:28). Even though this harmonious working was negatively affected by the fall (Gen. 3:16), it is being restored for Christian marriage partners as well as unmarried men and women who have experienced personal redemption from sin and possess the indwelling, transformative power of the Holy Spirit (Eph. 1:10; 5:18–33; 1 Corinthians 7).

This is the biblical pattern for fulfilled relationships, and any attempted alternatives, including Russell's postulate of liberation from oppression, are bound to fall short. Scripture calls Christian husbands not to abdicate their leadership but to love their wives sacrificially (Eph. 5:25–29) and calls Christian wives not to reject their husband's authority but to submit to it and be the glad recipients of their husband's provision, nurture, and guidance (Eph. 5:21–24). This, in turn, is in keeping with the scriptural mandate for all people to submit to the relevant authorities God has placed in their lives.

# 7

# ROSEMARY RADFORD RUETHER: WOMANGUIDES AND WOMEN-CHURCH

*Can a Male Savior Save Women?*
—Rosemary Radford Ruether, *Sexism and God-Talk* (1983)[1]

**Rosemary Radford** Ruether is one of the most prolific authors of the feminist movement, having authored or edited over thirty books to date. She grew up in Georgetown, Texas; her mother was Roman Catholic and her father Episcopalian. Her father passed away when she was twelve, and Rosemary and her mother moved to California. She attended Scripps College and married Herman Ruether during her last year there. They had three children. Ruether earned a master of arts in classics and Roman history and moved on to a doctorate in classics and patristics, both at the Claremont School of Theology.

Ruether became involved in the civil rights movement in the early 1960s. She taught at Howard University School of Religion for ten years. She served as the Georgia Harkness Professor of Theology at Garrett-Evangelical Theo-

1. R. R. Ruether, *Sexism and God-Talk: Toward a Feminist Theology* (Boston: Beacon, 1993 [1983]), 116: "Chapter 5: Christology: Can a Male Savior Save Women?"

logical Seminary in Evanston, Illinois, from 1976 until 2000 and is now Carpenter Professor of Feminist Theology at Pacific School of Theology.[2] While Ruether published her first work in 1967, it was not until the publication of *Womanguides* in 1985 that the full scope of Ruether's theological and hermeneutical program took shape.

---

### Fact Sheet 5: Rosemary Radford Ruether

**Born:** 1936 in Georgetown, TX

**Education:** M.A. in ancient history (1960), Ph.D. in classics and patristics, Claremont Graduate School (1965)

**Academic Position:** Georgia Harkness Professor of Theology at Garrett-Evangelical Theological Seminary in Evanston, IL (1976–2000); Carpenter Emerita Professor of Feminist Theology at Pacific School of Religion and Graduate Theological Union; currently Visiting Professor of Feminist Theology at Claremont School of Theology and Graduate University

**Religious Background:** mother Roman Catholic, father Episcopalian

**Major Works:** *Sexism and God-Talk* (1983); *Womanguides* (1985)

**Type of Feminist:** Reformist/Radical

**View of Jesus:** Jesus is a mere man, a religious seeker inspired by a vision; this-worldly vision of the kingdom; speaks of "feminism of Jesus"; Jesus is "paradigmatic liberator"; yet asks, "How can a male savior save women?"

---

### Ruether's Early Work

In her earlier work, Ruether sought to address Mary Daly's criticisms of reformist feminism.[3] In contrast to Daly, Ruether viewed feminism as part of a general movement for the liberation of all those who are subject to oppression, male as well as female, and continued to be committed to Christianity and "biblical religion." Concerning her studies of pagan, Hebrew, and Christian traditions she wrote, "I continued to believe that we need both spiritualities; both prophetic social transformations and encounters with the sacred depths of nature."[4]

In 1967 Ruether penned *The Church against Itself: An Inquiry into the Conditions of Historical Existence for the Eschatological Community*. In this

---

2. This chapter will include a survey of Ruether's major publications that are directly relevant to our study. There is broad relevance in these works in that they serve as a prolegomenon to her later writings on the subject and more specific relevance in others as they deal closely with Jesus and women. As will be seen, some of Ruether's earlier works provide the background for her ideology, which can later be seen to influence her hermeneutical approach.

3. See M. A. Kassian, *The Feminist Mistake: The Radical Impact of Feminism on the Church and Culture* (Wheaton, IL: Crossway, 2005), 268–73.

4. R. R. Ruether, *Women and Redemption: A Theological History* (Minneapolis: Augsburg Fortress, 1998), 222.

book she employs a "dialectical model" or "crisis theology" of ecclesiology. This involves a renaming process by which "realities that have falsely appropriated names . . . are . . . renamed according to their real nature."[5] Ruether emphasizes *naming* in order to change perception or understanding of terms and her suspicion toward the church's claiming authority on the basis of the apostolic witness. Her subsequent works develop these themes in considerably more detail.

In 1970 Ruether wrote *The Radical Kingdom: The Western Experience of Messianic Hope*. In this book she surveys historical movements and ideologies that sought to bring about the radical renewal and transformation of society, such as the Radical Reformation, the Enlightenment, and Marxism. While *The Radical Kingdom* is mostly descriptive, it reveals Ruether's interest in liberation movements as paradigmatic for the feminist movement.

Ruether's liberationist feminist ideology found its initial expression in the 1972 volume *Liberation Theology*. In 1974 Ruether edited *Religion and Sexism: Images of Woman in the Jewish and Christian Traditions*, a collection of essays dedicated to her mother. In one article, "Misogynism and Virginal Feminism in the Fathers of the Church,"[6] she chronicles the church fathers' views on women, ranging from misogynist to exalted virginity in high praise of women.

In 1975 Ruether published *New Woman, New Earth: Sexist Ideologies and Human Liberation*, a work dedicated to her three children. The book contains various lectures that study ideologies in support of sexism. In opposition to patriarchy, the women's movement is viewed as encompassing all other liberation movements.[7]

In this work Ruether identifies herself as one of the "implacable foes of those systems of ruling-class male power which have dominated human history."[8] Her struggle to "transform this entire social system in its human and ecological relationships" involves nothing less than the "transformation of consciousness."[9]

Ruether finds in the Gospels a startling contrast between "the feminism of Jesus and traditional Judaism."[10] In support of Jesus' unusually positive

---

5. R. R. Ruether, *The Church against Itself: An Inquiry into the Conditions of Historical Existence for the Eschatological Community* (New York: Herder, 1967), 5–6.

6. The New Testament article identifies Jesus as the "first 'feminist.'" R. R. Ruether, ed., *Religion and Sexism: Images of Woman in the Jewish and Christian Traditions* (New York: Simon and Schuster, 1974), 138, citing L. Swidler, "Jesus Was a Feminist," *Catholic World* 212 (1971): 177–83 and focuses on Luke–Acts.

7. R. R. Ruether, *New Woman, New Earth: Sexist Ideologies and Human Liberation* (New York: Seabury, 1975), xi.

8. Ibid., xiii.

9. Ibid., xiv.

10. Ibid., 63; the same expression, "feminism of Jesus," is found on p. 64.

view on women, Ruether cites Jesus' close relationships with women and his ministry to them, including: Jesus' female followers mentioned in Luke 8:1–3; Jesus' references to poor widows and outcast women (Luke 21:1–4; 7:36–50); his miracles for women (Matt. 8:14ff.; Mark 1:30–31; Luke 4:38–39; John 2:1–11); his feeling like a "mother hen" prior to the cross (Matt. 23:37; Luke 13:34); and his healing of the woman with blood flow (Mark 5:25–34). She also mentions Jesus' conversation with the Samaritan woman in John 4, his pronouncements on divorce, and the women as first witnesses of the resurrection.

Even more important, according to Ruether, is Jesus' model and teaching of servant leadership (citing Matt. 20:25–28), a theme that would surface regularly in later evangelical feminist literature on the subject. Ruether observes that, traditionally, the image of God as father was used to support sexism and hierarchicalism in a domination-subordination model, in which males were identified with God the Father in a manner that placed them in a hierarchical relationship over women and lower classes. Yet Ruether contends that Jesus opposed such an approach in his teaching when he told his disciples not to call anyone on earth their "teacher," "father," or "instructor" (citing Matt. 23:8–11).[11]

Ruether also finds support for this contention in Jesus' treatment of Mary and Martha, particularly his allowing Mary to sit at his feet to learn from him (Luke 10:38–42). She observed:

> The principles of Christian community are founded upon a role transformation between men and women, rulers and ruled. The ministry of the church is not to be modeled on hierarchies of lordship, but on the *diakonia* of women and servants, while women are freed from exclusive identification with the service role and called to join the circle of disciples as equal members.[12]

Ruether cites the parallelism of male and female examples in the parables as evidence that "women were included equally with men *as* students of the Christian catechesis."[13]

Later Ruether notes that feminism arose in the late eighteenth century as part of the ideology of liberalism and that in the mid-1800s feminism was identified with socialism. The liberation of women was envisioned by Marx and Engels as part of the communist revolution. Over against "the legacy of class, racist, imperialist, and sexist structures of domination"[14] and a Western capitalism that "is based on exploitation of people by people and

11. Ibid., 64.
12. Ibid., 66.
13. Ibid., 66–67.
14. Ibid., 183.

the rape of the earth," Ruether calls for the realization of a radical communism that could overcome economic oppression and the de-alienation of work and moved toward the kind of utopian society envisioned by Marx and others.[15]

This portion of her work is revealing. It clearly shows Ruether's view that the roots of feminism are found in liberalism, socialism, and communism and that feminism was wedded from the beginning to the notion of human liberation, not merely in economic terms but primarily in regard to gender. Ruether's vision is spelled out further in the final essay of the volume, "New Woman and New Earth: Women, Ecology, and Social Revolution," a theme developed more fully in her 1992 monograph, *Gaia & God: An Ecofeminist Theology of Earth Healing.*

## Branching Out

In 1976 a collection of essays cowritten by Eugene Bianchi and Rosemary Ruether appeared, titled *From Machismo to Mutuality: Essays on Sexism and Woman-Man Liberation.* Here Bianchi and Ruether discuss the challenge of sexism and women's liberation. Ruether's contributions to the volume, in particular her essay "Sexism and the Liberation of Women," reiterate her liberationist feminist agenda laid out in *New Woman, New Earth.*

In her work *Mary, the Feminine Face of the Church* (1979), Ruether sets out to reclaim the biblical narrative regarding Mary from what she considers to be the patriarchal mythology of Christian tradition, where, according to Ruether, Mary was a passive victim without any say in her own destiny. Ruether identifies Mary as a model of discipleship, whose faith was akin to that of Abraham and whose courage of self-giving reflected that of Christ. The Magnificat sounded the theme of social justice, where liberation theology and feminism met.[16]

In 1979 *Women of Spirit: Female Leadership in the Jewish and Christian Traditions* was published, coedited by Rosemary Ruether and Eleanor McLaughlin. In this collection of essays on leadership roles of women in the Jewish and Christian traditions, the editors and contributors seek the recovery of important chapters of women's history and the development of a new paradigm of female leadership. The editors claim at the outset that "in Christianity originally women seem to have been incorporated into the teaching role, but were eliminated early enough that the Church Fathers took for granted that women might never act as public teachers."[17]

15. Ibid., 182–83.
16. R. R. Ruether, *Mary, the Feminine Face of the Church* (Philadelphia: Westminster, 1979 [1977]), 32–34.
17. R. R. Ruether and E. McLaughlin, eds., *Women of Spirit: Female Leadership in the Jewish and Christian Traditions* (New York: Simon and Schuster, 1979), 17.

Ruether explores the topic of Christology and feminism in her 1981 work *To Change the World: Christology and Cultural Criticism*. Most noteworthy is the first chapter, "Jesus and the Revolutionaries: Political Theology and Biblical Hermeneutics."[18] The title was taken from the German New Testament scholar Oscar Cullmann's book by the same title. In his book, Cullmann, similar to Martin Hengel before him, opposed S. G. F. Brandon's thesis that Jesus was a political revolutionary, arguing instead that Jesus' messianism was eschatological and personal. Ruether sides with Brandon, contending that "Jesus's vision of the kingdom was essentially this-worldly, social and *political*, and not eschatological."[19]

## Ruether's Radical Turn

While Ruether's writings up to this point may still be viewed as expressive of a reformist type of feminism that regularly engages Scripture, her 1985 publication *Womanguides: Readings toward a Feminist Theology* reveals a considerably more radical approach. These readings evolved from the lectures Ruether gave in her first feminist theology classes in the 1970s. In the introduction Ruether boldly states her hermeneutical program as follows: "Feminist theology cannot be done from the existing base of the Bible."[20] The Old and New Testaments "have been shaped in their formation, their transmission, and, finally, their canonization to sacralize patriarchy."[21]

She states that Scripture "may preserve, between the lines, memories of women's experience. But in their present form and intention they are designed to erase women's existence as subjects and to mention women only as objects of male definition. In these texts the norm for women is absence and silence."[22] Reading between the lines of patriarchal biblical texts should be supplemented by reading extra-canonical texts. Nothing less than new texts, a new canon, and a new church are required as women "reconstruct meaning" for themselves by reading past writings and by creating new stories that are "revelatory" as well, in that they resonate with

18. R. R. Ruether, *To Change the World: Christology and Cultural Criticism* (New York: Crossroad, 1981), 7–18.
19. Ibid., 14.
20. R. R. Ruether, *Womanguides: Readings toward a Feminist Theology* (Boston: Beacon, 1985), ix.
21. Ibid. In her "method of correlation," Ruether advocates a prophetic critique of the patriarchal elements in Scripture, identifying the problem of "the patriarchal social order of men over women, masters over slaves, king (or queen) over subjects, nobility over peasants itself [as] seen [to be] reflecting the cosmic and heavenly order." "Feminist Interpretation: A Method of Correlation," in *Feminist Interpretation of the Bible*, 117.
22. Ibid.

their experience.[23] These statements indicate a clear rejection of Scripture as a basis for feminist theology.

Where should women go from there, then? What should take the place of the canon of Scripture? In the absence of an existing alternative canon, Ruether turns to a variety of sources. First, she proposes that women read between the lines of patriarchal texts about women in order to find fragments of women's experience that were not completely erased. Second, she suggests turning to extra-canonical texts that constitute "remains of alternative communities that reflect either the greater awe and fear of female power denied in later patriarchy or [the] questionings of male domination in groups where women did enter into critical dialogue."[24]

Once canonical texts are read critically in light of what Ruether calls that larger reality, i.e., feminism, "a new norm emerges on which to construct a new community, a new theology, eventually a new canon. That new norm makes women as subjects the center rather than the margin. Women are empowered to define themselves rather than to be defined by others. Women's speech and presence are normative rather than aberrant."[25]

*Womanguides* stays within the cultural matrix that has shaped Western Christianity, though Ruether states that creation stories from Australian aborigines or Amerindians, for example, could be revelatory.[26] Ruether says the time has come for women to start the work of their own theological reflection, and this work need not remain encapsulated in past symbols and texts, i.e., the Bible. New liberating experience empowers to write new stories, new parables, and new *midrashim* (expositions).[27]

According to Ruether, on the basis of this work of theological reflection issuing in new texts for women, a new feminist consciousness and movement would emerge: "We, too, can write new texts to express our new consciousness. We can read them in community gatherings of WomanChurch. They can become texts for teaching and preaching the vision."[28] Several such readings are feminist *midrashim*, such as those by Judith Plaskow on Lilith and Eve and those by several of Ruether's female students at Garrett-Evangelical Theological Seminary.

*Womanguides* represents a major shift in Ruether's thinking. No longer is she concerned to show egalitarian tendencies in the historical Jesus, as she had done in her earlier work. Instead, she begins advocating a form of a "hermeneutic of suspicion," rejecting Scripture as irremediably patriarchal.

23. See Kassian, *Feminist Mistake*, chap. 17.
24. Ibid., x–xi.
25. Ibid., xi.
26. Ibid.
27. Ibid., xii.
28. Ibid.

Ruether has become convinced that nothing less was required for fulfilling the feminist vision than new texts, a new canon, and a new church. Thus Ruether's radical turn brings her from a reformist approach to a radical, even revolutionary, form of feminism.

Although *Sexism and God-Talk* was published prior to *Womanguides* (in 1983), the readings published in the latter work formed the textual base of the former. As Ruether explains in the 1993 preface of the reissued *Sexism and God-Talk*, she encourages her students to write feminist parables, myths, and *midrashim*. According to Ruether, these exercises strike at the heart of her understanding of inspiration and religious authority: "God did not just speak once upon a time to a privileged group of males in one part of the world, making us ever after dependent on the codification of their experience."[29] Feminists must uncover repressed memories, she advocates, but they must also "reconstruct meaning" for themselves today in the "sparking of primal stories" that spring up from their experience.

*Sexism and God-Talk*, then, set forth in systematic-theology fashion Ruether's thought on the methodology, sources, and norms of feminist theology. We find here her view on God-language; woman, body, and nature (the theology of creation); humanity as male and female; Christology ("Can a Male Savior Save Women?"); Mariology; sin; the church; the new earth; and eschatology.

In the initial chapter, Ruether defends *experience* as the criterion of truth and the basic source for feminist theology. Scripture and tradition, she contends, are *themselves* codified collective human experience. In fact, human experience is the starting and end point of the hermeneutical circle. She claims that symbols are authoritative only to the extent and as long as they are experienced as meaningful by a given person. "If a symbol does not speak authentically to experience, it becomes dead or must be altered to provide a new meaning."[30]

Ruether's theology of revelation is firmly rooted in individual human experience: "By *revelatory* we mean breakthrough experiences beyond ordinary fragmented consciousness that provide interpretive symbols illuminating the means of the *whole* of life."[31] Ruether's critique of male-centered ecclesiastical tradition is fueled by the desire to "touch a deeper bedrock of authentic Being upon which to ground the self."[32]

29. Ruether, *Sexism and God-Talk*, xiv.
30. Ibid., 12.
31. Ibid., 13.
32. Ibid., 18, again reflecting Tillich.

Ruether postulates that the critical principle of feminist theology is *the promotion of the full humanity of women.* Whatever diminished women's full humanity was by this criterion judged "not redemptive."[33] Conversely, whatever did promote women's full humanity "is of the holy, it does reflect true relation to the divine, it is the true nature of things, the authentic message of redemption and the mission of redemptive community."[34] Ruether calls for the obliteration of all forms of sexism, including "humanocentricism," urging "a mutuality that allows us to affirm different ways of being."[35]

Ruether discusses Jesus in her construction of a feminist Christology. She proposes to start with Jesus' message and praxis and to strip off "the mythology about Jesus as Messiah or divine *Logos,* with its traditional masculine imagery."[36] This "historical Jesus," Ruether contends, engaged in criticism of the religious and social hierarchy of his day in a way that is remarkably parallel to feminist criticism. She notes the important role played by women in Jesus' vision of God's new order in which the lowly were exalted.

Ruether contends that women's role was different from "doctrines of romantic complementarity" and that the Gospels did not "operate with a dualism of masculine and feminine."[37] Jesus as liberator called for a dissolution of the web of status relationships by which people came to identify privilege and deprivation. Rightly understood, Jesus represented the "kenosis [self-emptying] of patriarchy."[38] Here she believes that Christ, as liberated humanity, is not confined to the earthly Jesus. Rather, as the paradigmatic liberator, Christ urges us on to realize the liberation of all where such liberation is yet to be accomplished.

In 1998 Ruether published *Women and Redemption: A Theological History* spanning from Jesus to the present. In the first chapter, "In Christ No More Male and Female? The Question of Gender and Redemption in the New Testament," Ruether reconstructs Jesus' career as follows: Jesus, a "religious seeker" and young man of artisan class, was attracted to John the Baptist's apocalyptic message of repentance. Later, however, he broke with the Baptist, inspired by a vision of Satan falling from heaven like lightning (Luke 10:18). This vision convinced Jesus that he did not have to wait for God's intervention in the future; Satan's power was already broken. Toward about A.D. 30 Jesus became convinced that the time of

33. Ibid., 19.
34. Ibid.
35. Ibid., 20.
36. Ibid., 135.
37. Ibid., 137.
38. Ibid.

fulfillment of his kingdom vision was near. He gathered his followers and went to Jerusalem, where he was arrested and crucified. Yet a few of Jesus' followers became convinced that Jesus was not dead but alive and present with them "in the Spirit." Hence the early church was born, with women playing an important role.[39]

Ruether includes a chapter with an almost identical title in her 1998 work *Introducing Redemption in Christian Feminism*. She states that, in her view of Jesus, she essentially followed John Dominic Crossan's *The Historical Jesus: The Life of a Mediterranean Jewish Peasant*, calling Jesus a "compelling healer and prophet."[40] As "examples of . . . iconoclastic egalitarianism and concern for women," Ruether cited Mark 5:25–34; 7:24–30; Luke 13:10–17; and Matthew 21:31.

## Evaluation

In her earlier work Ruether shared with Elisabeth Schüssler Fiorenza the conviction that women and men formed an egalitarian fellowship in Jesus' day and in the days of the early church, indicating that this kind of egalitarian relationship should be followed in today's church. However, it is not clear in what sense women were meant to be equal members of Jesus' circle of disciples. The Gospels universally attest to the fact that only men were chosen as members of the Twelve. Ruether contends that it should be the *diakonia* of women and servants only that is to make up the new paradigm rather than *diakonia* in general, whether by men *or* women. However, Jesus called *all* people to service (Mark 10:42–45; cf. Phil. 2:1–11), and Jesus himself, incarnated as a male, practiced servanthood.

Likewise, the link established by Ruether between male and female figures in Jesus' parables and their being equally students of Christian doctrine is not immediately evident. It is an inference drawn by Ruether, not a point made explicitly in Scripture. Though Jesus' use of both men and women in parables showed that he sought to identify with the life experience of both male and female, care should be taken not to press this observation beyond what may be warranted. In particular, Ruether does not compellingly address the crucial difference between women *learning* and women *teaching* or *serving in leadership positions* in the church.

Ruether's assessment of Jesus' agenda in her writings, particularly *To Change the World*, is heavily influenced by a feminist predisposition, which focuses on the transformation of political, socio-economic structures, particularly women's liberation. Yet Jesus' statement before Pilate, "My kingdom

---

39. Ruether, *Women and Redemption*, 16–20.
40. Ibid., 17.

is not of this world" (John 18:36), suggests that Jesus himself did not primarily pursue a political agenda. This is also indicated by Jesus' consistent refusal to be pressed into politics (e.g., John 6:14) or to define his mission in this-worldly terms (e.g., the temptation narratives in Matt. 4:8–10 and Luke 4:5–8). Therefore Jesus cannot be easily enlisted as an exemplar of a program of social liberation such as the one proposed by Ruether and other liberationist feminists.

Ruether's systematic theology, *Womanguides*, occupies a pivotal place in her thinking. Here she is no longer concerned to show egalitarian tendencies in the historical Jesus but has moved on to advocate a "hermeneutic of suspicion" and to reject Scripture as irremediably patriarchal, calling for new texts, a new canon, and a new church. The principle of a closed canon comprised of inspired and inerrant Scripture recognized historically and traditionally had been set aside. In this Ruether moves from a reformist to a radical, even revolutionary, brand of feminism.

In assessing Ruether's hermeneutic, we must ask whether it is proper to root the doctrine of revelation in human experience and to view Scripture as mere codified collective human experience. How can mere experience serve as an adequate criterion of truth? Scripture claims that God took the initiative to reveal himself to human beings, so the doctrine of revelation ought to be grounded in God and his initiative. Humans are the recipients and interpreters of revelation, not the creators and revealers. To say, as Ruether does, that revelation consists of human breakthrough experiences beyond ordinary fragmented consciousness excludes the possibility and reality of divine initiative in revelation and makes the human being the source and locus of revelation.

Also problematic is Ruether's comment that God did not just speak once upon a time to a privileged group of males in one part of the world, making us ever after dependent on the codification of their experience. As a feminist, Ruether may not have found acceptable that God's revelation in Jesus Christ occurred historically in the context of his apostolic circle of the Twelve, all of whom were male. However, this is an undisputable fact, attested to in Scripture.

Scripture also makes clear that God's revelation in Christ was final and definitive (John 1:17–18; Heb. 1:1–3) and for all future purposes it forms the pivotal moment in salvation history. This purpose was to unite all things in Jesus Christ (Eph. 1:10). For this reason it is unacceptable to diminish the unique stature of Christ and to level divine revelation as if God's self-disclosure in Christ were on the same level as feminist parables, myths, and *midrashim* of Ruether's disciples and other proponents of feminism.

Ruether's Christology raises concerns as well. In her effort to deemphasize Jesus' maleness Ruether questions Scripture's testimony to Jesus as the Messiah and the Word (*logos*), calling these titles "mythology." Yet Jesus was clearly incarnated as a male and fulfilled scriptural predictions of the Messiah, including his being the Son of David.

Ruether's distinction between the earthly Jesus and Christ at large is not borne out by Scripture's testimony. Although, she implies, the earthly Jesus did not fully implement his egalitarian or feminist vision, Christ, nevertheless, must be seen as the "paradigmatic liberator." However, Ruether fails to see that one should not drive a wedge between the earthly Jesus and the Christ, as if those were two separate individuals. Also, the Gospels feature men and women as distinct and show them fulfilling distinct roles, which does not support Ruether's statement that the Gospels do not "operate with a dualism of masculine and feminine."[41]

At the root of Ruether's reconstruction of the historical Jesus lies the notion that Jesus is a mere human. To characterize Jesus as a religious seeker who was inspired by a vision and later became convinced that the coming of God's kingdom was near, only to end up crucified, does not do justice to the Gospel witness that unequivocally states that Jesus claimed to be the Messiah and Son of God (e.g., Matt. 26:64; John 4:26) and was confessed as Lord and God by his first followers (e.g., John 20:28). The Jews' repeated attempt to stone Jesus clearly implies that Jesus' contemporaries understood Jesus' claim of divinity to be in direct conflict with their belief in only one God (see, e.g., John 5:18; 8:59; 10:31).

Jesus' resurrection, likewise, is presented by Scripture as a reality confirmed by evidence and numerous witnesses, not as a mere psychological, subjective perception in the minds of some of Jesus' followers (see esp. 1 Cor. 15:3–9). In fact, the actual reality of Jesus' resurrection is presented by the apostle Paul as an indispensable part of the Christian gospel (1 Cor. 15:12–20). Ruether's reconstruction of the "historical Jesus," therefore, falls short of Jesus' own actual claims and the Gospel witness. This lack of attention to Jesus' deity renders Ruether's Christology without foundation. This weakness also surfaces in her perception of Jesus in feminist and egalitarian terms.

Ruether is a prolific author and profound thinker. Her extensive writings reveal that she has a firm command of the major issues involved, and she has had a wide impact on the feminist movement. It is no coincidence that virtually all feminist writers in recent years take their point of departure from her. Clearly, on the premise that Scripture is patriarchal and a mere product of human religious experience, it would follow that, for a

41. Ibid.

feminist, there would be authoritative and relevant sources other than the Bible and that the canon should be expanded, if not replaced, by other writings more in keeping with feminist convictions. From the standpoint of a high view of Scripture, however, this cannot be accepted. Ruether's views are deficient primarily with regard to the nature of hermeneutics and Scripture.

In particular, her contention that feminist theology cannot be done from the existing base of the Bible is unacceptable, because it involves the substitution of alternate "revelatory" sources for the inspired, canonical Christian Scriptures. Ruether's call for new texts, a new canon, and a new church by and for women marks a sharp departure from historic Christianity. The role of experience in Ruether's approach as foundational and even revelatory is also inadequate, as is her view of Jesus as a mere human and religious seeker.

# 8

# Elisabeth Schüssler Fiorenza: Jesus' Alleged "Discipleship of Equals"

*The woman-identified man, Jesus, called forth a discipleship of equals that still needs to be discovered and realized by women and men today.*

—Elisabeth Schüssler Fiorenza, *In Memory of Her* (1983)[1]

*Elisabeth Schüssler* Fiorenza can rightly be considered the matriarch of North American feminism. She was born in Romania in 1938 and fled with her family to what would become West Germany during World War II. Fiorenza, who identifies herself as a Roman Catholic, earned her master of divinity degree from the University of Würzburg and her doctorate from the University of Münster, both in her native Germany. Her thesis was published in 1964 as her first book, titled *The Forgotten Partner: Foundations, Facts and Possibilities of the Professional Ministry of Women in the Church*. Originally her doctoral thesis bore the title "Priest for God: A Study of the Motif of the Kingdom and Priesthood in the Apocalypse."

1. E. S. Fiorenza, *In Memory of Her: A Feminist Theological Reconstruction of Christian Origins* (New York: Crossroad, 1983), 154.

Fiorenza has served for many years as the Krister Stendahl Professor of Divinity at Harvard Divinity School. Before assuming her position at Harvard, she taught as professor of New Testament studies at the University of Notre Dame and the Episcopal Divinity School. Fiorenza was the first woman elected to the post of president of the Society of Biblical Literature and has served on the editorial boards of many biblical journals and societies. Fiorenza is the cofounder (with Judith Plaskow) and editor of the *Journal of Feminist Studies in Religion* and a coeditor of *Concilium*, an international theological review in the Roman Catholic tradition. She has served with the Women's Ordination Conference; Sisters against Sexism; Feminist Theological Institute; Women Scholars in Religion; Women in Theology; and Women Moving Church.[2]

---

### Fact Sheet 6:  Elisabeth Schüssler Fiorenza

**Born:** 1938 in Romania as an ethnic German

**Education:** M.Div., University of Würzburg; doctorate, University of Münster

**Academic Position:** Professor of New Testament Studies at the University of Notre Dame and the Episcopal Divinity School; currently Krister Stendahl Professor of Divinity at Harvard Divinity School

**Religious Background:** Roman Catholic

**Major Works:** *In Memory of Her* (1983); *Jesus: Miriam's Child, Sophia's Prophet* (1995); *Jesus and the Politics of Interpretation* (2001)

**Type of Feminist:** Reformist/Radical

**View of Jesus:** Jesus is Sophia's prophet; Jesus launched renewal movement within Judaism, established "discipleship of equals"; wants to "decenter Jesus," focus on movement

---

## Fiorenza's Influence

While there were precursors in the 1970s, Elisabeth Schüssler Fiorenza's historical reconstruction of early Christian origins, particularly as it relates to Jesus' and the early church's treatment of women, has been by far the most influential in the past several decades. In her major work *In Memory of Her* (1983) which was translated into a dozen languages, Fiorenza proposes a fourfold hermeneutic:

---

2. Only Fiorenza's most relevant works can be considered below. Significant works articulating Fiorenza's hermeneutic not treated here include *But She Said: Feminist Practices of Biblical Interpretation* (Boston: Beacon, 1993); *Discipleship of Equals* (New York: Herder, 1993); *Bread Not Stone: The Challenge of Feminist Interpretation* (Boston: Beacon, 1995); *The Power of Naming* (Maryknoll, NY: Orbis, 1996); *Sharing Her Word: Feminist Biblical Interpretation in Context* (Boston: Beacon, 1999); *Rhetoric and Ethic: The Politics of Biblical Studies* (Minneapolis: Augsburg Fortress, 1999); and *Wisdom Ways: Introducing Feminist Biblical Interpretation* (Maryknoll, NY: Orbis, 2001).

1) a hermeneutic of suspicion toward traditional interpretations of biblical texts owing to patriarchal bias and assumptions;

2) a hermeneutic of remembrance that uncovers women's agency in foundational Christian tradition;

3) a hermeneutic of proclamation that relates this reconstruction to the Christian community; and

4) a hermeneutic of imagination that expresses feminism in ritual, prayer, hymns, banners, and art.[3]

In the book Fiorenza uses a form of the historical-critical method to reconstruct early Christian origins, particularly with regard to Jesus' treatment of women and the status of women in the early church. The questions Fiorenza and other early feminists addressed are: "What was the role of women in the life and ministry of Jesus?" and "What was women's status in the life of the early church?" This larger reconstruction, in turn, is subsequently used as a framework to interpret specific texts in keeping with their broad historical reconstruction of early Christianity.

In Fiorenza's own words, her primary objective in *In Memory of Her* is "to reconstruct early Christian history as women's history in order not only to *restore* women's stories to early Christian history but also to *reclaim* this history as the history of women and men."[4] The title alludes to Jesus' pronouncement regarding Mary of Bethany after she had anointed him for burial: "Truly, I say to you, wherever this gospel is proclaimed in the whole world, what she has done will also be told *in memory of her*" (Matt. 26:13; Mark 14:9).

Applying historical and sociological criticism to the Gospels, Fiorenza contends that the Gospels show Jesus standing in judgment over the kind of marginalization of women practiced today. Thus, female subordination is not part of the original gospel but a result of Christianity's accommodation to Greco-Roman culture. Fiorenza's hermeneutic is undergirded by the conviction that a text's life-setting is "as important for its understanding as its actual formulation. Biblical texts are not verbally inspired revelation [or] doctrinal principles but historical formulations within the context of

---

3. E. S. Fiorenza, "Emerging Issues in Feminist Biblical Interpretation," in *Christian Feminism: Visions of a New Humanity*, ed. J. L. Weidman (San Francisco: HarperSanFrancisco, 1984), 47–84; see Fiorenza, *In Memory of Her*, xxiii, 26–36; V. C. Phillips, "Feminist Interpretation," in *Dictionary of Biblical Interpretation*, ed. J. H. Hayes (Nashville: Abingdon, 1999), 393–94; M. A. Kassian, *The Feminist Mistake: The Radical Impact of Feminism on Church and Culture* (Wheaton, IL: Crossway, 1992), 131–38. For an application of Fiorenza's hermeneutic to a specific text of Scripture, Luke 10:38–42, see E. S. Fiorenza, "A Feminist Critical Interpretation for Liberation: Martha and Mary: Lk. 10:39–42," *Religion and Intellectual Life* 3/2 (1986): 21–36.

4. Fiorenza, *In Memory of Her*, xiv (emphasis added).

a religious community."[5] Thus, history precedes text and forms the focal point of scholarly investigation.

Taking her cue from Elizabeth Cady Stanton and *The Woman's Bible* (1895, 1898), Fiorenza affirms that biblical interpretation is a political act, and she espouses a liberation theology model of biblical interpretation with reference to the work of Letty Russell, Rosemary Radford Ruether, and Phyllis Trible.[6] For Fiorenza, "a feminist reconstitution of the world requires a feminist hermeneutic that shares in the critical methods and impulses of historical scholarship on the one hand and in the theological goals of liberation theologies on the other hand."[7]

Fiorenza concludes, "The revelatory canon for theological evaluation of biblical androcentric traditions and their subsequent interpretations cannot be derived from the Bible itself but can only be formulated in and through women's struggle for liberation from all patriarchal oppression."[8] In other words, "only those traditions and texts that critically break through patriarchal culture . . . have the theological authority of revelation."[9] Significantly, Fiorenza found "such revelation . . . in the life and ministry of Jesus as well as in the *discipleship community of equals* called forth by him."[10]

Fiorenza's model locates revelation not in texts but in Christian experience and community.[11] In keeping with the historical-critical method Fiorenza essentially embraces, her primary interest lies not in the text of Scripture but in phenomena *outside* of the scriptural text. What makes Fiorenza's task more difficult is the fact that "most of women's early Christian heritage is probably lost and must be extracted from androcentric early Christian records."[12]

Further on in her work *In Memory of Her*, Fiorenza attempts to reconstruct women's history as "the history of the discipleship of equals." Fiorenza understands the "Jesus movement" as a movement of renewal within Judaism that presented an alternative to the dominant patriarchal restrictions in that culture.[13] According to Fiorenza, Jesus' vision of the kingdom included the praxis of inclusive wholeness.[14] Jesus' healings, his table fellowship with sinners, and his accepting attitude toward all were cited as proofs of this new approach on his part.

---

5. Ibid., xv.
6. Ibid., 7–21.
7. Ibid., 29.
8. Ibid., 32.
9. Ibid., 33.
10. Ibid., 34 (emphasis added).
11. Ibid.
12. Ibid., 52.
13. Ibid., 107.
14. Ibid., 119, citing Luke 17:21; and p. 122, citing Luke 1:52–53.

After quoting Luke 7:35, "wisdom is justified by all her children," Fiorenza makes the claim that divine Sophia served as Israel's God and that "the Palestinian Jesus movement understood the mission of Jesus as that of the prophet and child of Sophia."[15] Sophia, the female deity, was also the driving force behind Jesus' pursuit of a "discipleship of equals." Fiorenza also, without further explanation, adduces the significance of texts such as the account of the Samaritan woman in John 4:1–42, the story of the Syrophoenician woman in Mark 7:24–30 and parallels, and the women followers of Jesus in Luke 8:1–3. Fiorenza concludes:

> As a feminist vision, the *basileia* [kingdom] vision of Jesus calls all women without exception to wholeness and selfhood, as well as to solidarity with those women who are the impoverished, the maimed, and outcasts of our society and church. It knows of the deadly violence such a vision and commitment will encounter. It enables us not to despair or to relinquish the struggle in the face of such violence. It empowers us to walk upright, freed from the double oppression of societal and religious sexism and prejudice. The *woman-identified man, Jesus, called forth a discipleship of equals* that still needs to be discovered and realized by women and men today.[16]

## Continuing on the Revisionist Feminist Path

In 1995 Fiorenza wrote *Jesus: Miriam's Child, Sophia's Prophet.*[17] At the outset, Fiorenza explains, "By naming Jesus as the child of Miriam and the prophet of Divine Sophia, I seek to create a 'woman'-defined feminist theoretical space that makes it possible to dislodge christological discourses from their malestream [*sic*] frame of reference."[18] In this work Fiorenza continues firmly in her revisionist feminist path, seeking to redefine, revision, reconceptualize, and otherwise recast conventional theological language, including language about Jesus, in feminist terms.

As she notes, "The hermeneutical-rhetorical creation of such a space intends to decenter hegemonic malestream [*sic*] christological discourses and to reframe them in terms of a critical feminist theology of liberation."[19] This also entails decentering Jesus himself. Thus Fiorenza seeks to replace the paradigm of Jesus as the divine Son, whom God the Father sent to redeem humans from their sins, with the image of Divine Wisdom's table and Mary's visitation of Elizabeth.

15. Ibid., 135. She developed this in book-length form in *Jesus: Miriam's Child, Sophia's Prophet: Critical Issues in Feminist Christology* (New York: Continuum, 1994).
16. Ibid., 153–54 (emphasis added).
17. New York: Continuum, 1995.
18. Ibid., 3.
19. Ibid.

Fiorenza makes clear that hers is neither another scriptural study of Jesus nor a "revolutionary biography" or even a "postpatriarchal christology."[20] As in her previous and subsequent work, Fiorenza is concerned here not merely with the reconstruction of historical data about Jesus but with the politics of Christological discourses. As such, Fiorenza seeks to expose the "commodification" (an expression taken from Marxist theory, where it denotes the capitalist marketing of things not previously thought of in economic terms) of Jesus and to keep before people's eyes the vision of radical equality and of liberation from (male) domination.

In this regard she sets herself in contrast to right-wing fundamentalism worldwide, which she considers to be the major force resisting women's emancipation. According to Fiorenza, this fundamentalism erroneously engages in a literalist interpretation and a dogmatic reading of Scripture.

But liberal scholars such as John Dominic Crossan fare no better, Fiorenza alleges, for they, too, by seeking to arrive at an accurate historical portrait of Jesus, are guilty of historical positivism, the view that facts are to be ascertained by empirical observation. Even feminist literary analyses of the Gospels fail to upset the rule of such scholarship.

For her part, Fiorenza rejects viewing feminism merely as a subjective, experiential vantage point from which to engage in biblical scholarship. Feminists, she says, must never relinquish the claim that their work has universal validity. She also reaffirms the importance of the "power of naming" for feminists, that of redefining conventional theology by assigning new names to familiar concepts.

Fiorenza notes that liberal Enlightenment Christologies of Jesus, those that view him as the greatest man who ever lived, as an exceptional hero, or as a religious genius, hark back to the notion of the *theios anēr* ("divine man") in ancient Greco-Roman thought, who was always conceived of in male terms. She seeks to show that the Christological Councils, likewise, presuppose and perpetrate patriarchy and androcentrism.

In the remainder of her book Fiorenza pursues a radical recasting of Jesus in feminist terms along the lines mentioned above. She claims that Luke's introductory statement, "Mary arose and went . . . into the hill country" (Luke 1:39), "does not function as a historical reference so much as a hermeneutical metaphor and interpretive key for a critical feminist theology."[21] Thus, feminist Christological discourses are wandering in the "hills," the "ups and downs" of the feminist struggle for liberation.[22] Fiorenza's role

---

20. Ibid., 4, with reference to the work of J. D. Crossan and D. W. Odell-Scott.
21. Ibid., 33.
22. Ibid.

is to remove "malestream" (her term) theological "roadblocks" impeding feminist progress.

In so doing, Fiorenza reiterates her contention that Jesus is "the prophet of Sophia sent to proclaim that the Sophia-G*d [sic] of Jesus is the G*d [sic] of the poor, the outcasts, and all those suffering from injustice."[23] Fiorenza locates this tradition in the hypothetical document commonly referred to as "Q" (from German Quelle, "source"), a hypothetical document containing material shared by Matthew and Luke. John's Gospel understands Jesus "as making Sophia present in and through her/his work."[24]

At the same time, Fiorenza acknowledges, and deplores, the fact that John presents Jesus predominantly as the Son sent by the Father, a fact she explains by a rhetorical situation in which the "Johannine community" defined itself over against contemporary non-messianic Judaism. This, in turn, has given occasion to centuries of anti-Semitism. Fiorenza also seeks to reconstruct the "historical Mary" to rescue her from the distortions of mariological (Roman Catholic) myths. Fiorenza concludes:

> Like the women of the resurrection narratives on the way to the tomb [feminists must] remove the "commonsense" stone that closes and contains potentially transformative readings within the preconstructed frame/tomb of the kyriarchal sex/gender system. . . . The very early, still open-ended Jesus traditions might be helpful for articulating feminist interreligious christological discourses today. These traditions understand John and Jesus as standing in a long line of messengers and prophets whom Divine Wisdom sent to announce "good news" not only to men but also to women. . . . Like John the Baptizer and Jesus the Galilean, or like Elizabeth of Ain Karim and Miriam of Nazareth, feminist theologians today continue the long line of Sophia's prophets and messengers that spans the centuries and points to an open-ended future.[25]

### The Politics of Jesus Scholarship

Almost twenty years after her groundbreaking work *In Memory of Her*, Fiorenza wrote a book, titled *Jesus and the Politics of Interpretation*, that specifically deals with the feminist interpretation of Jesus.[26] In this book, Fiorenza continues the argument from *Jesus: Miriam's Child, Sophia's Prophet*, focusing on the politics of Jesus scholarship. Fiorenza charges that modern scholarship has turned Jesus into a commodity of neo-capitalist culture. According to Fiorenza, the answer to the commodification of Jesus is not a rejection of Jesus scholarship as such but a critical examination of the

23. Ibid., 140 (adducing Luke 7:35 and Matt. 11:19).
24. Ibid., 152.
25. Ibid., 187.
26. E. S. Fiorenza, *Jesus and the Politics of Interpretation* (New York: Continuum, 2000).

ideologies themselves that drive historical Jesus research. Thus Fiorenza calls for an ethics of interpretation that undercuts anti-Jewish or anti-feminist interpretations of Jesus.

In its aims Fiorenza's book is similar to this volume in that it is conceived not primarily as a direct contribution to Jesus research but as an investigation of the presuppositions and hermeneutics underlying reconstructions of the historical Jesus and the early church. It seems ironic, however, that Fiorenza calls for a critical examination of the ideologies driving Jesus research when, quite transparently, her own work, including her reconstruction of Jesus' stance toward women, is itself heavily laden with feminist ideology—so much so that it has been recognized and critiqued even by other feminist scholars. In fact, as we will see in the following chapter, even those who share Fiorenza's feminist outlook have recognized that her ideological commitments have distorted both the procedure and results of her efforts at reconstructing Jesus' and the early church's stance toward women. It is also these same scholars, most notably Kathleen Corley, who have pointed out that Fiorenza has proven to be rather intransigent to critiques of her scholarship.

In *Jesus and the Politics of Interpretation* Fiorenza maintains that Jesus "was a member of the emancipatory *basileia* movement of Divine Wisdom for the well-being of all."[27] She writes that Christianity, as envisioned by Jesus, was "an egalitarian movement of Divine Wisdom for the healing of the downtrodden, an inclusive community of those who are powerless in the eyes of the mighty."[28] Fiorenza diagnoses an identity crisis in historical Jesus research, including the claim by scholars to have reconstructed the "real" Jesus from the historical data. Again, it must be noted, however, that Fiorenza's critique applied to herself as well, since in *In Memory of Her* she exuded great confidence to be able to do just that—reconstruct the "real" Jesus from historical data by means of redaction criticism and historical-critical methodology.

Consistently throughout this book Fiorenza lays the blame for capitalist distortions of the "real Jesus" primarily at the feet of males, though it is clear that men are not the only who that distort our understanding of Jesus. This anti-male undercurrent pervades the entire volume and is part of her overall feminist outlook.

Fiorenza charges that an emphasis on the "facts" of history "serves to promote scientific fundamentalism," a charge consistent with her previous critiques of conventional historiographic research.[29] There may be some

27. Ibid., 2.
28. Ibid.
29. Ibid., 6.

truth in Fiorenza's criticism, yet it does not invalidate historical research that is open to the data and takes seriously the fact that the canon of Scripture represents divine revelation of Jesus in the four Gospels. According to Fiorenza, the most adequate category here is that of memory, be it of Jesus as "dangerous" or as preserving the "status quo."[30]

Fiorenza notes that while in the nineteenth-century feminist movement the problem was seen to be man's and woman's sinfulness and need of redemption, recent feminist scholarship has focused on the problem of Jesus' maleness. She cites Rosemary Radford Ruether's question, "Can a male savior save women?" Fiorenza challenges what she calls the "ideology of gender dualism," i.e., male and female, alleging that in the ancient world a one-sex model was prevalent, one that saw women as having the same sex organs as men, just internally, and that viewed gender as a cultural construct rather than as a biological one. This, however, seems contradicted by Genesis 1 and 2, which speak of God creating man male and female (Gen. 1:27) and of God creating the woman from and for the man (Gen. 2:18, 20).

Fiorenza maintains that viewing Jesus as a great charismatic leader and as a heroic or divine man "reinforces the ideological power of androcentrism."[31] Even noting that women were disciples of Jesus does not break through the androcentric or, as Fiorenza calls it, "kyriocentric" (lord/master/father/husband-centered) framework of historical Jesus studies. She says that only men can identify with a male-hero Jesus.

It is this "dualistic gender lens" constituting the framework of modern Jesus research that Fiorenza sets out to question. Invoking Albert Schweitzer's book on the quest for the historical Jesus, Fiorenza concurs that scholars tend to create Jesus in their own image, but she adds that this has important political and ideological ramifications. Her goal is to challenge the "elitist, anti-Jewish, colonialist, racist, and anti-feminist tendencies of positivist Historical-Jesus scholarship."[32]

As she engages in the construction of an alternative historical-Jesus discourse, Fiorenza reenvisions Jesus as an alternative in which women's emancipation is the declared goal. The paradigm shift called for by Fiorenza is away from Jesus as "exceptional man and charismatic leader" to "the emancipatory Divine Wisdom movement of which he was a part."[33]

Fiorenza reiterates her program in *In Memory of Her* as (1) writing "a feminist history of the Jesus movements in Palestine and in the Greco-Roman cities by placing wo/men at the center of attention"; (2) moving beyond a

30. Ibid., 7.
31. Ibid., 11.
32. Ibid., 14.
33. Ibid., 21.

description of the world "as it is"—something feminists are not interested in—to changing the world to fit women's own experience of being in the world as "wo/men"; (3) focusing not on the historical Jesus but on the historical people who joined an "emancipatory *basileia*-movement"; and (4) seeking to imagine the beginnings of early Christianity differently, in feminist terms.

Fiorenza admits that different construals of the evidence are possible, but she claims that her reading is completely viable, especially when applying a "hermeneutics of suspicion." Adapting the work of Patricia Hill Collins, Fiorenza posits three criteria in Jesus research:

1) Does a reconstruction of the historical Jesus speak truth to people about the reality of their lives?
2) What is the stance toward freedom in a particular source text?
3) Does a particular reconstruction move people to struggle or does it advocate the *status quo*?[34]

In interaction with current Jesus research, especially that done by John Dominic Crossan and Luke Timothy Johnson, Fiorenza maintains that "a feminist reconstruction of Jesus must adopt both a sociopolitical frame of conflict and struggle and a theological-inclusive frame of radical equality and well-being as its reconstructive framework of interpretation."[35] To this end, she urges a method of *re-membering* and *re-vision*.

Fiorenza also responds rather defensively to a critique by another feminist scholar, Kathleen Corley. Corley strongly objects to Fiorenza's historical reconstruction of Jesus as establishing an egalitarian community on historical grounds. In turn, Fiorenza claims that Corley has misrepresented her argument and charges that Corley's historical imagination is inhibited.[36]

At the end of her book Fiorenza contends that "a feminist Christian identity is to be articulated again and again within the emancipatory struggles for the vision of God's *basileia*, which spells well-being and freedom for all in the global village."[37] Significantly, Fiorenza's feminist vision of Wisdom-Sophia involves decentering Jesus from his central role in Christianity. As Fiorenza explains:

34. Ibid., 54.
35. Ibid., 73.
36. Ibid., 129–37, with reference to K. Corley, "The Egalitarian Jesus: A Christian Myth of Origins," *Forum New Series* 1–2 (1988): 291–325.
37. Ibid., 173.

> By focusing not on the Historical-Jesus as the great (male) individual and charismatic leader but on the vision and praxis of the movement gathered in his name, such a reconstructive model . . . seeks to avoid the cultural romantic trap of wo/men's sado-masochistic attachment to the man Jesus.

In the end, the only view of Jesus acceptable to Fiorenza is one that undermines relations of domination: "The one biblical G*d of Jews, Christians, and Muslims today still calls wo/men of faith to engage in the prophetic-messianic vision of justice, freedom, love, and salvation that has inspired our ancestors in their religious-political struggles for a more just world."[38]

## Evaluation

Fiorenza's reconstruction of early Christianity has held virtually paradigmatic status among feminist biblical scholarship for the better part of two decades. This status is apparent also from the fact that other feminist and egalitarian scholars routinely take their point of departure from Fiorenza's reconstruction. As will be seen in the next chapter, however, Fiorenza's paradigm has come under increasing fire even by other feminist scholars, both male and female. It appears that her feminist ideology has unduly influenced her handling of the available evidence.

Fiorenza speaks of her enlarged Scripture as "the open, cosmic house of divine Wisdom"[39] that allows her access to divine revelation; yet, arguably, by diluting the church's historical canon, she leaves behind the inspired sources that alone can provide access to divine revelation. Fiorenza supports her notion of divine Wisdom by citing Luke 7:35, contending that "the Palestinian Jesus movement understood the mission of Jesus as that of the prophet and child of Sophia."[40] Yet while wisdom is personified in this passage, there is no evidence that Jesus or the early church understood wisdom as divine Sophia or Jesus as her "prophet and child," and Fiorenza's use of Scripture is of doubtful value exegetically.[41]

In context, Luke 7:35 is the final statement in a portion of Luke's Gospel that deals with the question of Jesus' relationship with John the Baptist.[42] Luke 7:18–23 narrates John's question to Jesus; 7:24–30 provides Jesus' assessment of John and speaks of the greatness of the kingdom; and 7:31–35 contains a parable rebuking Israel for failing to respond to both John and Jesus. According to Jesus, their failure to respond is a case of "damned if you do, damned if you don't." People did not like John's austere lifestyle

---

38. Ibid.
39. E. S. Fiorenza, ed., *Searching the Scriptures* (New York: Crossroad, 1994), 2:11.
40. Fiorenza, *In Memory of Her*, 135.
41. See Kassian, *Feminist Mistake*, 209–11.
42. See D. L. Bock, *Luke*, BECNT (Grand Rapids, MI: Baker, 1994), 1:656–58.

and took umbrage at Jesus' fraternizing with sinners. Yet both John and Jesus were sent by God as part of his salvation-historical plan: John as the herald announcing the arrival of the Messiah, Jesus as that Messiah. Israel should have received both but they received neither. They were preoccupied with the style and mode of John's and Jesus' presentation and thus failed to discern the truthfulness of their underlying message.

Jesus' statement in Luke 7:35—"Yet wisdom is justified by all her children"—harks back to Luke 7:29: "When all the people heard this, and the tax collectors too, they *declared* God *just*, having been baptized with the baptism of John." In this context, "wisdom" refers to God's plan and message as proclaimed and realized by John the Baptist (and Jesus), a personification of God's wise salvific counsel.[43]

The parallel in Matthew 11:19 speaks of wisdom's *works*; the passage in Luke refers to the *results* of these works in people's response. In Luke 7:31–35, Jesus compares contemporary Israel to spoiled brats at play who complain when others refuse to play by their rules; it's "my way or no way." This was precisely the way it was with Israel's stance toward Jesus: unless he conformed to their expectations with regard to the Messiah, they would not accept him. Clearly, this was unacceptable, and indeed foolish, because God does not conform to man's expectations; it must be the other way around.

All of this is to show that Fiorenza's interpretation of Jesus as "Sophia's prophet" lacks adequate support from Luke 7:35. This passage does not talk about Sophia as a female deity that sent Jesus as her prophet. Rather, the passage harks back to the personification of wisdom used, for example, in the book of Proverbs that presents wisdom as a divine attribute that was expressed in the missions of John the Baptist and Jesus but rejected by Israel. As Paul said elsewhere, even God's "folly" is greater than man's "wisdom"; how much greater is God's wisdom than man's folly (1 Cor. 1:18–25).

To move on to a related point, Fiorenza's location of "revelation not in texts but in Christian experience and community"[44] constitutes an unacceptable departure from Scripture's testimony to itself as inspired and authoritative (2 Tim. 3:16; 2 Pet. 1:21) and unduly shifts the locus of revelation to a sphere that is relative and thus in no way able to exercise any meaningful authority. Also, embarking on a quest for "alternative theological self-understanding" cannot be affirmed as legitimate apart from truth as conveyed in Scripture. If historical reconstruction is no longer conducted on the basis of actual historical sources and evidence but fueled by historical

---

43. See Prov. 1:20–33; 8:1–9:6 (esp. 8:32–33); and apocryphal passages mentioned in Bock, *Luke*, 1:684, n. 36.
44. Fiorenza, *In Memory of Her*, 34.

imagination on the basis of feminist presuppositions, this does not conform to conventional notions of *historical* or *research*.

In response, Fiorenza has strongly argued against a Rankean understanding of history that seeks to determine what really happened, contending that such is an impossibility.[45] Contrasting an objectivist-realist approach to history (von Ranke) with a constructionist one (her own approach), she stresses the "time-boundedness" and "linguisticality" of history, which, according to Fiorenza, make it impossible to know the real past.[46]

The cautions and concerns raised by Fiorenza are real and should not be lightly dismissed. Nevertheless, regardless of our inability to determine what really happened with absolute certainty, an approximation of this ought to remain our goal. Fiorenza's own constructionist approach utilizing historical imagination renders history far too vulnerable to revisionism. As Colleen Conway shows, this "new historicism," which argues that all interpretation is invariably ideological, irremediably subjective, and inescapably relative, is itself on uncertain footing.[47]

While containing an element of truth, Fiorenza's contention that history is always history *for a certain purpose* and *a certain group* does not adequately recognize the value of the available sources.[48] As John Elliott aptly observes, the reconception of history as revisioning and reimagining of the past in line with one's own preferred version of reality does not properly distinguish between a given ideal and its real-life actualization in the form of concrete historical social structures.[49]

In light of these insights, Fiorenza's historical reconstruction of the Jesus movement and of early Christianity requires significant revision. The arguments registered above further caution against accepting Fiorenza's reconstruction of an egalitarian Jesus community. Over the past few decades, Fiorenza's model has served as a powerful "myth of Christian origins" for the feminist movement. Adopting her model would necessitate the development of an alternative broad understanding of Jesus' approach to women and of the early church's practice with regard to women, particularly as far as their participation in roles of leadership is concerned.

---

45. E. S. Fiorenza, "Remembering the Past in Creating the Future: Historical-Critical Scholarship and Feminist Biblical Interpretation," in *Feminist Perspectives on Biblical Scholarship*, ed. A. Y. Collins, *Feminist Perspectives*, 43–63; see esp. 44–48.
46. Ibid., 48–55.
47. C. M. Conway, "The Production of the Johannine Community: A New Historicist Perspective," *Journal of Biblical Literature* 121 (2002): 494.
48. Fiorenza, "Remembering," 7.
49. J. H. Elliott, "Jesus Was Not an Egalitarian. A Critique of an Anachronistic and Idealist Theory," *Biblical Theology Bulletin* 32/3 (2002): 75–91; and "The Jesus Movement Was Not Egalitarian but Family-Oriented," *Biblical Interpretation* 11/2 (2003): 173–210. This critique also applies to Fiorenza's *Jesus and the Politics of Interpretation*.

This is not to say that Fiorenza's basic quest for a proper historical understanding of Jesus' treatment of women is illegitimate. However, any position on this subject must be based on a plausible reconstruction of the words and actions of Jesus based on the available sources. There is a need for a study of all the available sources toward that end. Jesus' example and teaching are central in this regard, but a comprehensive study would need to include also the book of Genesis, the sweep of Old Testament history, and the New Testament Epistles, particularly those of Paul.[50]

By comparing Fiorenza's earlier work with her more recent contributions, we can conclude that, first, Fiorenza seems to have moved from her initial assertion of Jesus' "discipleship of equals" (1983) to a stance that calls for a decentering of Jesus in light of his incontrovertible maleness (2001). Does this indicate a tacit acknowledgment on Fiorenza's part that, even if Jesus had established an egalitarian community, this would still not satisfy her and her fellow feminists?

Second, how is it possible to decenter Jesus and still retain his centrality in the Christian faith? By focusing on the community rather than on Jesus in order to diminish the offense created by his maleness, Fiorenza jettisons what is rightly, and inextricably, central to the Christian faith. It is not membership in an egalitarian movement that saves anyone but faith in Jesus' finished work at the cross.

Third, not only does Fiorenza marginalize Jesus by saying that Jews, Christians, and Muslims all can be part of a great movement of love, justice, and concern for the poor, but she also dilutes the concept of God. Thus theology proper, soteriology, and ecclesiology are all redefined in a way that no longer is Christian, in the sense this has been affirmed by historic Christianity on the basis of biblical teaching. Jesus said, "I am the way, and the truth, and the life. No one comes to the Father except through me" (John 14:6). The church does not consist of those belonging to an egalitarian movement of love, justice, and concern for the poor but of believers in Christ who have been regenerated by the Holy Spirit.

Fourth, by saying she is not interested in how things actually were in the first century but in what she can *imagine* things to have been, and faulting those feminists who disagree with her for an "inhibited imagination," Fio-

---

50. As mentioned, this comprehensive study is beyond the scope of the present work, in which the focus is only on Jesus and women. Though see the attempts by S. B. Clark, *Man and Woman in Christ* (Ann Arbor, MI: Servant Books, 1980); W. Neuer, *Man and Woman in Christian Perspective* (Wheaton, IL: Crossway, 1991); S. J. Grenz with D. M. Kjesbo, *Women in the Church: A Biblical Theology of Women in Ministry* (Downers Grove, IL: InterVarsity, 1995); and D. K. Patterson, "Aspects of a Biblical Theology of Womanhood" (Th.D. thesis, University of South Africa, 1997). See also the survey of the material on Jesus and women in the Gospels in chapter 14 of this volume.

renza seems to have moved away from her initial efforts in *In Memory of Her*, to reconstruct Jesus' program of establishing a discipleship of equals, to a more utopian vision that, by her own admission, may not be adequately grounded in historical precedent. Her shift may be the result of the stringent response, even from fellow feminists. Or it may be due to her own realization that even if Jesus did establish an egalitarian community, he was still male, and, with Ruether, "How can a male savior save women?" For this reason Fiorenza's more recent work has focused more on the politics of Jesus research. Yet Fiorenza, too, reconstructs Christianity in view of her feminist presuppositions and beliefs.

Fifth, major questions remain regarding the primary role of feminist experience in Fiorenza's hermeneutic, which leads to a marginalization of Scripture in her scholarly work. As preeminent ethicist and egalitarian R. B. Hays rightly notes, "The danger of Fiorenza's work is that her approach might ultimately undermine the authority of the New Testament so thoroughly that its liberating power would also be lost."[51] W. Spohn concurs: "One wonders whether there is much scripture left for Christian ethics in this approach. . . . The end result of Fiorenza's complex project is a moral argument that seems minimally religious."[52]

Sixth, calling biblical wisdom a "female deity" is without scriptural warrant. The central confession of Judaism affirms that there is one God (Deut. 6:4), and he is the one consistently called "Father" by Jesus. Wisdom, according to Proverbs 8:22–31 and other passages, is an attribute of this one God rather than a separate, independent female deity that was at his side at creation. Wisdom is personified as a woman in Proverbs, as is folly—a literary device humanizing important ethical principles designed to teach important theological truths.

From the vantage point of one who takes Scripture seriously as a source for Christian theology, therefore, we must conclude that Fiorenza's related work is valuable only to the extent that it accurately represents the historical Jesus. In fact, it is the aim in interpretation to recover exactly what Jesus and the early church taught and practiced regarding women. If the early church practiced egalitarianism, this should be the norm for the church. The question, then, is, "Does Fiorenza's reconstruction accurately describe Jesus' approach to women as far as this can be discerned by historical research?" That is the subject of the next chapter.

---

51. R. B. Hays, *The Moral Vision of the New Testament* (New York: Harper, 1996), 282.
52. W. Spohn, *What Are They Saying about Scripture and Ethics?* (New York: Paulist, 1995), 73.

# 9

# Kathleen Corley and Others: The Case of the Crumbling Paradigm

*The notion that Jesus established an anti-patriarchal movement or a "discipleship of equals" is a myth posited to buttress modern Christian social engineering.*

—Kathleen Corley, *Women and the Historical Jesus* (2002)[1]

**As we've** seen, Elisabeth Schüssler Fiorenza's reconstruction of Jesus and early Christianity held enormous sway in feminist circles for a considerable amount of time and enjoyed near-paradigmatic status. In recent years, however, many, even in feminist circles, have begun to question the historical merits of Fiorenza's proposal. The following discussion summarizes the contributions toward this historical reconstruction offered by Kathleen Corley, John Elliott, Esther Ng, and Amy-Jill Levine. These contributions will be integrated into a critique of Fiorenza's reconstruction of Jesus' stance toward women.

1. K. E. Corley, *Women and the Historical Jesus: Feminist Myths of Christian Origins* (Santa Rosa, CA: Polebridge, 2002), 1.

## Kathleen Corley: Mounting a Challenge

Kathleen Corley, who holds a master of arts and a doctor of philosophy in religion from Claremont Graduate School, mounts a major challenge to Fiorenza's paradigm of Jesus as a first-century Jewish feminist in her book *Women and the Historical Jesus* (2002). Corley, who serves as Oshkosh Northwestern Distinguished Professor at the University of Wisconsin-Oshkosh, where she has taught since 1992, forcefully contends that Fiorenza unduly imposes her feminism onto the biblical and historical record, and other feminists agree.

What is particularly significant is that these critiques are coming from within the feminist movement. Not only non-egalitarians are questioning the notion that Jesus was an egalitarian, but also feminists themselves who are committed to responsible historical research. Corley and others have come to the realization that the view of a feminist Jesus is historically unsustainable.

Thus at the very outset of her book *Women and the Historical Jesus: Feminist Myths of Christian Origins* (2002), Kathleen Corley, in a reference to Fiorenza's landmark work *In Memory of Her*, calls the notion that Jesus established a discipleship of equals a "feminist myth of Christian origins."[2] Summarizing her own conclusions, Corley writes:

> While this study affirms the role of women in Jesus' own community and in subsequent Jesus movements, it challenges both the assumption that Jesus himself fought ancient patriarchal limitations on women and the hypothesis that the presence of women among his disciples was unique within Hellenistic Judaism. Rather, an analysis of Jesus' teaching suggests that while Jesus censured the class and status distinctions of his culture, that critique did not extend to unequal gender distinctions. The notion that Jesus established an anti-patriarchal movement or a "discipleship of equals" is a myth posited to buttress modern Christian social engineering.[3]

It is significant that Corley—a member of a scholarly group of critical scholars called the Jesus Seminar known for its unconventional approach, such as casting colored beads to vote on the historicity of Jesus' words and deeds—reached her conclusions on the basis of *historical research*, the very method that led Elisabeth Schüssler Fiorenza to the diametrically opposite conclusion that Jesus was in fact pursuing an egalitarian agenda.

According to Corley, while Jesus was concerned for Jewish monotheism and expressed an interest in class and rank, "he did not address the concern

---

2. See already K. Corley, "The Egalitarian Jesus: A Christian Myth of Origins," *Forum New Series* 1–2 (1988): 291–325 and the discussion in the previous chapter.
3. Corley, *Women and the Historical Jesus*, 1.

most central to modern women—inequality between the sexes."[4] Rather, Corley notes, Jesus reaffirmed marriage, "the major hierarchical social relationship between a man and a woman that was considered the bedrock of the state in antiquity" (Mark 10:1–12).[5]

---

**Fact Sheet 7: Kathleen E. Corley**

**Education:** M.A. and Ph.D. in religion, Claremont Graduate School
**Academic Position:** Oshkosh Northwestern Distinguished Professor at the University of Wisconsin-Oshkosh, where she has taught since 1992
**Major Work:** *Women and the Historical Jesus* (2002)
**Type of Feminist:** Jesus Seminar (Historical)
**View of Jesus:** Notion that Jesus established "discipleship of equals" (Fiorenza) is itself a feminist myth of Christian origins; Jesus reaffirmed traditional marriage

---

Corley observes that the reigning consensus among the members of the Jesus Seminar, many of whom were influenced by the scholarship of Schüssler Fiorenza, affirms that "Jesus preached a kind of social egalitarianism that pitted him against the social and religious hierarchies of his day."[6] Corley cites a litany of scholars who refer to Jesus as a feminist, labeling his acceptance of women as revolutionary, radical, unique, reformational, or unprecedented in the ancient world, including Palestine.[7]

However, while the vision of an egalitarian "society of Jesus" that eventually gave way to a patriarchal backlash by the second- and third-century institutional church may provide an ideal rallying point as a "foundational myth for Christian feminism," Corley argues that this reconstruction is historically untenable and unsupported by the available sources, including the Gospels.

Corley identifies five specific problems with Fiorenza's work. (1) The radical distinction between Jesus' attitude and practice toward women and that of his Jewish contemporaries is not borne out by concrete historical evidence. (2) The reconstruction of Jesus' "discipleship of equals" remains without real parallel in first-century Palestine; however, this would be a problem only if Jesus were limited to imitating other contemporary Jewish rabbis. (3) The contention that Jesus preached *wholeness* in contrast to *holiness* is questionable. (4) The insistence that Jesus founded an egalitarian community seems out of step with both first-century Judaism and Greco-Roman culture. (5) The attribution of the decline of women's status in early Christianity to Greco-Roman social institutions is doubtful.

---

4. Ibid., 4.
5. Ibid.
6. Ibid., 7.
7. Ibid., 10; see p. 148, notes 13–18.

In the conclusion to *Women and the Historical Jesus*, Corley summarizes her major findings. First, she writes, "The group around Jesus cannot be characterized as a 'discipleship of equals,' since probably only a few women were members of the predominantly male group; . . . the limited participation of women does not suggest a group focused on equality or equal representation."[8] Second, Jesus' concern was more broadly for the poor and the marginalized in society than for women's rights specifically: "The women seem to be around Jesus more as a matter of course than as a result of a gender-equal vision of the Kingdom of God." Any such concerns came to the fore only subsequent to Jesus' ministry.[9] Third, women around Jesus continued to be involved in traditionally female roles such as mourning the dead and participating in funerary rites and gravesite rituals. Corley believes that Jesus sought to discourage this involvement, and thus she locates a feminist or "resistant impulse," not in Jesus but in some of the women around him.[10]

These comments show considerable more historical nuancing than the reconstruction by Fiorenza. Overall, Corley finds a certain amount of common ground with Fiorenza while remaining largely critical of her basic paradigm.

It should also be noted that in her work *Jesus and the Politics of Interpretation*, Fiorenza responded to an earlier essay by Corley. However, Fiorenza did not advance any significant new evidence in support of her historical reconstruction of Jesus' stance toward women in *In Memory of Her*. For this reason Corley's main critique continues to be valid, and other voices have added further critiques that undermine the validity of Fiorenza's paradigm of the "egalitarian Jesus," all of which contribute to the "case of the crumbling paradigm."

### John H. Elliott: Debunking the Historical Jesus

John Elliott is another who critiques the notion that Jesus instituted an egalitarian community. Elliott, professor emeritus of theology and religious studies at the University of San Francisco, contends that Fiorenza's theory is implausible both socially and politically in light of the available textual and historical evidence. According to Elliott, the notion of the egalitarian Jesus does not square with the actual historical and social nature of the nascent Jesus movement and represents an instance of the "idealist fallacy," that is, the improper practice of confusing one's own preferred ideology with actual reality. Elliott summarizes his concerns as follows.

8. Ibid., 143.
9. Ibid., 144.
10. Ibid., 144–45.

1) The concept of equality is of modern origin and alien to the thought world and social reality of the ancient world:

> The notion that all persons are created equal and endowed with certain inalienable rights is a construct of the modern Enlightenment and thoroughly alien to the thinking of the ancient world. There the prevailing notion was rather that humans were by nature born unequal and this unalterable inequality was evident physically, socially, and ethnically.[11]

2) *Equality* terminology (*iso-*) is never used in the New Testament to convey the notion of gender or other equality but rather that of equity or sameness.[12]

3) Those who find egalitarianism in the New Testament interpret texts anachronistically by imposing a post-Enlightenment concept onto the first-century world. One example is Jesus' call to discipleship (e.g., Mark 1:16–20; 10:29–30), which involved a renunciation of one's natural ties where they conflicted with supreme allegiance to Jesus. However, not all were called to leave their natural families, and those who were may have done so only temporarily. Hence, Jesus' call for repentance and a radical reorientation of priorities sought exclusive allegiance and unconditional trust in God in light of the imminence of God's reign and the urgency of Jesus' message but did not entail an explicit critique of the family as such. The same is true for Jesus' anticipation of conflict and division within biological families as a result of his call to discipleship (e.g., Mark 13:12).

4) The biblical texts cited in support of Jesus' establishment of an egalitarian society are better interpreted on the presumption of inequality of social status. Jesus' teaching regarding the reversal of status presumes the existence of status in the first place (e.g., Mark 9:35–37; see Mark 10:13–15). This includes differences in status between disciple and teacher (Luke 6:40; Matt. 10:24–25; John 13:16; 15:20); parents and children (Mark 7:11–13; 10:19); and husbands and wives (Matt. 5:31–32; 19:9).

5) No concrete historical or social evidence exists that Jesus instituted a community of equals. There is no evidence in the writings of Josephus, Pliny, Tacitus, Suetonius, or any other extrabiblical author.

6) The primary New Testament text cited in support of egalitarianism, Galatians 3:28, pertains to the unity of believers in Christ, not their equality,

---

11. J. H. Elliott, "Jesus Was Not an Egalitarian. A Critique of an Anachronistic and Idealist Theory," *Biblical Theology Bulletin* 32/3 (2002): 77.
12. Ibid., 78, 84, citing the instances of *isos* in Matt. 20:12; Mark 14:46, 59; Luke 6:34; John 5:18; Acts 11:17; Phil. 2:6; Rev. 21:16; of *isotēs* in 1 Cor. 8:13–14; Col. 4:1; of *isotimos* in 2 Pet. 1:1; and of *isopsychos* in Phil. 2:20.

affirming inclusivity with regard to ethnic, social, and gender boundaries rather than leveling all status distinctions.

7) The equation between patriarchy and dominance customarily made by feminists does not hold.

8) The egalitarian hypothesis is unsupported by the available historical evidence but constitutes an instance of the "idealist fallacy."

9) Insufficient thought is given to the practical implementation of an egalitarian vision into concrete social reality. From a sociological point of view, Jesus' establishment of an egalitarian community would have required dramatic changes in the social structures of his day.

10) The thesis has been rejected by feminist scholars such as Mary Rose D'Angelo (1992), Amy-Jill Levine (1994), and Kathleen Corley (1998, 2002) owing to its lack of historical support.

11) The notion of Jesus' establishment of a community of equals fails to account for Jesus' reaffirmation of the family as the primary social structure instituted by God.

Elliott concludes the first part of his study:

> By imputing to the biblical authors a modern concept of equality that is not found in the Bible and the ancient world and by allowing this imputed concept to determine their interpretation of the New Testament, they have produced an interpretation that distorts and obscures the actual content and thrust of these texts. Such an interpretative procedure appears [to be] more eisegesis than exegesis and deserves to [be] rejected as a[n] unhappy example [of] interpretive method. An anachronistic imputation of modern notions to the biblical authors should be challenged and resisted in the name of historical honesty wherever and however it occurs. To be sure, let us expend every ounce of energy it takes to reform the ills of society and church. But let us do so with historical honesty, respecting the past as past and not trying to recreate it with modern constructs or re-write it with new ideological pens.[13]

In his sequel, Elliott investigates Fiorenza's theory with regard to circumstances subsequent to Jesus' death. According to Elliott, "The egalitarian theory fares no better in clarifying the structure of the Jesus movement after Jesus' death than it does in explaining the nature of the community established by Jesus."[14] Not only is the concept of equality or egalitarianism historically incompatible with first-century conditions, but there is

13. Ibid., 90.
14. J. H. Elliott, "The Jesus Movement Was Not Egalitarian but Family-Oriented," *Biblical Interpretation* 11/2 (2003): 204.

no evidence of egalitarianism in the New Testament or any other ancient source. Elliott concludes:

> On a personal note, I must confess that I have not enjoyed mounting this critique. With every fibre of my egalitarian being I wish it were demonstrable that the Jesus movement had been egalitarian, at least at some point in its early history. This surely would make it easier for today's advocates of equality, among whom I count myself, to appeal to our past as a source of inspiration and moral guidance for the present. But, as the historical and ideological critic in all of us insists, wishing and politically correct ideology cannot not [sic] make it so. Ultimately, this well-intentioned theory is an unhappy example of anachronism and idealist thinking that must be challenged not just because it is indemonstrable or an example of flawed interpretation but also because it is so seductive. The notion that the Jesus movement ever formed a "community of equals" founded by Jesus is a phantasm, a *fata morgana*, a wish still awaiting incarnation. If the church were ever to put an egalitarian vision into practice, it would be a first-time event and an accomplishment that eluded even Jesus and his first followers.[15]

### Esther Yue L. Ng: Challenges Raised

Yet another recent critique of Fiorenza's work comes from Esther Yue L. Ng, *Reconstructing Christian Origins? The Feminist Theology of Elisabeth Schüssler Fiorenza: An Evaluation* (2002), originally a doctoral dissertation completed under the supervision of the British egalitarian scholar I. Howard Marshall in 1999. In her discussion of Fiorenza's work, Ng challenges Fiorenza's treatment of the so-called androcentric texts in Judaism and her depiction of the female figure of divine Sophia. She also questions the alleged presence of emancipatory impulses within Judaism that provide the plausibility structure for the emergence of an egalitarian vision among the early Christians.

With regard to the Greco-Roman world, Ng suggests that Fiorenza's picture of emancipation is too rosy while her portrayal of patriarchalism is too gloomy.[16] Ng concludes:

> The plausibility of true egalitarianism in early Christian groups is very small, if they took their models from their contemporary Graeco-Roman society, since the best kind of egalitarianism that can be found . . . falls short of our modern standards. If . . . early Christian groups met in households, we have even more reason to believe that, if these groups took Graeco-Roman house-

15. Ibid., 205–6.
16. E. Y. L. Ng, *Reconstructing Christian Origins? The Feminist Theology of Elisabeth Schüssler Fiorenza: An Evaluation* (Carlisle: Paternoster, 2002), 108.

holds as their model, they would be hierarchical and patriarchal in nature, rather than egalitarian.[17]

Ng also evaluates Fiorenza's contention that the burden of proof rests with those who dispute the presence and agency of early Christian women and concludes that a fair approach would examine the available evidence to see whether one's hypothesis does justice to the available texts.[18]

Ng also notes that Fiorenza operates under a "canon within a canon." She limits revelation to those texts that in her view break through patriarchal structures.[19] Apparently, Fiorenza awards canonical status to her own reconstruction of early Christianity, insulating her against any further criticism by those who differ with her reconstruction, including other feminists. Since her reconstruction is only one of several possible alternatives, this leaves her with a precarious foundation.

With regard to the appeal to women's experience as a norm for determining whether a text has potential for liberation, Ng observes that any such appeal has its limitations since women's experience varies according to culture and a variety of other factors. Finally, Ng identifies a degree of circularity in any approach that starts out with a particular ideology, finds its ideal expressed in a particular historical reconstruction, such as Jesus' discipleship of equals, and then locates evidence that supported its conclusions.

## Amy-Jill Levine: Questions Posed

In her article "Second Temple Judaism, Jesus, and Women," Amy-Jill Levine, a Jewish feminist professor of New Testament at Vanderbilt University and editor of the fourteen-volume *Feminist Companion to the New Testament and Early Christian Writings*, seeks to provide a nuanced and evidence-based assessment of Jesus' treatment of women against the backdrop of how others treated women in first-century Judaism.[20] Against the stereotype that "the Jesus movement . . . was good for women" and "Second Temple Judaism . . . was . . . generally bad for women," Levine contends that (1) Second Temple Judaism was not as patriarchal as often alleged, speaking of a "critical feminist impulse" already present; and (2) that the Jesus movement was not as egalitarian as is commonly held.[21]

---

17. Ibid., 110.
18. Ibid., 125.
19. Ibid., 329.
20. A.-J. Levine, "Second Temple Judaism, Jesus, and Women: Yeast of Eden," *Biblical Interpretation* 2/1 (1994): 8–33.
21. Ibid., 12–13.

In her article Levine opposes the notion that "Jewish women of course were attracted to the 'community of equals' of the Sophia-Christ."[22] According to Levine, in Second Temple Judaism, Levitical purity legislation was not as "all-consuming" as often alleged,[23] and women participated in synagogal activities more than frequently realized.[24]

---

**Fact Sheet 8: Amy-Jill Levine**

**Education:** Ph.D. in religion, Duke University (1984)

**Academic Position:** E. Rhodes and Leona B. Carpenter Professor of New Testament Studies, Vanderbilt University

**Major Work:** Editor, *The Feminist Companion to the New Testament and Early Christian Writings* (14 vols.)

**Type of Feminist**: New (Jewish) Feminist

**View of Jesus:** Judaism more diverse; Jesus movement less egalitarian than alleged by Fiorenza; feminism has priority over Scripture; critical stance toward Scripture; variety of literary methods

---

As a result, Levine questions the notion of women being liberated by Jesus from an oppressive, patriarchal Judaism. After an extensive study of the hypothetical "Q" document, Levine opposes the view that women in the Jesus movement "were 'liberated' from a purity-obsessed, institutionally restricted, patriarchal Judaism."[25] If Jesus "proclaimed the elimination of gendered heirarchies [*sic*]," according to Levine, he failed. "The past may not be able to reveal the ideal, egalitarian community, but investigation of the texts (if not the texts themselves) offer[s] a means of creating one yet."[26]

While one wonders to what extent Levine's historical work is motivated by her desire to present Judaism in a more positive light than has previously been done, her reconstruction differs significantly from Fiorenza's. Levine concludes that the historical and textual evidence does not support Fiorenza's hypothesis of an "egalitarian Jesus." Nevertheless, she holds out hope that feminist investigation of biblical texts—albeit not necessarily from the texts—may aid in bringing about the feminist ideal in our day, all but abandoning the notion that feminists can find support for their ideal in the practice of Jesus and directly in the biblical texts.

22. Citing J. D. Crossan, *The Historical Jesus: The Life of a Mediterranean Jewish Peasant* (San Francisco: HarperSanFrancisco, 1991), 298, following Fiorenza.

23. Levine, "Second Temple Judaism," 15, citing E. P. Sanders, *Judaism: Practice and Belief, 63 BCE–66 CE* (Philadelphia: Trinity Press International, 1992), 71, 76; contra B. Witherington, "Women (NT)," in *Anchor Bible Dictionary*, ed. D. N. Freedman (Garden City, NY: Doubleday, 1992), 6.957.

24. Citing B. J. Brooten, *Women Leaders in the Ancient Synagogue: Inscriptional Evidence and Background Issues*, Brown Judaic Studies 36 (Chico, CA: Scholars Press, 1982).

25. Levine, "Second Temple Judaism," 32.

26. Ibid., 33.

Table 9.1: Major Feminist Critiques of Fiorenza's Theory of Jesus' "Discipleship of Equals"

| Proponent | Critique |
| --- | --- |
| Kathleen Corley | Lacks adequate historical foundation; "myth of early Christian origins" |
| John Elliott | Improper anachronistic imputation of modern notion of "equality" |
| Esther Ng | Picture of emancipation too rosy, of patriarchalism too gloomy |
| Amy-Jill Levine | First-century Judaism more diverse; Jesus movement less egalitarian |

## Evaluation

The critiques of Fiorenza's paradigm by Kathleen Corley, John Elliott, Esther Ng, and Amy-Jill Levine are on the whole persuasive. As Kathleen Corley compellingly shows, Fiorenza's historical reconstruction of Jesus lacks an adequate historical foundation and is itself a "myth of early Christian origins." As John Elliott demonstrates, Fiorenza improperly imputes the modern notion of "equality" onto Jesus and the biblical record. As Esther Ng aptly notes, Fiorenza's picture of emancipation in the Jesus movement is too rosy, and her portrayal of first-century Jewish patriarchalism is too gloomy. And as Amy-Jill Levine helpfully points out, historical research shows that first-century Judaism was more diverse than Fiorenza's monolithic presentation, and the Jesus movement was less egalitarian than she contends.

The major conclusion, therefore, is this: Fiorenza's theory that Jesus, as a first-century Jewish feminist, established a "discipleship of equals" is not sustainable any longer by serious historical research. To put it bluntly, Jesus was not a feminist, nor did he establish a radically egalitarian community. Perhaps the realization that Fiorenza's system is ultimately unsustainable has driven even Fiorenza herself to look for other texts that are more in line with her feminist ideology. She contends, "Only those traditions and texts that critically break through patriarchal culture . . . have the theological authority of revelation,"[27] and such revelation is to be found "in the life and ministry of Jesus as well as in the discipleship community of equals called forth by him."[28] By this she sets up a "canon within a canon" based on her feminist presuppositions.[29]

It is understandable that Fiorenza, when finding insufficient warrant for her feminist ideology in Scripture, discards portions of the biblical record that she views as having a "patriarchal bias" and instead includes extrabibli-

27. Fiorenza, *In Memory of Her*, 33.
28. Ibid., 34.
29. See esp. E. S. Fiorenza, "Emerging Issues in Feminist Biblical Interpretation," in *Christian Feminism: Visions of a New Humanity* (ed. J. L. Weidman; San Francisco: HarperSanFrancisco, 1984), 44–47; Fiorenza, "Toward a Feminist Biblical Hermeneutics: Biblical Interpretation and Liberation Theology," in *The Challenge of Liberation Theology: A First World Response*, ed. B. Mahan and L. D. Richesin (Maryknoll, NY: Orbis, 1981), 107–8.

cal texts. Not only does this unduly blur the line between inspired Scripture and later non-inspired writings, but also her rationale for revisioning the feminist canon is itself untenable.[30] Fiorenza is driven by a search for "a different theological self-understanding and historical imagination." She advocates "transgressing the boundaries" of the recognized Christian canon in order to include writings she judges to be more favorable toward her feminist perspective.

By this Fiorenza has moved from a revisionist stance to an increasingly more radical position. Her search for a new canon and new texts amounts to an implicit admission that her quest to find in Scripture an "egalitarian Jesus" has been unsuccessful. The reformist feminist effort to show that Jesus was a feminist has largely failed, as is recognized even by many feminists themselves. As a result, many reformist feminists have moved on to expand their canon, look for new texts, and establish a new church.

This, however, is not an option for egalitarians. Because of their commitment to an inerrant Scripture, they must show that Jesus was egalitarian and thus can be used as a paradigm for contemporary church practice. This, in turn, places egalitarians in the difficult position of defending a paradigm—that of the egalitarian Jesus—that has largely been discarded by other feminists.

Yet before taking up this issue it will be helpful to take a closer look at more recent developments in the feminist non-evangelical world. How have feminists dealt with the case of the crumbling paradigm? What is the current state of affairs in the feminist movement? What, if anything, has taken the place of Fiorenza's paradigm of the egalitarian Jesus? Or is there in fact no prevailing paradigm in the feminist movement in our day? It is to this fascinating question that we now turn.

---

30. E. S. Fiorenza, ed., *Searching the Scriptures* (New York: Crossroad, 1994), 2:8; see also R. R. Ruether, *Womanguides: Readings toward a Feminist Theology* (Boston: Beacon, 1985); and compare the section on "Toward a New Canon" in Kassian, *Feminist Mistake*, 200–201.

# 10

# THE FEMINIST COMPANION
# AND THE NEW FACE OF FEMINISM

*The task of feminist exegesis . . . is to bring to front stage the female
characters of the text, to draw attention to their absence, and to examine the textual presuppositions that shape their characterization.*

—Dorothy Lee, *A Feminist Companion to John* (2003)[1]

*The new* face of feminism is not that of any one person in the feminist
movement. Unlike previous eras in the movement, which were marked by
strong personalities, feminism in our day does not have any one recognizable
spokeswoman. Instead, feminism is significantly diversified into a variety
of strands, many literary in nature. Searches for grand paradigms such as
Fiorenza's have largely ceased, and scholars are widely engaged in studies of smaller pericopes with no attempt to assemble their findings into a
larger synthesis. In many ways, interpretive realism—closer attention to the
biblical text—has replaced ideological fervor, though, of course, feminist
presuppositions remain a functional nonnegotiable.

In the early years of modern feminism, scholars utilized primarily historical or sociological approaches, probing into the most likely orientation of
Jesus' followers and the role of women in that movement. Many though

---

1. D. A. Lee, "Abiding in the Fourth Gospel: A Case Study in Feminist Biblical Theology," in
*A Feminist Companion to John*, ed. A.-J. Levine (Cleveland, OH: Pilgrim, 2003), 2:65.

not all reformist feminist scholars, whether revisionist or liberationist or both, drew on some form of the historical-critical method, such as redaction criticism, primarily to see *historically* whether Jesus was patriarchal or egalitarian or to understand his approach to women in relation to first-century Judaism and the Greco-Roman world.

Over time some feminist scholars began to follow a mainly literary or narrative approach to scriptural interpretation, bringing their feminist outlook to the text in an effort to *reread* Scripture in light of their concerns and interests. This method is found in the work of the Old Testament scholar Phyllis Trible, especially in her influential contribution *Texts of Terror*. The method can also be seen in the 1983 issue of the journal *Semeia*. The most recent expression of this literary approach is located in the multi-volume *Feminist Companion* edited by Amy-Jill Levine, where the term *feminist* encompasses all types of feminism with no distinction between radical and reformist approaches or further subtypes.

### The New Feminism

The development over the past several decades from a historical to a literary approach in feminist biblical interpretation has included some literature on Jesus and women.[2] This development is essentially in keeping with trends in the field of hermeneutics in general.[3] While literary feminist approaches often take their starting point from the work of Elisabeth Schüssler Fiorenza and other feminist writers who utilize historical approaches, such as Rosemary Radford Ruether, their ultimate interest lies in the interpretation of particular biblical texts rather than in reconstructing the historical setting underlying those texts.

Adele Reinhartz writes that she follows "along a path that has been cleared by others before me over the last quarter century or more," listing Fiorenza and others.[4] Dorothy Lee likewise takes her point of departure from the work of Fiorenza yet seeks to transcend it in significant ways.[5] She writes:

> Elisabeth Schüssler Fiorenza has given perhaps the most thorough response to these questions, developing a methodology arising from women's historical and political experience of marginalization. The hermeneutical methodology

2. This is not to say that literary readings were not found in earlier periods, but that the focus shifted from a predominantly historical to a literary paradigm.
3. See esp. K. J. Vanhoozer, *Is There a Meaning in This Text?* (Grand Rapids, MI: Zondervan, 1998).
4. A. Reinhartz, "Women in the Johannine Community: An Exercise in Historical Imagination," in *A Feminist Companion to John*, 2:15.
5. Lee, "Abiding in the Fourth Gospel," 2:64.

she has developed is based on a revisioned historical criticism that endeavors to enter the text imaginatively and critically, making contact with women's hidden traditions. Employing a "hermeneutic of suspicion," Fiorenza's model incorporates remembrance and re-actualization of women's reclaimed history in the struggle to develop a community of equality and liberation. This struggle has led, for her, to include other texts from the ancient world that contain resources for women's liberation.

However, as Lee observes, this method of historical criticism means that Fiorenza's "interest in the text as a literary and theological whole is generally secondary to its interest in the world *behind the text*, despite some rhetoric to the contrary." Lee herself is suspicious of Fiorenza's hermeneutic of suspicion, because "it regards women's experience as the ultimate norm for authority in interpreting the text, creating arguably an 'alternative magisterium [teaching office],'" and uses suspicion as the primary exegetical tool for exposing the alleged patriarchal bias reflected in the text of Scripture.[6]

A better approach, according to Lee, studies the presence or absence of female characters and their mode of presentation within specific biblical texts.[7] She writes:

> [Such a] feminist re-reading examines various biblical documents in order to draw women from the shadows, exploring the roles they play (or don't play) and assessing their literary and theological function. . . . Thus the task of feminist exegesis, in this view, is to bring to front stage the female characters of the text, to draw attention to their absence, and to examine the textual presuppositions that shape their characterization.[8]

In order to evaluate this feminist literary approach, special emphasis will be given in this chapter to three representative and influential collections of literary feminist studies over the past two decades: the 1983 issue of the journal *Semeia* published by the Society of Biblical Literature (SBL); the 1994 commentary collection *Searching the Scriptures*; and the five-volume *Feminist Companion to the Gospels* published in 2003 and 2004.

### Semeia (1983)

The journal *Semeia* devoted an entire issue (vol. 28 [1983]) to the Bible and feminist hermeneutics from a literary vantage point. This is a sign of

6. Ibid., 2:65; see D. A. Lee, "Reclaiming the Sacred Text—Christian Feminism and Spirituality," in *Claiming Our Ties: Studies in Religion by Australian Women Scholars*, ed. J. Morny and P. Magee (Sydney: Australian Association for the Study of Religion, 1994), 80–84; Lee, "Beyond Suspicion? The Fatherhood of God in the Fourth Gospel," *Pacifica* 8 (1995): 140–54.
7. Lee, "Abiding in the Fourth Gospel," 2:65.
8. Ibid.

the increasing attention given to feminist interpretation in the larger world of scholarship and to literary approaches within feminist interpretation as a whole. The volume, edited by Mary Ann Tolbert, gathers several papers originally presented at the 1981 meeting of the American Academy of Religion (AAR) and SBL in Dallas. The two essays that are relevant for the present discussion are Janice Capel Anderson's, which is included in the *Feminist Companion to Matthew*, and "Fallible Followers: Women and Men in the Gospel of Mark" by Elizabeth Struthers Malbon.

The introductory essay by Tolbert is devoted to a discussion of "the problem of the Bible and feminist hermeneutics."[9] Tolbert is a reformist feminist who is committed to operating within the framework of the Christian tradition. She expresses a bias in favor of the Bible though she is prepared to dismiss it if necessary.[10] At the outset, she states her four commitments in descending order:

1) a commitment to feminism and its critique of oppressive structures, including those of Christianity;

2) a commitment to operate within the framework of the Christian tradition, thus marking her as a "reformist feminist";

3) a bias in favor of the Bible, though one that must of necessity "be open to judgment and, if necessary, dismissal";[11] and

4) a commitment to the canons of academic discourse.

Identifying feminism as essentially a liberation movement, Tolbert distinguishes between the "ascendancy position," which argues that women are superior to men, so that power structures that currently place men in power over women ought to be reversed, and the "equality position," which aims for the replacement of all suppressive structures and advocates reconciliation between the sexes. The latter is the more common approach.

With regard to feminist hermeneutics, Tolbert affirms that not only feminist but all biblical interpretation is subjective: "Interpretation, then, is always a subjective activity, in the sense that it is always influenced by the conscious and unconscious concerns of the interpreter."[12] Thus, for Tolbert, "all hermeneutical perspectives are advocacy positions."[13] Yet, the fact that

9. M. A. Tolbert, "Defining the Problem: The Bible and Feminist Hermeneutics," *Semeia* 28 (1983): 113–26.

10. Ibid., 114.

11. Ibid.

12. Ibid., 117.

13. Ibid.; see esp. Fiorenza, "Toward a Feminist Biblical Hermeneutics: Biblical Interpretation and Liberation Theology," in *The Challenge of Liberation Theology: A First World Response*, ed. B. Mahan and L. D. Richesin (Maryknoll, NY: Orbis, 1981), 91–112.

all scholarship is advocacy does not necessarily invite anarchy. Rather, the criteria of public evidence, logic, reasonableness, and intellectual sophistication still apply in distinguishing acceptable from unacceptable positions. Nevertheless, different reading communities will employ different canons of validity.

Feminist hermeneutics, then, positions itself over against patriarchal hermeneutics, which advocates a "male-oriented, hierarchically established present cultural power system."[14] Patriarchal hermeneutics can be defined as a reading of a text or reconstruction of a history in light of the oppressive structures of patriarchal society. Feminist hermeneutics may aim primarily at exposing the androcentric bias or oppressive intention underlying a given text, demonstrating that such a text is unalterably patriarchal and thereby without authority or value (the ascendancy view), or at uncovering the "hidden liberation potential" of certain texts for women, a practice more common among the proponents of the equality position.[15] In all this, feminist hermeneutics is grounded self-consciously in women's experience of oppression.

What is more, according to Tolbert, feminist hermeneutics is profoundly paradoxical, because in seeking to dismantle the patriarchal bias of Scripture, it employs as its tool for liberation the very Scriptures containing the bias it seeks to dismantle. In keeping with her reformist stance, Tolbert eschews the notion of a feminist revolution, advocating instead incremental changes over a long period of time, brought about by "small, often unnoticed acts of subversion,"[16] something that calls for patience.

Within the reformist position, according to Tolbert, there are at least three relatively distinct approaches to Scripture. First, one may look for a *trajectory of liberation* in biblical events such as the exodus, the message of the prophets, or the message of Jesus. This trajectory then becomes the central core of the biblical witness that determines which other texts are or are not authoritative—a "canon within a canon" approach. This strategy, which finds the essence of Christianity in its prophetic call of liberation for the oppressed, is ideal for the equality approach.

Second, one may look for biblical texts, however few, that bear the seeds of the *counter-cultural affirmation of women*. This involves the rereading of texts that historically have been understood from a male-centered perspective. Third, one may engage in a *reconstruction of history* that shows that the earliest phases of Christianity were egalitarian.

Tolbert does not favor the first approach, conceding that "the prophets never argued for the liberation of women" and arguing that "some of the

14. Tolbert, "Defining the Problem," 118.
15. Ibid., 119.
16. Ibid., 121.

most misogynistic passages in the Bible" are found in the prophetic books of Scripture.[17] The second approach, too, according to Tolbert, is less than satisfying because it involves merely "the discovery of the occasional or exceptional" in an otherwise "patriarchal religion." She is more favorable toward the third approach but notes that "the crucial question is . . . whether or not *any* historical reconstruction can form the basis of Christian faith and practice."[18] Thus Tolbert asks:

> If one is convinced, as I am, of the pervasively patriarchal nature of the Bible and yet not persuaded that reconstructions of history can replace the canon [which essentially is Fiorenza's solution], is it still possible to stay within the Christian tradition?[19]

This statement well captures the paradoxical—some might say inconsistent—nature of the reformist feminist position. Realizing that history is an inadequate basis of authority, reformist feminists ground biblical interpretation not in the biblical texts themselves but in their own experience, engaging in the circular enterprise of identifying texts "with hidden liberation potential" on the basis of their feminist commitment. Experience varies from person to person and from community to community, as feminists themselves readily acknowledge; however, it hardly constitutes a firm basis for authority or even validity of scriptural interpretation.

Tolbert's final attempt at a solution has Rudolf Bultmann's program of demythologization as a point of reference. Recognizing that the miracles of the Bible were unacceptable for modern "enlightened" people in a scientific age, Bultmann sought to identify an "existential core" in the myths of Scripture. To be sure, Tolbert acknowledges that feminists' task is more radical, since "the Bible is not only intellectually unintelligible [Bultmann's view] but actively evil. . . . Yet, the hermeneutical and theological dilemma Bultmann struggled to address still remains: how does one deal with a biblical text that is so completely saturated in an unacceptable perspective?"[20] Tolbert holds out the hope that feminists may yet succeed in separating the *kerygma*, the core biblical message, from the text, and even suggests that feminism is the future of New Testament theology.

Tolbert's essay raises some concerns. The first pertains to how Tolbert positions her approach over against patriarchal hermeneutics. Her categorization presupposes that any approach that finds Scripture enjoining male leadership is guilty of supporting male oppression of females and starts with

17. Ibid., 123.
18. Ibid., 124.
19. Ibid.
20. Ibid.

a predetermination of the Scriptures' message. However, this is arguably not the case. In fact, non-feminist interpretations contend that Scripture enjoins the male exercise of authority in the context of loving, caring, self-sacrificial relationships.

Non-feminist interpretations, as mentioned, follow the pattern of patri-centrism, which places the father and head of the household at the center of the life of his family but views his exercise of authority in the larger context of his care and concern for the members of his family, rather than viewing all forms of paternal authority as an inexorably autocratic, harsh, or abusive "rule of the father." If Scripture can be shown to teach this kind of male leadership, it would not be patriarchal hermeneutic that is responsible for this teaching. Rather, it is loving male leadership that is determined from the reading of Scripture itself, properly interpreted. In this context, it may be helpful to emphasize the need for a "listening hermeneutic" that perceives what is there in the biblical text rather than elevating one's own ideology—feminist, patriarchal, or otherwise—above the scriptural message.

Tolbert's call for a feminist revolution brought about by "small, often unnoticed acts of subversion" reflects well the feminist movement's anti-authority stance that pits women as the oppressed against men as the op-pressors. This is class warfare language borrowed from Marxist economic theory and applied to gender. However, such rhetoric and the ensuing strategy of launching a revolution through acts of subversion are unduly simplistic and perpetrate gender division.

It is just not true that only women are oppressed and all men are op-pressors. Women are capable of oppressing men, too. It is not accurate to label an entire gender—males—as oppressors and to seek to undermine their domination. As Scripture makes clear, the pervasive and universal human predicament is sin, extending to both men and women (Genesis 3; Rom. 3:23), and both men and women are offered salvation in Christ on the basis of faith in him (Gal. 3:28).

The Christian gospel does not call on Christian women to take an antago-nistic stance toward men and to "subvert their rule" but enjoins Christian wives to submit to their husbands (Eph. 5:22–23; Col. 3:18; 1 Pet. 3:1–6). And all believers are to live together harmoniously in the church as God's family (e.g., Eph. 4:1–6; Phil. 2:1–11). Therefore, the feminist call of all women to arms to subvert male domination, with its anti-authority bias, is deeply at odds with the truth of the Christian gospel. To be sure, male domination and abuse of authority have been, and continue to be, a real problem. Yet the biblical solution is demonstrably not the obliteration of all authority nor is it gender revolution and warfare.

Also in the 1983 issue of *Semeia* is Elizabeth Struthers Malbon's study, "Fallible Followers: Women and Men in the Gospel of Mark." In this essay Malbon seeks to isolate texts in Mark's Gospel that possess liberative potential for women, emphasizing the feminist agenda of women's liberation. Malbon finds that women characters supplement and complement Mark's portrayal of the disciples, forming a composite portrait of fallible followers of Jesus. She observes that women or girls who appear in Mark's narrative "seem *almost* incidental to it."[21] Two healed daughters contribute little (Mark 5:22–24; 7:24–30); Peter's mother-in-law is slightly more prominent in that she is shown to serve Jesus and his disciples (Mark 1:31).

Also in Mark are two women who are healed by Jesus: the woman with blood flow and the Syrophoenician woman, and two who sacrifice for Jesus: the poor widow and the woman anointing Jesus. In each case, the woman takes the initiative and Jesus responds. Mark 15:40–41 mentions a group of women at the cross. Malbon disagrees with Munro's contention that Mark is aware of women's presence in Jesus' ministry but obscures it, suggesting instead that Mark delays explicit reference to the women followers until the true meaning of discipleship can be understood.[22]

Here Malbon believes to have found a text possessing liberative potential for women. Nevertheless, she observes that not all women in Mark are followers of Jesus, just as not all followers of Jesus in Mark are women. While women characters are not as frequent, nor are they named as often as men, their significance is determined not by their sex or numbers but by their relationship to Jesus. In the end, "women and men . . . all contribute to the development of a composite and complex image of what it means to be a follower of Jesus."[23] Overall, Malbon's mostly descriptive study follows the text rather closely. Her search for texts with liberative potential in Mark is in keeping with a reformist feminist agenda and hermeneutic.

### Searching the Scriptures

Another representative work of the new feminist interpretation of the Bible is the two-volume *Searching the Scriptures*. The first volume contains essays on the history of feminist interpretation in different socio-historical locations as well as several methodological contributions. The second volume, which, apart from an introductory essay by the editor, features commentaries

21. E. S. Malbon, "Fallible Followers: Women and Men in the Gospel of Mark," *Semeia* 28 (1983): 34 (emphasis added).
22. Ibid., 42; see W. Munro, "Women Disciples in Mark?" *Catholic Biblical Quarterly* 44 (1982): 234.
23. Malbon, "Fallible Followers," 47.

on biblical and nonbiblical books, including (in this order) the Gospels of Mark, John, Matthew, and Luke, each approximately thirty to forty pages in length.

### Commentary on Mark

The commentary on Mark by Joanna Dewey considers the themes of androcentrism and liberation. While Mark has included powerful stories of women, "what we have left in Mark is only a remnant of a once much richer women's tradition."[24] The mention of women in Mark 15 and 16 is "too little too late" in an otherwise androcentric narrative. Mark has used women as needed for the plot and to teach men. Today's feminists must go beyond Mark in order to create "a true discipleship of equals in which women—and all marginalized groups—are full participants."[25] The commentary on Mark is an example of a reformist feminist hermeneutic employing a "hermeneutic of suspicion" and criticizing Scripture for its patriarchal bias.

### Commentary on John

The commentary on John is written by Adele Reinhartz, who holds that it was not the apostle John but a later community, tracing its origin from the apostle, that was responsible for the Gospel in its final form. Reinhartz notes that John includes portraits of women who are "honored and empowered," such as the mother of Jesus, the Samaritan woman, Mary and Martha, and Mary Magdalene.[26] Reinhartz notes negatively the emphasis on Jesus as the "Son of God" and the prevalence of "Father-Son" language in John's Gospel. Reinhartz is even more offended by the portrayal of the Jews as archenemies of Jesus. In her unbelief, Reinhartz rejects the central tenet of the Gospels—that Jesus is the Messiah—and this unbelief compounds Reinhartz's negativity toward the Gospel both on account of her feminism and her Jewishness.

### Commentary on Matthew

Elaine Wainwright, the author of the commentary on Matthew, employs a hermeneutics of suspicion and remembrance with special focus on women characters in Matthew's Gospel. The first stage of investigation is literary, drawing on insights from narrative and reader-response criticism. The second stage employs the historical-critical method, especially redaction criticism, in an effort to reconstruct the socio-historical situation inscribed within the

24. J. Dewey, "The Gospel of Mark," in *Searching the Scriptures*, ed. E. S. Fiorenza (New York: Crossroad, 1994), 508.
25. Ibid.
26. A. Reinhartz, in *Searching the Scriptures*, 594–97.

narrative. In a third stage, other historical and sociological data are used to supplement the findings from the previous two stages of research and to reconstruct the community behind the Gospel.

### Commentary on Luke
The commentary on Luke by Turid Karlsen Seim reveals an attempt at discerning patterns of gender in the Lukan composition. The author finds that Luke draws fairly strict boundaries for women's activity. Yet, at the same time, Luke also preserves strong traditions about women and attributes a positive function to them. Since Luke among the Gospel writers shows the most overt interest in women, Seim has the easiest task of locating women's contributions in the Gospel. Seim's work is mostly descriptive.

### The Feminist Companion to the Gospels
The most recent comprehensive literary work of feminist scholarship is the multi-volume *Feminist Companion* edited by Amy-Jill Levine. This series spans the entire New Testament, assembling what the editor judges to be the most important feminist scholarly contributions of the past two decades. Included are several essays first printed in *Semeia* 28 (1983) as well as those produced by participants in the annual meetings of the SBL and AAR. The volumes span the whole range of feminist approaches, from text-oriented and more descriptive to revisionist and even radical.

The editor revels in the multiplicity of viewpoints represented in these volumes, noting that "feminist biblical commentary is remarkably diverse in its practitioners, its methods, its subjects, and its results."[27] Looking to biblical women as "their foresisters and their inspiration," the authors seek to appropriate and utilize their insights to argue for a variety of feminist-type models and conclusions in order to engender "the narrative's potential ... for liberation, not just for women, but for anyone denied rights, denied voice, denied authenticity."[28]

What follows is a brief survey of the relevant contributions found in the five volumes of *The Feminist Companion to the Gospels*. There is one volume each on Matthew, Mark, and Luke; two volumes are on John's Gospel.

### The Feminist Companion to Matthew
Janice Capel Anderson's contribution is devoted to exploring the symbolic significance of gender in the Gospel. She notes that although women, with the exception of Herodias and her daughter in Matthew 14:1–12, are portrayed favorably, they assume subordinate and auxiliary positions.

27. Levine, *A Feminist Companion to John*, 2:1.
28. Ibid.

Gail O'Day discusses the account of the Canaanite woman in Matthew 15:21–28, claiming that the Canaanite woman holds Jesus accountable to his mission of wholeness. In this way the woman becomes a model of persistence and faith for the readers of the Gospel. Stephenson Humphries-Brooks presents Herodias as a success story, in that Herodias was successful in bringing about the death of John the Baptist.

### The Feminist Companion to Mark

Contributor Deborah Krause examines the portrayal of Peter's mother-in-law in Mark 1:29–31. Krause is suspicious of the glorification of women's domestic service by earlier feminists, who saw in this woman a prototypical disciple if not deacon. Seeking to navigate the tensions between gender-determined servitude and egalitarian discipleship, Krause finds that, once healed, this woman is not truly liberated but instead returns to fulfill her domestic duties.

Sharon Ringe recasts Jesus' initial refusal to help the outcast woman in Mark 7:24–31a as a guarding of the limited resources Jesus wished to preserve for his own Galilean people. The primary issue is no longer the woman serving as a model of faith and Jesus moving from sexist to teachable but rather economic factors.

### The Feminist Companion to Luke

In this volume Turid Karlsen Seim finds that the definition of motherhood is moved from biological procreation to ascetic and communitarian relationship as part of the Lukan theme of ascetic practice as a rehearsal of the life to come. Barbara Reid views the sinful woman in Luke 7:36–50 not as a sexual sinner but as a potential disciple and even a Christological prefiguration. For Reid, the text is sexist and the evangelist's presentation shortsighted; feminists today must ask, "What is wrong with this picture?" in order to arrive at a more satisfying interpretation.

Teresa Hornsby, in a study of Jesus' anointing by a "sinful woman," contends that Luke is concerned to portray Jesus as an ideal male, and she is critical of the designation "sinner," which fixes the woman in her feminine role while leaving Jesus' masculinity undisturbed. Esther de Boer focuses on women followers of Jesus in Luke 8:1–3, observing that these three women were with Jesus consistently throughout his ministry rather than appearing only at the end. Nevertheless, in the end the women proclaiming the resurrection are not believed, because they lack authority. Gender bifurcation is maintained here.

Warren Carter proposes that Martha and Mary (not her real sister) were "missionary women partners" and that Martha was distracted by relational problems with her ministerial colleague. Jesus' prescription, writes Carter, is to cultivate single-mindedness.

### The Feminist Companion to John, Volume 1

In this volume F. Scott Spencer concludes that Jesus, as a hierarchical male, was possibly rude to women. Stephen Moore deconstructs traditional readings of the Samaritan woman in John 4 and concludes that Jesus' desire, rather than the woman's, is central to the narrative. Concerning the same passage, Jerome Neyrey argues that the narrative subverts gender expectations concerning men in that the woman frequently disobeys Jesus: she does not call her husband, does not give him a drink, and does not go "home" but returns to the public square. Holly Toensing discusses the Samaritan woman also, observing that Jesus is guilty of applying a double standard by holding women to a higher code of ethics than men.

Ingrid Rosa Kitzberger seeks to show that some of the female characters in John's Gospel regularly transcend gender roles. Mary, by washing Jesus' feet, becomes a role model for Jesus' footwashing. Kitzberger enlists Lazarus in support of her feminist convictions in that he is presented as a model of "untying and the empowering of the silenced and marginalized" so they can "speak up for" themselves.[29]

### The Feminist Companion to John, Volume 2

In her essay Dorothy Lee contends that, for John, "indwelling" conveys the notion of mutuality between human and divine, with the result that alienation, competition, and hierarchy are overcome. In feminist terms, "abiding" as a relational category provides liberation and forges the pathway for achieving authenticity and self-realization free from the constraints of hierarchy.

Colleen Conway contends that, for John, women are superior to men, for while Jesus frequently corrects men, he reveals himself to women and commissions them. Despite her feminist findings, Conway concludes that Jesus is portrayed as the ideal male who supplants the feminine notion of "Jesus Sophia." Thus, the Fourth Gospel is found to articulate a traditional view of gender roles.

### Unifying Themes

On the whole, these essays from the five volumes of *The Feminist Companion to the Gospels* span the range from reformist feminist to rather radical. Nevertheless, there are several things they share in common. The first is a *commitment to feminism over Scripture* as guiding authority. Together

29. Ibid., 1:177.

with this comes a quest for women's liberation from the constraints of male hierarchy and a search for positive female role models in Scripture.

The second common feature is a *critical stance toward Scripture*. Both Reid and Hornsby, for example, criticize Luke's portrayal of the "sinful woman" in 7:36–50 as sexist. Spencer contends that Jesus was rude to women. Toensing charges Jesus with applying a double standard toward women and men.

The third common element is the use of a *variety of literary methods*. Moore employs deconstructionism; several other authors, such as Neyrey and Kitzberger, engage in reader-response readings. Most of the essays analyze fairly closely the text of a particular biblical narrative dealing with one or several female characters.

Some of the studies included in these volumes, such as those by Anderson and Malbon, are rather restrained and follow the text quite closely. While their feminist orientation is readily apparent, these writers' contributions are mostly descriptive and can best be classified as reformist. The focus on women characters and women disciples in the Gospels is in keeping with the feminist agenda of identifying positive contributions of women that may have been overlooked or may not have been adequately appreciated.

One possible problematic aspect in some of the essays included in *The Feminist Companion* is their unilateral focus on scriptural passages about women. This focus might lead to a neglect of the study of all the relevant texts, including those featuring male characters and passages of general human concern, and thus fail to capture the comprehensive teaching of Scripture. A certain ambivalence in some of the essays points to the possibly self-contradictory nature of authors who study Scripture yet are critical of its portrayal of women or Jesus' behavior toward them.

In other cases, the authors employ unlikely readings, judging by the standards for hermeneutics set forth later in this volume. Ringe's argument that Jesus' interaction with the Gentile woman in Mark 7 was driven by economics, not theology, and that Jesus sought to preserve his limited resources for his own Galilean people, is a reconstruction of the historical background without adequate basis in the text or context. Carter's contention that Mary and Martha were women ministers is founded on an anachronistic construal of the Greek term meaning "to serve." Kitzberger's view that Lazarus serves as a role model for the oppressed, likewise, lacks textual and contextual support; the raising of Lazarus is shown in John's Gospel to validate Jesus' own claims and to anticipate Jesus' resurrection.

Overall, it should be noted that many of these essays evidence a considerable degree of sophistication in literary analysis. Nevertheless, the feminist commitment of these writers seems to influence the interpretive process and their conclusions in a direction that tends to magnify the role of women and characterizes men—including Jesus—as rude, patriarchal, and sexist. None of these essays provides a larger paradigm for apprehending the biblical message regarding men and women. Rather, each represents individual readings of texts that do not claim compelling authority or greater validity than other equally legitimate readings, feminist or otherwise.

### Understanding New Feminist Literary Approaches

The new feminist literary approaches must be credited with a proper emphasis on the text of Scripture itself. The text of Scripture, rather than conjectural background reconstructions, should constitute the final point of reference for biblical interpretation. Having said this, our main concern is that these feminist literary approaches seem to proceed from the notion of textual autonomy while neglecting the notion of authorial intention.

In interpreting a given text, appropriate hermeneutical procedure involves the discovery of the authorial intention as conveyed in the text. Severed from authorial intention, the interpretation of texts is destined to result in eisegesis and in a transformation of the original purpose of Scripture based on the ideology and interpretative strategy of the reader. However, this is not responsible interpretation. It deprives the author of his right to communicate his intentions through his text. Anyone interpreting a given text, regardless of her perspective—patriarchal, feminist, or otherwise—must recognize that authors, texts, and readers should all be treated with respect. Moreover, these rights should be balanced, with the rights of the author of a particular text being primary, since the author is the one who produced the document with an intention to convey a certain message.

While the focus on the text in literary feminist approaches is therefore affirmed, the strategy of exposing androcentric bias and of uncovering the hidden liberation potential of texts may have the effect of transposing the textual message in keeping with the reader's own vision, ideals, and ideological commitments. This is clearly seen when Mary Ann Tolbert states her commitment to both feminism and Christian tradition yet makes clear that when these are in conflict, her commitment to feminism is foundational.[30] Tolbert conceives of feminism as the critique of oppressive structures, among which she includes Christianity. While as part of her commitment to Christian tradition she cites a "bias in favor of the Bible," she acknowledges that she is "open to judgment and, if necessary, dismissal" of the Christian

---

30. Tolbert, "Defining the Problem," 113–26.

Scriptures.[31] An interpreter who is prepared to eliminate a given text on the basis of her feminist commitment does not accept proper boundaries of biblical interpretation. The text itself as intended by the author must remain the center of discussion.

Tolbert's acknowledgment that feminist hermeneutics is paradoxical should also be evaluated. Feminist hermeneutics may more correctly be perceived as inconsistent. It would be consistent for new feminists to reject the Bible altogether, as radical feminists do, rather than to continue engaging in what Tolbert calls a "profoundly paradoxical" enterprise misrepresenting the author's intended meaning. How can a given interpreter be highly suspicious of Scripture and yet use that of which she is highly suspicious as a tool for reconstruction? Many feminists have commented on this challenge but have continued to have difficulty reconciling these countervailing notions.

Another important item to note is the "canon within a canon," which is evidenced by the selection of certain texts and not others for scholarly study in texts. The focus on certain select pericopes for their "hidden liberation potential" and the setting aside of other texts owing to their "androcentric bias" is too narrowly conceived. The procedure of selecting a passage that favors one's viewpoint while neglecting others that are judged to be countervailing does not meet the set standards for hermeneutics.

Additionally, the division of humanity by way of gender into two distinct "classes," women and men, implicit in many of these feminist literary studies, and in fact much of feminism as a whole, is dichotomistic. This procedure appears to favor antagonism when many passages of Scripture do not dichotomize between men and women but rather show what they share in their common humanity—salvation, growth in Christ, sacrificial self-giving, and so on. Even in Christ not all role distinctions are eliminated, and the scriptural vision for male-female relationships is one of harmony rather than one of mutual antagonism and struggle for power.

### Evaluation

Two of the major underlying purposes of feminism as a movement—the affirmation of the equal value and worth of women and the redressing of injustices toward women in the past—are valid goals. In the area of the interpretation of Scripture, too, feminists have given new impetus to a fresh study of relevant biblical passages on Jesus and women and in some cases have served as correctives to established readings of the text (e.g., abusive notions of male headship). At the same time, our survey of feminist literature dealing with Jesus and women has revealed several areas of weakness.

31. Ibid., 114.

The feminist critique of the Bible is itself open to critique. Properly understood, the Old Testament narratives reflect a pattern of male-female relationships that may be more adequately labeled "patricentrism." It is true, however, that the negative notion of patriarchy as an abusive and illegitimate control of authority is itself an offensive ideology and represents a sinful abuse of God's true intentions. Yet since the Bible does not teach or advocate this abusive notion of patriarchy, it is unnecessary to reject the teaching of Scripture or parts of it in this regard.

As we have seen, feminism appears to be in a state of transition. Fiorenza's historical reconstruction of the Jesus movement has been dismantled by recent feminist authors. At this time no new, overarching paradigm has taken its place. The current scene shows an accepted diversity of feminist readings by practitioners of the new feminism. This new feminism, for its part, operates largely on the foundation of its reformist/liberationist precursors, including the hermeneutics of suspicion, while eschewing labels such as "reformist" or "liberationist," holding to its precursors' critique of Scripture as patriarchal and deficient. Yet the new feminism goes beyond older feminist models. It is more textually focused, more literary in its methodology, and characterized by a large variety of approaches and presentations.

# PART 4

# JESUS AND EVANGELICAL FEMINISM (EGALITARIANISM)

*Is it true to say that the God of the Bible is a male deity who demands to be served by a male priesthood? Is the patriarchal ordering of Church, society and family absolutely concomitant with the expression of biblical faith? Is it correct to assume that the Bible clearly and consistently casts woman in the role of the "subordinate partner" and permanently excludes her from the exercise of ministerial authority?*

—Mary Hayter, *The New Eve in Christ* (1987)[1]

The 1970s saw the birth of what is called *evangelical feminism* or *biblical feminism*, a movement also termed *egalitarianism*. The movement places emphasis on the full equality of men and women while professing commitment to scriptural inspiration and authority. This movement represents an effort within evangelicalism to revisit the traditional interpretation of gender passages in the Bible, including Jesus' perspective on women, in order to align it with a notion of gender equality. Within an inerrantist framework, this movement considers itself to be evangelical-biblical and feminist.

While radical and reformist feminists rally around the notion of *liberation from oppression*, evangelical feminists adopt *equality* as their central tenet. The teaching of Galatians 3:28, that in Christ "there is no male and female," serves as the key biblical text by which all other teachings of Scripture are to be measured.

1. M. Hayter, *The New Eve in Christ: The Use and Abuse of the Bible in the Debate about Women in the Church* (Grand Rapids, MI: Eerdmans, 1987), 1.

As we will see, the inconsistencies of evangelical feminism lie not so much in its hermeneutical *theory*, with its apparent high view of Scripture and affirmation of inerrancy and inspiration, but in the evangelical feminist *execution* of its hermeneutics in arriving at specific interpretations of passages dealing with Jesus and women.

# 11

# THE EARLY YEARS: EMANCIPATION

*The Bible, properly interpreted, teaches the fundamental equality of men and women of all racial and ethnic groups, all economic classes, and all age groups, based on the teaching of Galatians 3:28—There is neither Jew nor Greek, there is neither slave nor free, there is neither male nor female; for you are all one in Christ Jesus.*

—Statement by Christians for Biblical Equality (1989)[1]

*From the* beginning, evangelical feminists used strong language to denounce a traditional understanding of male and female roles. Letha Scanzoni and Nancy Hardesty maintain that "equality and subordination are contradictions."[2] Paul Jewett echoes this concern, posing the question, "But how can one defend a sexual hierarchy whereby men are over women . . . without supposing that the half of the human race which exercises authority is superior in some way to the half which submits?"[3] According to Jewett, any interpretation of Scripture that does not align with "Paul's fundamental statement of Christian liberty" (see Gal. 3:28) is "incongru-

1. Christians for Biblical Equality, "Men, Women and Biblical Equality" (Minneapolis, 1989), http://www.cbeinternational.org.
2. L. Scanzoni and N. Hardesty, *All We're Meant to Be: A Biblical Approach to Women's Liberation* (Waco, TX: Word, 1974), 110.
3. P. K. Jewett, *Man as Male and Female: A Study of Sexual Relationships from a Theological Point of View* (Grand Rapids, MI: Eerdmans, 1975), 71.

ous" with the Bible, for it "breaks the analogy of faith."[4] Virginia Ramey Mollenkott contends that the hierarchical model is unhealthy and carnal, while Dorothy Pape asserts that hierarchical roles indicate superiority and inferiority.[5]

## The Early Years (1966–1986)

### Definition of Evangelical Feminism (Egalitarianism)

The evangelical feminist group Christians for Biblical Equality (CBE) holds that all believers, without regard to gender, race, and class are free and encouraged to use their God-given gifts in families, ministries, and communities. References to Jesus and the Gospels are rather infrequent in CBE's discussion of biblical truths, yet the assertion that both "men and women are divinely gifted and empowered to minister to the whole Body of Christ, under His authority" is supported by references to Mark 15:40–41; 16:1–7; Luke 8:1–3; and John 20:17–18. The only other Gospel references are found in its attempts to define the function of leadership as the empowerment of others for service rather than as the exercise of power over them.

So it appears that CBE's primary support for evangelical feminism is derived from the Pauline writings rather than from the Gospels. In order to set the stage for an understanding of evangelical feminism, therefore, we will briefly engage other New Testament texts. Setting evangelical feminism within this larger framework will, in turn, aid in our understanding of their treatment of passages in the Gospels.

Like most feminists, evangelical feminists hold to the complete equality of men and women in both personal identity and role. But unlike most feminists, evangelical feminists hold to a high view of Scripture. Evangelical feminists believe that the words of the Bible are inspired by God and free from error. Whereas most feminist writers view the Bible as reflecting a patriarchal bias that should be exposed, evangelical feminists typically maintain that the Bible itself, "properly interpreted," teaches egalitarianism.

Evangelical feminists find support for this conviction in Paul's statement that in Christ "there is no male and female" but all are "one in Christ Jesus" (Gal. 3:28). They say that the few isolated texts that appear to restrict the full redemptive freedom of women, such as 1 Corinthians 11:2–16; 14:33–36 or 1 Timothy 2:9–15, must be interpreted in relation to this central text and other similar texts.

4. Ibid., 134.
5. D. Pape, *In Search of God's Ideal Woman: A Personal Examination of the New Testament* (Downers Grove, IL: InterVarsity, 1978), 173.

Evangelical feminists cite some Gospel texts in support of the notion that both men and women are divinely gifted and empowered to minister to the whole body of Christ. Mark 15:40–41 mentions several women at the cross who were watching from a distance. These women had followed Jesus and had cared for his needs, which shows that Jesus did indeed have women followers during his ministry who were an integral part of his group. Mark 16:1–7 refers to three of these women as being those who brought spices to anoint Jesus' body. Although the women are fully engaged in loving and serving Jesus, these passages are not adequate support for the notion of unmitigated participation of women in all forms of ministry.

Luke 8:1–3 mentions some women who were with Jesus and the disciples, traveling about from one village to another as Jesus proclaimed the good news of the kingdom of God, helping to support them out of their own means. Again here women are shown to be sacrificially engaged in Jesus' mission and an integral part of it. However, this passage likewise does not provide adequate support for the argument that women should be involved in all forms of ministry without any restrictions.

In John 20:17–18 a particular woman, Mary Magdalene, is instructed by Jesus to relay a message to his disciples that Jesus is ascending to his Father, yet this does not provide a mandate for a sweeping pronouncement on women's leadership, nor does it address a broad base of ministry possibilities for women.

Both Mark 10:42–45, dealing with servant leadership, and John 13:13–17, discussing servants not being greater than their masters with regard to service, constitute generic statements about ministry. Though evangelical feminists use these passages to support women's leadership, the passages do not deal directly with women's issues. Nevertheless, the two passages are included in the CBE statement to support a view of ministry in terms of service rather than authoritarian dominance on the part of leaders.

However, the fact that leaders must have a servant attitude does not imply that authority is completely removed from those serving in positions of church leadership. Arguably, the contrast is between humility on the one hand and an arrogant abuse of authority on the other. The model of Christian leadership is not one of service without authority, but one of a responsible exercise of authority in a spirit of humility and servanthood.[6]

6. See W. Grudem, *Evangelical Feminism and Biblical Truth* (Sisters, OR: Multnomah, 2004), 167–68.

Table 11.1: Evangelical Feminism: The Early Years (1966–1986)

| Proponent | Major Work (Date) |
|---|---|
| Krister Stendahl | *The Bible and the Role of Women* (1966)* |
| Letha Scanzoni, Nancy Hardesty | *All We're Meant to Be* (1974) |
| Paul Jewett | *Man as Male and Female* (1975) |
| Dorothy Pape | *In Search of the Ideal Woman* (1978) |
| Mary Evans | *Woman in the Bible* (1983) |
| Ben Witherington | *Women in the Ministry of Jesus* (1984) |
| Gilbert Bilezikian | *Beyond Sex Roles* (1985) |
| Aida Besançon Spencer | *Beyond the Curse* (1985) |
| Richard Longenecker | Essay in *Women, Authority and the Bible* (1986) |

*Note that Stendahl is not an evangelical feminist as far as his view of Scripture is concerned. He is included here as a proponent of egalitarianism who has had a significant impact on the evangelical feminist movement. It should also be noted that there is a certain amount of variety among other proponents of evangelical feminism/egalitarianism discussed in chaps. 11–13, though for the most part these writers hold to a high view of Scripture.

### Krister Stendahl

Krister Stendahl's 1966 work, *The Bible and the Role of Women*, had an enormous impact on evangelical feminism and served as "the precursor of much modern egalitarian thinking."[7] Stendahl takes up the issue of Jesus choosing twelve men as his apostles.[8] Arguing against a "museum-minded conservatism," he raises the question of what constitutes ancient Near Eastern thought patterns and what constitutes revelation.[9] What, in Stendahl's words, is the "translatability" of the event of Jesus' choosing twelve men as his apostles?

Stendahl, a strong, early advocate of an egalitarian view of gender roles, devotes a short three pages to women in the Gospels and their relationship to Jesus.[10] Stendahl observes that even in Luke's Gospel, the most women-friendly of the four canonical Gospels, there is little support for an egalitarian viewpoint, noting that "the circle around Jesus is a circle of men," the story of Martha and Mary in Luke 10:38–42 notwithstanding.[11] The Last Supper was a meal with the Twelve, who were all men, and men were in charge even of the preparations (Luke 22:12–13). Stendahl concludes

7. Grudem, *Evangelical Feminism and Biblical Truth*, 359. See also R. W. Yarbrough, "The Hermeneutics of 1 Timothy 2:9–15," in *Women in the Church: A Fresh Analysis of 1 Timothy 2:9–15*, ed. A. J. Köstenberger, T. R. Schreiner, and H. S. Baldwin (Grand Rapids, MI: Baker, 1995), 178–82.

8. K. Stendahl, *The Bible and the Role of Women*, Facet Books (Philadelphia: Fortress, 1966), 19–23.

9. Ibid., 22.

10. Ibid., 25–28.

11. Ibid., 25.

that nothing in the Gospels indicates that Jesus transcended or stood in conscious opposition to the traditional patriarchal Jewish understanding of male-female relations.[12]

| Egalitarian Profile 1 |
| --- |
| **Proponent:** Krister Stendahl |
| **Title:** *The Bible and the Role of Women* (1966) |
| **Contribution:** Egalitarian model of ministry on basis of "breakthrough verse" Gal. 3:28 |
| **View of Jesus:** patriarchal, traditionalist |

Stendahl, however, argues for an egalitarian model of ministry in today's church on other grounds—most notably on the "breakthrough" verse, Galatians 3:28—in spite of acknowledging the centrality of men in Jesus' inner circle and the fact that Jesus did not distance himself from the traditional Jewish patriarchal model.[13] According to Stendahl, seeking to enshrine permanently the principle of male leadership in the church was to fall prey to a "descriptive realism"; in other words, just because male leadership was the norm in that time does not mean it must be so today. Doing so, according to Stendahl, is to establish "an archaizing deep freeze" and to "display serious hermeneutical naïveté."[14]

### Letha Scanzoni and Nancy Hardesty

Letha Scanzoni and Nancy Hardesty anticipate many standard, evangelical feminist, exegetical arguments that arose in the following decades in their 1974 volume. Their quest is for the "liberated Christian woman" who is "free to know herself, be herself, and develop herself in her own special way."[15] They define the goal of women's liberation as women's attainment of full humanity,[16] which also entails women's right to privacy and choice, thus supporting the 1973 US Supreme Court ruling legalizing abortion.[17]

The authors deny the eternal subordination of the Son, saying that Jesus' words "I and the Father are one" (John 10:30) and "Whoever has seen me has seen the Father" (John 14:9) balance "The Father is greater than I" (John 14:28), and that all these passages relate solely to Jesus' earthly ministry.[18]

12. Ibid., 27.
13. Ibid., 32–35.
14. Ibid., 35.
15. Scanzoni and Hardesty, *All We're Meant to Be*, 12.
16. Ibid., 206.
17. Ibid., 143.
18. Ibid., 22.

According to Scanzoni and Hardesty, Paul's words, "submitting to one another out of reverence for Christ" (Eph. 5:21–33), teach the mutual submission of husband and wife, since "in Christ there is no chain of command but a community founded and formed by self-giving love."[19]

Paul's teaching on male-female interdependence in 1 Corinthians 11:11–12, "Nevertheless, in the Lord woman is not independent of man nor man of woman," is seen to override his words in 1 Corinthians 11:8–9, "For man was not made from woman, but woman from man. Neither was man created for woman, but woman for man."[20]

With regard to the woman being called a "helper" in Genesis 2:18, Scanzoni and Hardesty note that God is called a "helper" in Psalm 121:1–2 and Psalm 146:3, 5; they say that because it is impossible to think of God as subordinate to man, in the case of the woman, too, "helper" cannot convey the notion of subordination.[21] The conventional argument that the man's creation prior to the woman implies his headship is said to be a "traditional rabbinic (and one might add 'Christian') understanding that is not supported by the text." First Timothy 2:13, referring to God's creation of Adam first and then Eve, is set aside.[22] The reference to man created as male and female in Genesis 1 precludes any notion of female subordination in Genesis 2.[23] The term *kephalē* means "source," not "head."[24] Male rule is a consequence of the fall.[25] Jesus is "woman's best friend,"[26] and the early church witnessed women's "full participation."[27]

The authors note that Lydia was the first European convert (Acts 16:14–15); ten out of twenty-nine persons greeted in Romans 16 are women; and there were female Old Testament prophets, New Testament teachers, especially Priscilla (Acts 18:24ff.), and administrators, especially Phoebe. Scanzoni and Hardesty claim that 1 Timothy 5:1–2 refers not merely to older women but to women elders, on the grounds that Paul here talks about "established orders of ministry." They take Junia (Rom. 16:7) as a female apostle, referring to her in the same vein as the twelve apostles.

In interpreting 1 Timothy 2:12, "I do not permit a woman to teach or to exercise authority over a man," *authentein* ("to exercise authority") is viewed

19. Ibid.; see also p. 99.
20. Ibid., 28.
21. Ibid., 26.
22. Ibid., 28.
23. Ibid., 28–30.
24. Ibid., 30–32, 100.
25. Ibid., 32–36.
26. Ibid., 54–59.
27. Ibid., 60.

negatively as "to interrupt" or "to domineer." According to Scanzoni and Hardesty, Paul's concern in 1 Timothy 2:12 is to preserve the cultural status quo of male dominance in the church.[28] However, the authors claim that the conservatism of 1 Timothy 2:12 is transcended by the radical egalitarianism of the programmatic pronouncement of Galatians 3:28.[29] To refuse women ordination is seen as quenching and grieving the Holy Spirit.[30]

Letha Scanzoni and Nancy Hardesty quote Galatians 4:4–5, where Paul says that God sent forth his Son in order to redeem those under the law, noting that no one was bound more by the law than women: "Jesus' life on earth from beginning to end outlines a paradigm for women's place." They conclude that ever since Jesus' day "the church has struggled . . . to cut through the barbed wire of cultural custom and taboo to emulate the one who promised both men and women, 'If the Son makes you free, you will be free indeed.'"[31]

---

**Egalitarian Profile 2**

**Proponents:** Letha Scanzoni and Nancy Hardesty

**Title:** *All We're Meant to Be* (1974)

**Contribution:** quest for "liberated Christian woman," gender equality required for women's attainment to "full humanity"

**View of Jesus:** treated women as equals; contrast to patriarchal culture

---

According to Scanzoni and Hardesty, Jesus' behavior toward women was truly extraordinary in light of the patriarchal culture surrounding him. He never made jokes about women; he took them seriously and treated them as human beings without condescension or sentimentality. Jesus associated with all kinds of women, whether wealthy and prominent or poor and morally disreputable. Jesus taught women openly in the Temple Court of Women (Luke 21:1–4), considering them capable of comprehending spiritual truth. He identified himself as the Messiah to the Samaritan woman and taught her about proper worship. This stood in contrast to other Jewish rabbis of his day who refused to teach women. Jesus also identified himself to Martha as the resurrection and the life and comforted her in her grief.

As to his teaching methods, Jesus incorporated women or activities relevant to women's experience in his illustrations, be it grinding corn, putting yeast in bread, lost coins, or wedding feasts. Jesus also touched women and called them daughters of Abraham (e.g., Luke 13:16), a highly unusual designation. When the woman with blood flow touched Jesus, he did not

28. Ibid., 71.
29. Ibid., 71–72.
30. Ibid., 180.
31. Ibid., 59.

ridicule her but told her that her faith had made her well (Mark 5:34). Jesus also accepted intimate gestures of love from women at several occasions without rebuking them, instead commending them for their devotion (John 12:1–8: Mary of Bethany; Luke 7:36–50: the sinful woman who anointed Jesus).

Women followed Jesus to the end, risking life and virtue. They found the tomb empty, heard the angels announce that Jesus had risen, and bore witness to the fact that Jesus was alive (Mark 16:6–7). Jesus' first resurrection appearances were to women, and it was women who were first instructed to bring the gospel of his resurrection to others.

Overall, Scanzoni and Hardesty closely follow the Scripture and make some astute observations about the value and worth of women in Jesus' eyes; however, they often exceed the evidence, such as when they claim that Jesus' promise of liberation conveys the notion of such liberation in feminist terms. Yet all that can be conclusively determined by a survey of Jesus' treatment of women is that Jesus treated women well and with respect, awarding them great value. Jesus never gave any indication that women were to be teachers or to be free to take whatever role they might aspire to in the church or home. In this context, it should also be noted that Scanzoni and Hardesty do not address Jesus' choice of twelve men as his apostles and his commissioning of these men as the core leadership group representing the church.

### Paul Jewett

Paul Jewett, professor of systematic theology at Fuller Seminary, wrote the widely influential *Man as Male and Female* in 1975. In his treatment of Jesus and women, Jewett notes that while Jesus never clashed with the rabbinic authorities over women's rights, he was truly revolutionary in the way he treated women. According to Jewett, Jesus *"treated women as fully human, equal to men in every respect; no word of deprecation about women, as such, is ever found on his lips."*[32]

Jesus "broke through the barriers of tradition and custom in a way that put women completely at ease in his presence."[33] Relatively early in his Galilean ministry, mention is made of women disciples who followed him along with the Twelve. Jewett maintains this was "an unprecedented happening in the history of that time," and that "Jesus knowingly overthrew custom when he allowed women to follow him."[34]

---

32. Jewett, *Man as Male and Female*, 94 (emphasis in original).
33. Ibid., 97.
34. J. Jeremias, *Jerusalem in the Time of Jesus* (Philadelphia: Fortress, 1969), in ibid., 376.

Similarly, Martha and Mary were not followers like these other women. Although they stayed at home, they were truly disciples of Jesus. Jesus fellowshiped with these women the same way he did with his male disciples. Mary, similar to the woman in Luke 7:36–50, is a liberated first-century Jewish woman who felt free to behave in a way that only a male slave would have done, anointing Jesus' feet with her hair. Jesus' relationships with women were characterized not only by intimacy and openness but also by social breadth.[35] Included were upper-class women such as Joanna, wife of Herod's steward (Luke 8:3) as well as lower-class women such as the unnamed sinful woman in Luke 7 or the woman in John 4, who was not only a woman but also Samaritan and sinful.

Jesus' interactions with women demonstrate that he "conceived the commandment to love one's neighbor as knowing no boundaries of the sort that prejudice erects."[36] Jewett also cites Jesus' praise of the poor widow's mite (Mark 12:41–42; Luke 21:1–2); his commendation of the faith of the Syrophoenician woman (Matt. 15:28); and his healing of women in need such as Peter's mother-in-law (Mark 1:30–31), the infirm woman in Luke 13:10–11, and the desperate woman with blood flow in Mark 5:25–26. Jesus' parables draw significantly on illustrations relevant to women's experience (Matt. 13:33; 25:1; Luke 15:8; 18:1–8).

As a result, it is not surprising that women followed him all the way to the end (Luke 23:27; Mark 16:1). Even on his way to the cross, Jesus had words of comfort for women (Luke 23:28). Women were the first witnesses of Jesus' resurrection (Matt. 28:9–10; Mark 16:9–11; John 20:11–18). "His male disciples first proclaimed the resurrection to the world; but his female disciples first received the revelation on which this proclamation was based."[37] According to Jewett, to argue for the priority of the man is also to argue for his superiority.[38] Jewett takes as his starting point Genesis 1:26–27, which affirms that man was created in God's image as male and female.

---

**Egalitarian Profile 3**

**Proponent:** Paul Jewett
**Title:** *Man as Male and Female* (1975)
**Contribution:** equated female subordination with inferiority
**View of Jesus:** revolutionary; Jesus "treated women as fully human, equal to men in every respect"

---

35. Jewett, *Man as Male and Female*, 101.
36. Ibid.
37. Ibid., 103.
38. Ibid., 14.

Jewett also examines Pauline texts such as 1 Corinthians 11:2–16; Ephesians 5:22–33 and the parallel passage Colossians 3:18–19; 1 Corinthians 14:34–35; and 1 Timothy 2:11–15 and then offers a survey of the related teaching of Aquinas, Luther, Calvin, and Barth, as well as a sketch of women in the Old Testament and Judaism and of Jesus and women.

Jewett notes that Paul consistently refers to Genesis 2 rather than Genesis 1 and claims that Paul is here dependent on "incorrect" rabbinic teaching.[39] Jewett argues that if temporal sequence conveys superiority, woman should be considered superior to man because she was created last, since clearly creation moved from inanimate creation to animals to humans.[40] Yet, despite following supposedly incorrect rabbinic teaching, Paul possessed "remarkable insights for a former Jewish rabbi" because he wrote what Jewett refers to as the "Magna Carta of Humanity" in Galatians 3:28.[41] In conclusion Jewett, like Scanzoni and Hardesty, calls for the ordination of women.[42]

Similar to the comment on Scanzoni and Hardesty above, Jewett's scriptural focus is commendable. Indeed, there is much in the Gospel witness to Jesus' treatment of women indicating that Jesus included women among his followers and awarded them great dignity and respect. Jewett's discussion seems to be somewhat at variance with Stendahl, however. While Stendahl concluded that Jesus nowhere transcended the patriarchalism of his day, Jewett said Jesus treated women as equal in every respect.

### Dorothy Pape

Dorothy Pape's 1978 volume *In Search of God's Ideal Woman* is a popularly written work by a missionary wife and mother organized into three parts: women in the Gospels, Acts, and Epistles. Pape notes that Proverbs 31 is often seen as a depiction of "God's ideal woman," and she asks whether this is really the final word on the subject.

In her discussion of the Gospels, Pape says that Jesus epitomizes Galatians 3:28, "There is . . . no male and female, for you are all one in Christ Jesus." He did not call a woman among the Twelve because to call a single woman would have led to unsavory suspicions, and married women were busy with their families.[43] Pape also highlights Jesus' courtesy to women, confidence in women, and compassion for women.

39. Ibid., 119, similar to Scanzoni and Hardesty's argument.
40. Ibid., 126–27.
41. Ibid., 142.
42. Ibid., 170.
43. Pape, *God's Ideal Woman*, 25.

| Egalitarian Profile 4 |
| --- |
| **Proponent:** Dorothy Pape |
| **Title:** *In Search of Ideal Woman* (1978) |
| **Contribution:** popularly written work by missionary wife and mother |
| **View of Jesus:** epitome of Gal. 3:28 |

In the book of Acts, Pape finds women functioning as full members of the church. They joined in prayer meetings (Acts 1:14); served as Spirit-filled prophets (Acts 2:15–18); helped establish and support local churches (Lydia, Acts 16:40); performed acts of charity (Acts 9:39, 41); received miraculous healing (Acts 16:18); and were held responsible for their sin (Acts 5:1–10). Studying the Epistles turned out to be a "much less pleasant" task for her than studying Jesus and the early church,[44] for there are in Paul "a few restrictive instructions for female believers, suggestive of an inferior status." Pape deals with 1 Timothy 2:11–14 under the heading, "Women's Church Role: Mute Benchwarmer?" She thus acknowledges that there are in Paul's teaching certain restrictions placed on women, but she expresses only discomfort with these; there is no sustained argument.

### Mary Evans

In 1983 Mary Evans, a lecturer in biblical studies at London Bible College, published *Woman in the Bible*, a book hailed by the North American evangelical feminist scholar David Scholer as "the best book in support of women in ministry written from an evangelical perspective with a commitment to careful exegesis."[45] The third chapter of Evans's book is devoted to material in the Gospels.[46] Evans contends at the outset that Jesus' approach to women is without precedent in contemporary Judaism[47] and revolutionary.[48]

In every source, Jesus' attitude toward women comes across clearly: in parables, miracles, and discourses. All the Gospels, not just Luke, present Jesus in the same way. According to Evans, Jesus taught that women were to be treated as subjects, not objects. She states that Jesus makes clear that he expects his followers to control their sexual desires and includes women among his disciples, because they are to be not just the objects of men's desires (Matt. 5:28). She also draws attention to the fact that Jesus considers

44. Ibid., 103.
45. Back cover of M. J. Evans, *Woman in the Bible* (Downers Grove, IL: InterVarsity, 1983).
46. Ibid., 44–60
47. Ibid., 44, citing W. Forster, *Palestinian Judaism in New Testament Times* (Edinburgh: Oliver & Boyd, 1964), 127; and J. Jeremias, *New Testament Theology* (London: SCM, 1971), 1:27.
48. Ibid., 45.

"leaving a sister" as great a sacrifice as leaving one's parents, children, or houses (Matt. 19:29; Mark 10:29). However, this is not explicitly stated in the text; it constitutes an inference drawn by Evans.

Certainly, sisters are considered important as members of one's family, but in Jesus' statement they are included *alongside* all other family members. There seems to be no good reason to draw particular attention to leaving one's sister. Jesus' point is not that leaving one family member is more or less important than leaving another, but just that a sacrifice is made when a person leaves one's family and embarks on being a disciple. Beyond this, it may be true that part of Jesus' message is that sisters are not any less important family members to leave behind than others, but this is probably not his major point.

Additionally, she quotes Luke 13:16, where the crippled woman is identified as a "daughter of Abraham," and notes that Jesus deliberately chose the title to bring out the value he placed on this woman. Evans observes that Jesus talked freely with women in contrast to the practices of Judaism, which instructed men to avoid any unnecessary contact with women, and notes that Jesus, again in contrast with contemporary Judaism, completely ignored concerns of purity in his healings of women such as the woman with blood flow (Matt. 9:18–26). Rabbinic parables avoided mention of women, while Jesus pointedly includes them. The term "daughter of Abraham" indeed seems to have been chosen deliberately by Jesus to emphasize the value he placed on this woman. This does appear to stand in contrast with first-century Judaism where this expression is virtually unknown.

---

**Egalitarian Profile 5**

**Proponent:** Mary Evans

**Title:** *Woman in the Bible* (1983)

**Contribution:** because women were taught by Jesus along with men, they are equally his disciples and equally equipped to teach God's people in the future

**View of Jesus:** revolutionary; without precedent in Judaism

---

Evans also comments on the fact that Jesus chose twelve men and no women to be his apostles. Many times, she notes, Jesus went against contemporary custom and convention, and he clearly could have done so in this case as well, if he had chosen to do so. However, Evans believes that Jesus here chose to remain within the constraints of his patriarchal Jewish culture, and thus his choice of twelve *men* as apostles is only of temporary significance. But Evans neglects to mention that Scripture does not state or suggest in any way that Jesus intended this to be a mere temporary pattern. As a matter of fact, if Jesus' general approach was to be countercultural while living within his culture, as Evans herself acknowledges, why was Jesus willing to accommodate himself to Jewish culture at this point?

Indeed, one could see how Jesus might have accommodated himself when no major principle was at stake such as paying the temple tax or observing religious festivals. In the present case, however, it could be argued that there is in fact a major principle at stake, and although Jesus has gone against Jewish tradition in his general dealings with women thus far, here is one point where he deliberately chooses to follow the pattern laid out in the Hebrew Scriptures.

Apart from this, Evans contends that women were included "in the true discipleship of Jesus" alongside men because of "active Christian love for the neighbour."[49] Evans understands the meaning of the Greek term *diakonein*, "to serve," as conveying the sense of "very personally the service rendered to another."[50] As a result, she connects all forms of service mentioned in Acts and the Epistles, including prophecy, preaching, and taking up collections, under the rubric of service to be rendered equally by men and women. However, not all kinds of service mentioned in Scripture are the same. To level all New Testament passages referring to "serving" without regard to their respective referents is committing the "referential fallacy" or what D. A. Carson calls an "unwarranted linking of sense and reference."[51]

Evans asserts that "the woman also shared with the rest of the disciples in other activities such as their teaching sessions"[52] and implies that because women were taught by Jesus along with men, they were equally his disciples and equally equipped to teach God's people in the future. Yet this does not necessarily follow from the biblical evidence. Even if women were included in Jesus' teaching sessions alongside of Jesus' male disciples, this would not by itself prove that they are called to serve as teachers and have authority over the church. In fact, both of these encounters are private interactions with Jesus, not "teaching sessions" where women are instructed by Jesus alongside of the rest of the disciples.

Evans notes that Jesus held women responsible for their actions and saw them as intelligent and capable of engaging in in-depth theological conversation. In her discussion of women in the passion narratives, Evans draws attention to two functions of women—witness to and proclaimer of

49. Ibid., 51.
50. Ibid.
51. D. A. Carson, *Exegetical Fallacies*, 2nd ed. (Grand Rapids, MI; Baker, 1996), 63–64; see G. R. Osborne, *The Hermeneutical Spiral: A Comprehensive Introduction to Biblical Interpretation*, rev. and exp. ed. (Downers Grove, IL: InterVarsity, 2006), 94–96.
52. Evans, *Women in the Bible*, citing Luke 10:39; John 11:28.

the resurrection message.[53] She concludes by stating that "it is . . . difficult to find any difference in the approach of Jesus to women and to men."[54] However, when she refers to women as "first proclaimers" of the message of the resurrection, she exceeds the evidence. In Luke 24:9–10, the women merely report to the eleven all that has happened to them; they relay a message, but do not preach a sermon or the like.

In John 20:18, Mary Magdalene likewise simply reports to the disciples that she has seen the Lord and tells them what Jesus had told her. In Matthew 28:10, the women are instructed to tell the disciples that Jesus will meet them in Galilee. In her discussion of women in the passion narratives Evans exercises remarkable restraint when she notes that it is possible that the women were the first to see the risen Jesus only because they happened to be at his tomb first.[55]

Overall, Evans draws a rather sharp distinction between Jesus' approach to women and first-century Judaism. As discussed earlier, however, the feminist scholar Amy-Jill Levine rejects this characterization, contending that first-century Judaism was not as monolithically patriarchal as is often claimed, while Jesus was not as egalitarian as is sometimes maintained. Not all first-century Jews or Jewish rabbis treated women solely as sex objects or excused men indulging in lust.[56] As to divorce, there clearly was a range of views from conservative to liberal (see Matt. 19:3–12; Mishna, *Gittin* 9:10).

Concerning the radical difference Evans claims existed between Jesus and his Jewish contemporaries, research does suggest that many Jews in Jesus' day were legalistic and patriarchal in orientation. In this regard Jesus does indeed provide a contrast. He was not a legalist and did not feel bound by rabbinic purity regulations and similar concerns that caused rabbis to limit contact with women. At the same time, to use this to support the notion that Jesus not only welcomed women among his followers but treated them as equals to men in terms of leadership roles exceeds the evidence.

Evans's argument can be summed up as follows: (1) Women were equal to men in terms of worth and dignity. (2) Women were equal to men in terms of following Jesus and discipleship. (3) Women were equal to men in terms of service. Because of this progression, and because Evans essentially levels all forms of service, both those involving the exercise of authority

53. Ibid., 54.
54. Ibid., 56.
55. Ibid., 54.
56. A.-J. Levine, "Second Temple Judaism, Jesus and Women: Yeast of Eden," *Biblical Interpretation* 2/1 (1994).

and those that did not, there is an implication that women are equal to men also in terms of leadership.

### Ben Witherington

In *Women in the Ministry of Jesus* (1984), Ben Witherington provides a study of Jesus' attitudes toward women. He also deals with Jesus' views on marriage, the family, and singleness, and Jesus' teaching on adultery and divorce. Although seeking to magnify Jesus' positive stance toward women, Witherington concludes that Jesus was neither a chauvinist nor a feminist.

Focusing on how women fit into Jesus' teaching, deeds, and ministry, this is a thorough, book-length study of Jesus' attitude toward women. Witherington provides for the most part helpful treatments of all the major passages in the Gospels that pertain to the topic. On the whole, however, Witherington goes beyond the clear teaching of certain biblical passages in an apparent effort to underscore women's status as equal to that of men.

| Egalitarian Profile 6 |
| --- |
| **Proponent:** Ben Witherington |
| **Title:** *Women in the Ministry of Jesus* (1984) |
| **Contribution:** comprehensive study of Jesus and women |
| **View of Jesus:** granted women "equal right to participate fully in the family of faith" |

Overall, Witherington helpfully notes how Jesus' teaching on subjects relevant to women, such as adultery, divorce, and singleness, was countercultural. However, Witherington's evangelical feminist outlook appears to unduly flavor his assessment of the biblical evidence. A case in point is Witherington's assertion that "the community of Jesus, both before and after Easter, granted women *together* with men . . . an equal right to participate fully in the family of faith."[57] At the very least, "equal right" and "participate fully" need careful definition. "Equal rights" terminology improperly retrojects post-Enlightenment concerns into first-century Judaism.

Also, it is unclear how Witherington can say that the community of Jesus, before Easter, acknowledged women's equal right to participate fully in the life of community, in light of Jesus' choice of twelve men as his apostles. Witherington can make this claim only if serving in positions of leadership is not part of his definition of "full participation" and "equal rights." If that is the case, it seems contradictory to call women's participation "full" if it excludes positions of leadership.

Witherington similarly insists that "Luke especially seems determined to drive home his point about the equal place and new roles of women in

---

57. B. Witherington, *Women in the Ministry of Jesus*, SNTSMS 51 (Cambridge: Cambridge University Press, 1984), 127.

the community of Jesus by utilizing the techniques of male-female parallelism [and] male-female role reversal, and by giving space to stories about
women not found in the other Gospels."[58] Again, speaking of women's
"equal place" without further qualification may be misleading in light of the
fact, attested also by Luke, that Jesus' inner circle consisted of men (Luke
6:12–16). While the Lukan evidence does suggest that women along with
men were accepted by Jesus as his followers, this does not mean that there
were no differences in role.

### Gilbert Bilezikian

Bilezikian, professor emeritus of Wheaton College, authored a basic book
on gender roles. He sets his discussion of gender within the creation-fall-
redemption pattern in Scripture. In his treatment of creation and the fall,
Bilezikian denies any reference to headship and submission, claiming that
God's original creation is "equalitarian." He describes the old covenant era
as dominated by the "dark side" of polygamy, patriarchal oppression, a
double standard on adultery, and compromise divorce legislation. On the
"bright side," he discerns women's assumption of positions of rulership (e.g.,
Deborah) and "the recovery of the goodness of monogamous, equalitarian
marriage."[59] According to Bilezikian, the new creation in Christ reverses
the effects of the fall, most notably male headship.

---

**Egalitarian Profile 7**

**Proponent:** Gilbert Bilezikian
**Title:** *Beyond Sex Roles* (1985)
**Contribution:** God's original creation is "equalitarian" [sic]
**View of Jesus:** instituted principle of full access of both men and women to all posi-
tions of church leadership; "Jesus smashed the pyramidal concept of ecclesiastical
authority and replaced it with participatory consensual community rule"

---

   In his treatment of Jesus, Bilezikian paints a picture of Judaism that mercilessly oppressed women and strictly segregated them from men.[60] Jesus,
on the other hand, "took a firmly countercultural stance on many issues,"[61]
affirming creation and repudiating the fall. He sought to restore women's
dignity to that of Eve's condition prior to the fall and thrust them to center
stage in the drama of redemption with "the spotlights of eternity beaming
upon them, and He immortalizes them in sacred history."[62] Bilezikian also

58. Ibid., 129.
59. G. Bilezikian, *Beyond Sex Roles*, 2nd ed. (Grand Rapids, MI: Baker, 1985), 69.
60. Ibid., 81.
61. Ibid.
62. Ibid., 82.

provides brief treatments of unnoticed women, women as faith models, equal opportunities, privileged opportunities, and the abrogation of rulership.

Bilezikian notes Jesus' mention of "sisters" among his disciples in Matthew 12:46–50 and claims that Jesus, in calling his mother "blessed" (Luke 11:27–28), "catapulted women along with men, both shoulder to shoulder, to the cutting edge of God's program for the redemption of the world."[63] Bilezikian also notes Mary's adopting the stance of a disciple in Luke 10:38–42 and the reference to women disciples in Luke 8:1–3.

Bilezikian mentions the "privileged opportunities" some women were given, such as those in Jesus' genealogy (Matt. 1:3, 5–6). Others include Mary's role in the incarnation and her part in Jesus' first miracle; the first Samaritan and Gentile convert; women who were "first" in receiving Jesus' resurrection teaching; those who saw Jesus at the cross; and those who witnessed the resurrection. With regard to the wine miracle at Cana, Bilezikian's argument is that because both a man and a woman (i.e., the groom and the bride) were equal beneficiaries of the miracle, "a woman became instrumental in providing with her spouse the occasion for the first manifestation of Jesus' eschatological glory."[64]

In his discussion of Jesus' abolishing rulership, Bilezikian points to Jesus' teaching on servant leadership in passages such as Matthew 18:1–5, 15–20; 20:20–28; or 23:1–12. He claims that "true kingdom greatness is not to be achieved through rank, position, and leadership but by accepting the placement of oneself in a position of inferiority and dependency in regard to others."[65] Bilezikian concludes, "According to Jesus, the appropriate locus for authority rests within the congregation and not in a leader above it. Jesus smashed the pyramidal concept of ecclesiastical authority and replaced it with participatory consensual community rule."[66]

Bilezikian summarizes his conclusions as follows:

Jesus intruded into the sin-laden institutions of the world in order to release a new kind of life, an irrepressible ferment that would change men and women and empower them with the effervescent dynamic of the Spirit. Endowed with new powers, they would personify the new creation and establish the new community. In this community, men and women are called by God to occupy kingdom functions and to assume kingdom roles at maximum levels of involvement and visibility tolerable within their contemporary cultures. In multiple ways, Jesus established the principle of full access of both men and women to the responsibilities attendant to the harmonious functioning of

63. Ibid., 95.
64. Ibid., 99.
65. Ibid., 106.
66. Ibid., 107.

the new community. Jesus taught His followers in word and deed to consider the gender difference irrelevant to the concerns and to the processes of the kingdom of God.[67]

Bilezikian validates his model of church leadership from Paul's epistles, casting his discussion in terms of equal rights in Christian marriage (1 Cor. 7:1–5), in mixed marriages (1 Cor. 7:14), and in Christian service (1 Cor. 7:32–35), and speaking of wives' and husbands' mutual submission (Eph. 5:22).

The question of why Jesus chose only men among the Twelve is treated by Bilezikian in a lengthy footnote.[68] He links the all-male composition of the Twelve to the intended target audience of Jesus' mission, which was Jewish. According to Bilezikian, all members of the Twelve had to be Jews and all of them male. The exclusion of women, Samaritans, and Gentiles in this initial phase was required by the dynamic of Jesus' mission. Later on, however, all these people groups were included in the church's missionary force, which can only point to the fact that "pragmatic considerations of accommodation determined the composition of the first apostolic group."[69] The exclusion of women was "a temporary but necessary expedient."[70] Those who contend today that women should be excluded from leadership positions in the church might just as well argue that Gentiles should be excluded.[71]

Even allowing for the popular nature of Bilezikian's work, his exegesis of the relevant passages is often thin. Although he claims that both bride and groom were equal recipients of the wine miracle at Cana, the fact is that the text mentions the groom only briefly in passing, and the bride is not mentioned at all. The inference Bilezikian draws is clearly different from the biblical author's intended message, which was to present Jesus' first sign of his messianic identity. Bilezikian imports his evangelical feminist presuppositions into the text.

Bilezikian's picture of Judaism as mercilessly oppressing women and as strictly segregating them from men, although true in essence, paints Judaism in extreme terms, perhaps in order to magnify the contrast between Jesus and contemporary Judaism. This kind of exaggeration is also seen in Bilezikian's claim from Luke 11:27–28 that "Jesus catapulted women along with men . . . to the cutting edge of God's program for the redemption of the world." What in the text is essentially a rebuke of the woman for her sentimental elevation of motherhood and an affirmation of the priority of

67. Ibid., 118.
68. Ibid., 273, n. 14.
69. Ibid., 274.
70. Ibid.
71. However, see the refutation of this argument by J. A. Borland, "Women in the Life and Teachings of Jesus," in *Recovering Biblical Manhood and Womanhood: A Response to Evangelical Feminism*, ed. J. Piper and W. Grudem (Wheaton, IL: Crossway, 1991), 121–22.

Christian discipleship has, in Bilezikian's hands, become an endorsement of an egalitarian role relationship between men and women. Yet there is no indication that Jesus intended to comment on the question of whether or not women should serve in church leadership on equal terms with men.

Finally, Bilezikian's argument that Jesus' teaching on servant leadership precludes any meaningful notion of "rank, position, and leadership" in the church is questionable as well. Bilezikian exaggerates when he claims that "Jesus smashed the pyramidal concept of ecclesiastical authority and replaced it with participatory consensual community rule."[72] The true biblical contrast is more likely between an improper and a proper use of authority, not between the use of authority and the lack thereof.

### Aida Besançon Spencer

Aida Spencer's *Beyond the Curse* (1985) includes discussion on Jesus' teachings and practices concerning women. Spencer argues that male-female role distinctions are a function of the fall rather than part of the created order. She takes her starting point from the torn curtain in the temple, something signifying open access to God for all, Gentiles as well as Jews, women as well as men. Spencer claims that Jesus' choice of twelve men as apostles was designed to represent the twelve tribes of Israel. Spencer contends, "If Jesus' choice of twelve male disciples signifies that females should not be leaders in the church, then, consistently his choice also signifies that Gentiles should not be leaders in the church."[73]

In order to demonstrate the extent to which Jesus broke the traditional barriers between men and women, Spencer provides a treatment of first-century Jewish thought and practices concerning women. She also discusses Luke's account of Mary and Martha, which, according to Spencer, shows "Jesus' new principle of encouraging women to seek religious training."[74] Spencer thus urges seminaries today to encourage women on equal terms with men to come and learn the Scriptures.

---

**Egalitarian Profile 8**

**Proponent:** Aida Besançon Spencer
**Title:** *Beyond the Curse* (1985)
**Contribution:** male-female role distinctions a function of the fall
**View of Jesus:** broke traditional barriers between men and women, encouraged women to learn

---

72. Ibid., 107.
73. A. B. Spencer, *Beyond the Curse: Women Called to Ministry* (Nashville: Thomas Nelson, 1985), 45, n. 5 (see the preceding discussion of Bilezikian). But see Borland, "Women in the Life and Teachings of Jesus," 121–22.
74. Ibid., 61.

Spencer's treatment of Jesus and women is not comprehensive; it focuses on the different treatments of women among Jesus and contemporary Judaism. Because Jesus encouraged women to seek religious training, Spencer contends that today they should be allowed to serve as ministers on par with men. However, her reasoning is unpersuasive for several reasons. First, the torn temple veil most likely signifies equality of *access* to God rather than equality of *opportunity* to serve as minister. Second, Jesus' encouragement to women such as Mary to learn does not necessarily imply that he supported their equal participation in positions of church leadership. Seminaries today should certainly encourage women to enroll as students, but the encouragement to learn does not necessarily entail equality of access to the pastoral office.

Beyond this, Spencer's treatment is too brief to serve as an adequate apologetic for an evangelical feminist approach to gender roles. Her 2004 essay will be the subject of a thorough critique later on in this volume.

## Richard Longenecker

There is no essay on Jesus and women in the evangelical feminist volume *Women, Authority and the Bible* edited by Alvera Mickelsen in 1986. Included in the book, however, are two short paragraphs devoted to Jesus and women in an essay by Richard Longenecker.[75] Longenecker maintains that Jesus was perfectly at ease in the company of women since "for him equality between the sexes was . . . a rather self-evident fact."[76] In contrast to other rabbis, who doubted women's ability to learn Scripture and depreciated their worth, he granted women the right to learn the good news and to participate in his ministry.

| Egalitarian Profile 9 |
|---|
| **Proponent:** Richard Longenecker |
| **Title:** "Authority, Hierarchy and Leadership Patterns in the Bible" (1986) |
| **Contribution:** "developmental hermeneutic" |
| **View of Jesus:** redemption in Christ suggests freedom, mutuality, and equality |

Longenecker sets forth a "developmental hermeneutic,"[77] an approach that "clarifies the fullness of the redemptive note sounded in the New Tes-

75. R. N. Longenecker, "Authority, Hierarchy and Leadership Patterns in the Bible," in *Women, Authority and the Bible*, ed. A. Mickelsen (Downers Grove, IL: InterVarsity, 1986), 71–72.
76. Ibid., 71, citing C. E. Carlston, "Proverbs, Maxims, and the Historical Jesus," *Journal of Biblical Literature* 99 (1980): 96–97.
77. Referring also to his previous work: "On the Concept of Development in Pauline Thought," in *Perspectives on Evangelical Theology*, ed. K. S. Kantzer and S. N. Gundry (Grand Rapids, MI: Baker, 1979), 195–207; and *New Testament Social Ethics for Today* (Grand Rapids, MI: Eerdmans, 1984), esp. chap. 2, pp. 16–28.

tament."[78] According to Longenecker, Paul and the early church worked from two categories of thought when dealing with the roles of the sexes: (1) God's *created order*, indicating hierarchy, subordination, and submission; and (2) God's *redemptive work*, where freedom, mutuality, and equality "take prominence." Longenecker contends that while hierarchical order is built into creation by God and must be respected, "a hierarchical ordering of life is not always fixed, particularly when redemptive concerns overshadow what is true because of creation."[79] While both creation and redemption categories must be taken into account in the Christian life, priority is to be given to the latter.

As to a proper hermeneutical starting point, Longenecker contends that we must begin studying any issue at the point where progressive revelation has reached its zenith—in this case, with Jesus as portrayed in the Gospels and with the apostolic interpretation of his ministry in the New Testament. From there one can trace lines of continuity and development back into the Old Testament and forward into the patristic period and beyond. This is why, according to Longenecker, a study of the role of women must begin with Jesus and the apostolic period. And this, too, is why Galatians 3:28 is so important: "For there the gospel is clearly stated as having revolutionary significance for the cultural, social and sexual areas of life."[80]

Longenecker agrees with Jewett that a distinction must be made between the New Testament proclamation about life in Christ and its first-century implementation: "We should look to the passages which point beyond these first-century attitudes toward women to the ideal of the new humanity in Christ. Only thus can we harness the power of the gospel to make all history, not just first-century history, salvation history."[81] Such a hermeneutic "compels us as Christians to stress the redemptive notes of freedom, equality and mutuality that are sounded in the New Testament."[82]

Overall, Longenecker's discussion is not very specific. He bases his case on vague references, such as the recorded attitudes of Jesus toward women and the principles of the gospel, and the claim that freedom, mutuality, and equality should take prominence in God's redemptive order. His categories of creation and redemption are set up in an unduly dichotomous manner. In truth, however, God's redemptive work does not nullify God's created order but, to the contrary, reaffirms it. God and his purposes in creation and redemption are not divided or contradictory.

---

78. Longenecker, "Authority, Hierarchy and Leadership Patterns," 81.
79. Ibid., 82.
80. Ibid., 83.
81. Jewett, *Man as Male and Female*, 147–48.
82. Longenecker, "Authority, Hierarchy & Leadership Patterns," 84.

According to Longenecker, redemption suggests freedom, mutuality, and equality. Yet redemption as a theological category must properly be understood as salvation from sin through Christ. Freedom in redemption, rightly conceived, means freedom from the power of sin, not freedom from all submission to the authority God has built into the structure of human existence. Likewise, equality in Christ does not mean the removal of all distinctions of role; it means there is only one way of salvation for both men and women: confessing one's sin and trusting in Christ for salvation; in this there is no difference.

A developmental hermeneutic is helpful if one observes scriptural restraint. Longenecker, however, introduces terms such as *freedom* and *equality* into his discussion of the biblical teaching on women in such a way that his interpretation supersedes scriptural teaching. Rather than developing his understanding of redemption in Christ from the relevant biblical passages, he asserts his own understanding, which falls outside the central concept of what redemption in Christ really means. The scriptural ideal of a new humanity in Christ does not encompass equality in every sense, if by this one means leveling all distinctions, particularly in role.

## Evaluation

There are several areas of difficulty in the hermeneutic of these evangelical feminist proponents. The first concerns Jesus' relationship with his rabbinic contemporaries. Stendahl is alone in this group in claiming that Jesus did not transcend his Jewish surroundings. Scanzoni and Hardesty, Jewett, and Evans all contend strongly that Jesus differed radically from other Jewish rabbis of his day in how he treated women. Bilezikian and Evans, in particular, draw a fairly sharp distinction between Jesus' approach and that of first-century Judaism. To be sure, unlike many of his Jewish contemporaries Jesus was not a legalist and thus did not feel bound by the rabbinic purity regulations that led to an avoidance of contact with women.

However, Evans's and Bilezikian's treatments unduly generalize about first-century Jews' treatment of women. Bilezikian, especially, fails to distinguish between the ways *different* Jews treated women.[83] Additionally, Bilezikian's treatment exceeds the evidence.

A second difficulty with some of these interpreters is their apparent presupposition of a particular worldview of liberation, freedom, and equality that is independent from Scripture. Scanzoni and Hardesty, for example, claim that Jesus' promise of liberation conveys the notion of liberation in feminist terms. Yet Jesus never gave any indication that women were free to take whatever role to which they may aspire in the church or the home. Jewett's comment that Jesus treated women as "equal to men in every respect" is

---

83. See Levine, "Second Temple Judaism."

potentially misleading; it can be easily taken to suggest that women were and are equally as welcome to serve in the role of teachers or leaders as men. Yet as has been seen, even most recent feminist historical scholarship has concluded that Jesus did not come to establish an egalitarian community where role distinctions no longer applied.

A third difficulty for an egalitarian interpretation of Scripture arises with regard to Jesus' choice of twelve men as his apostles and his commissioning of these men as the core leadership of the church. Scanzoni and Hardesty do not address this. Bilezikian also does not comment on this in his work and limits his discussion about it to a single endnote. Both Evans and Bilezikian suggest the leadership of the Twelve was merely a temporary pattern. However, as Evans and Bilezikian acknowledge, it seems unlikely that Jesus would have accommodated himself to the surrounding culture if an important principle were at stake.

A fourth difficulty is the exaggerated claims made on the basis of limited evidence or observation.[84] Examples include:

- Jesus denounced male lust (Matt. 5:28) to make way for female disciples.
- Leaving one's sister is considered equally sacrificial as leaving other family members; therefore, women are equal to men.
- Because women engaged in certain kinds of service, they should be able to perform all kinds of service, including teaching and preaching.
- Because women were taught by Jesus along with men, they are equally his disciples and equally equipped to teach God's people in the future.
- Women are equal because they were the "first proclaimers" of the message of the resurrection.

A fifth concern relates to the following line of reasoning intimated by Evans: (1) women were equal to men in terms of worth and dignity; (2) women were equal to men in terms of following Jesus and discipleship; (3) women were equal to men in terms of service. Because of this progression, and because Evans essentially levels all forms of service, there is (4) an implication that women are now equal to men in terms of leadership. However, while few would argue with the first point, the subsequent points are subject to debate.

---

84. See the two major categories in the "Non-Feminist Response" by J. Cottrell, *Gender Roles and the Bible: Creation, the Fall, and Redemption* (Joplin, MO: College Press, 1994), 176–88: (1) exaggerated radicalness; and (2) feminist hyperexegesis.

# 12

## THE MATURING MOVEMENT: INCREASING COMPLEXITY

*Women have an equal place in the mission of Christ to the world.*
—Grant R. Osborne, "Women in Jesus' Ministry" (1989)[1]

*The second* phase of evangelical feminism comes across as a maturing movement. Its writers exhibit increasing complexity in their argumentation. After the pioneering work of Krister Stendahl, Letha Scanzoni and Nancy Hardesty, Paul Jewett, Mary Evans, Ben Witherington, Richard Longenecker, and others (1966–1986), the years 1987 to 1999 witnessed the contributions of Grant Osborne, Ruth Tucker, R. T. France, and Stanley Grenz.

Table 12.1: Evangelical Feminism: The Maturing Movement (1987–1999)

| Proponent | Major Work (Date) |
| --- | --- |
| Grant Osborne | "Women in Jesus' Ministry" (1989) |
| Ruth Tucker | *Daughters of the Church* (1987); *Women in the Maze* (1992) |
| R. T. France | *Women in the Church's Ministry* (1995) |
| Stanley Grenz | *Women in the Church* (1995) |

1. G. R. Osborne, "Women in Jesus' Ministry," *Westminster Theological Journal* 51 (1989): 287.

## The Maturing Movement (1987–1999)

### Grant Osborne

In his 1989 article "Women in Jesus' Ministry," Grant Osborne covers Jewish and Hellenistic attitudes toward women, Jesus' relationship with women, and attitude correspondences between Jesus and Paul. Osborne notes that there is no early evidence (prior to AD 70) to support the notion that women served as synagogue rulers. He also points out that there is little evidence that Jesus was consciously breaking Jewish conventions regarding women or that his Jewish contemporaries considered his relationship with women a threat to their beliefs as they did his fellowship with sinners.[2]

Osborne's discussion of women in Jesus' ministry follows a redaction-critical approach, assuming Markan priority and noting ways in which Matthew or Luke respectively alter the material in Mark or share common material ("Q").[3] Women in John are also treated. Overall, based on the data he uses, men are mentioned three times more often than women, a ratio that roughly holds true in the various Gospels and traditions, whether the individuals are named or unnamed.

---

**Egalitarian Profile 10**

**Proponent:** Grant Osborne
**Title:** "Women in Jesus' Ministry" (1989)
**Contribution:** redaction-critical treatment of Jesus and women in four Gospels
**View of Jesus:** while refusing to challenge the "patriarchal matrix," "consciously planted a seed of change"

---

In his treatment of Mark, Osborne notes that a woman's sacrificial act of service at Jesus' anointing renders her "a model for true discipleship" but says that he does not want to overstate Mark's emphasis, "as if he portrays Jesus as a radical egalitarian."[4] Osborne draws attention to the fact that in his teaching Jesus "distinctly reaffirms the traditional Jewish values of hearth and home," including the childbearing role of women. Concluding his treatment of women in Mark, Osborne acknowledges that "Mark accepts the basic patriarchal structure of Judaism but within that framework uses women in a remarkably positive role as valid disciples of Jesus and even as models of faith."[5]

Moving on to Matthew, Osborne notes that the first evangelist adds mention of just one woman not referenced in Mark. Also, he observes that

2. See S. B. Clark, *Man and Woman in Christ* (Ann Arbor, MI: Servant Books, 1980), 242.
3. See W. Munro, "Women Disciples in Mark?" *Catholic Biblical Quarterly* 44 (1982): 226.
4. Osborne, "Women in Jesus' Ministry," 268.
5. Ibid., 270.

Matthew tends to shorten Mark's stories of women, as he does most other stories. Osborne notes small redactional changes introduced by Matthew, assuming that Matthew used Mark as one of his sources. He notes that women are used in kingdom parables and that "Jesus used men and women equally as role models."[6]

He comments that after Jesus' resurrection the women in Matthew are portrayed more positively than in Mark. Osborne casts it this way: "The women have temporarily replaced the Twelve and function similarly to the righteous remnant of the prophetic period in calling the disciples back to God."[7] Osborne concludes that while in Mark the women "finalize the theme of discipleship failure," in Matthew they "summarize the overcoming power of Jesus' presence in discipleship."[8] According to Osborne, "They become the archetypal disciples who succeed even when the disciples fail" as well as a group of outcasts "reinstated to their proper place in God's economy by the redemptive presence of Jesus."[9]

Osborne notes that Luke features many of the same women as Mark and Matthew but adds several significant passages, thus indicating Luke's special interest in the role of women in Jesus' ministry. Luke alone mentions what Osborne infers to be women's presence in Jesus' "inner circle of disciples" and participation in Jesus' mission (Luke 8:1–3).[10] Unique to Luke are also the raising of the widow's son (Luke 7:11–17) and Jesus' anointing by a "sinful woman" (Luke 7:36–50), and Osborne notes that Jesus had compassion on these women.

Osborne reiterates that he does not want to overstate the case, noting that "if Jesus had been a revolutionary feminist, he would have included a woman among his inner circle of twelve disciples."[11] He claims that while "Jesus clearly accepted the basic patriarchal matrix of his time, the roles of women were redefined within rather than outside that structure."[12] Osborne adds, "Clearly [women's] importance as bridge-builders between Jesus and the early church . . . is great indeed."[13] Nevertheless, Osborne acknowledges that "it is certain that Jesus continued to reserve the place of leadership for men even in Luke, the most outspoken proponent of women's rights."[14]

6. Ibid., 275.
7. Ibid.
8. Ibid., 276.
9. Ibid.
10. Ibid., 280.
11. Ibid.
12. Ibid.
13. Ibid., 282.
14. Ibid., 283.

Yet while Jesus stayed within the patriarchalism of his day, Osborne contends that Luke the evangelist "goes out of his way to stress the equality of men and women in the kingdom."[15] What is more, Osborne cites Tucker and Liefeld, who have contrasted the moral weaknesses of men to the spiritual strength of women.

Turning to women in John, Osborne discusses Mary the mother of Jesus, Mary and Martha, and Mary Magdalene. For Osborne, Jesus' mother "becomes a model for the woman disciple whose very relationship to her son is transformed at the 'hour' of Jesus' triumph."[16] Mary's act of anointing Jesus marks her as a "devoted disciple."[17] Jesus' words to Mary Magdalene in John 20:17—"go and tell my brothers"—are interpreted by Osborne as a clear apostolic commission to proclaim a message with both redemptive and theological overtones.[18] Osborne concludes that "women have an equal place in the mission of Christ to the world."[19]

Osborne claims that Jesus, while refusing to challenge the patriarchal matrix, consciously planted a seed of change. According to Osborne, "Paul and Jesus alike began a social revolution, the results of which are still felt."[20] For Osborne, therefore, the Gospels provide a bridge to Paul in that the concerns expressed by the evangelists are similar to those of Paul. Osborne speaks of the elevation of women to a ministerial role as "a sign of the inbreaking kingdom," even though he concedes that first-century women did not have a pastoral role.[21]

Overall, while much of Osborne's discussion of the various passages in this work stays within conventional parameters, his conclusions do not demonstrably follow from his interpretation of the textual data. Rather, there is a tendency toward general statements that encompass more than what is in the text. The result is unsubstantiated claims of women's being equal to men or coming alongside men in kingdom ministry.

### Ruth Tucker

For the most part, Tucker traverses by-now familiar territory in terms of the women she discusses. Her treatment of Martha's confession of Jesus as the Christ and the Son of God (John 11:27) notes the verbal similarity with Peter's confession of Jesus at Caesarea Philippi, and from this she draws the implication that "Martha seems to have a status as a spokesperson in

15. Ibid.
16. Ibid., 285.
17. Ibid., 286.
18. Ibid., 287.
19. Ibid.
20. Ibid., 290.
21. Ibid.

John similar to that of Peter in the Synoptics. Certainly her role is greater than his in the fourth Gospel."[22]

Tucker also provides a brief discussion of Jesus' appointing only male apostles. She asks, "What would have happened if Jesus had appointed a female apostle?"[23] Tucker gives a fourfold response: (1) it would have been logistically difficult for women to travel alone as itinerant missionaries in the first century; (2) women would not have found acceptance as religious teachers in most areas; (3) women were not accepted as witnesses; (4) the apostles symbolically represented the twelve tribes of Israel. She summarizes:

> Jesus had women learning from him as disciples and traveling with him in service. He engaged in theological dialogue with women. He helped women in need and in sin without demeaning them. He treated men and women alike with regard to their failings. He encouraged both men and women in their faith.[24]

Many of Tucker's observations are valid. However, her contentions that Martha's status as a spokesperson in John was similar to that of Peter in the Synoptics and that "certainly her role is greater than his in the fourth Gospel" raise questions. As in the Synoptics, Peter is presented in John's Gospel as the spokesman of the Twelve (see esp. John 6:68–69, a passage Tucker does not discuss; see also John 13:6–11, 36–38). From Peter's call to discipleship, which is narrated in John 1:40–42, to his final commissioning by Jesus in John 21:15–19, he is portrayed as the primary apostle among the Twelve in keeping with the Synoptic portrait. Martha, by contrast, appears only in John 11. Without diminishing the significance of her confession of Jesus in John 11:27, Martha hardly rivals Peter's status in John's Gospel as the spokesman of the Twelve, and her role is certainly not greater than his.

---

**Egalitarian Profile 11**

**Proponent:** Ruth Tucker

**Titles:** *Daughters of the Church* (1987); *Women in the Maze* (1992)

**Contribution:** ministry entails servanthood, not exercising authority; hence any male-female role distinctions with regard to church offices are moot

**View of Jesus:** revolutionary; "showed an unusual sensitivity to women and their needs"

---

22. R. A. Tucker and W. L. Liefeld, *Daughters of the Church: Women and Ministry from New Testament Times to the Present* (Grand Rapids, MI: Baker, 1987), 28.
23. Ibid., 46.
24. Ibid., 47.

In her book *Women in the Maze: Questions and Answers on Biblical Equality* (1992), Tucker contends that in contrast to first-century Palestinian Judaism, which regarded women as inferior, Jesus' approach to women was "nothing less than revolutionary." Tucker acknowledges that applying the label "feminist" to Jesus is debatable, but she states that "it is safe to say that he showed an unusual sensitivity to women and their needs."[25] As examples Tucker cites Jesus' interaction with the Samaritan woman (John 4) and his relationship with his mother. Jesus' treatment of his mother demonstrates that "all his followers, whether male or female . . . had equal status in his sight."[26] Yet this argument is not clear. If by "equal status" she means that all are equally saved and equally members of God's kingdom in Christ, she is in keeping with the biblical message. If, however, she extends "equal status" to roles in the church, that is another matter.[27]

In addition to Tucker's discussions of Jesus' marital status, the women Jesus referenced in his parables, and his abolishing the double standard in his teaching on divorce, she argues that Jesus had women disciples (Luke 8:1–3). In doing so she quotes Grant Osborne at length, reaffirming his claim that women became part of the inner circle of disciples and participated in the mission of Jesus.[28]

Why, then, according to Tucker, did Jesus not include a woman among the Twelve? The "most compelling explanation for Jesus' failure to call women to be among the twelve has to do with decorum. The potential for scandal was too great that . . . the gospel message might be slandered because of rumors of sex scandals was a risk he could not justify."[29] But this is an argument from silence. More likely, as Tucker notes, "the twelve disciples were perhaps representative of the twelve tribes of Israel, and only males could symbolically fill these roles."[30] Tucker disavows, however, that this constitutes an abiding principle, since none of the Twelve was Gentile, which would mean that only Jews could serve in church leadership today.

Tucker notes that the debate over women in ministry is really a debate over women and authority. She rightly acknowledges that no one argues against women in ministry; rather, the argument is against women's performing ministry that entails authority. According to Tucker, Jesus taught that ministry entails servanthood, not the exercising of authority (citing Matt.

25. R. A. Tucker, *Women in the Maze: Questions and Answers on Biblical Equality* (Downers Grove, IL: InterVarsity, 1992), 80.
26. Ibid., 83.
27. See the comments on Jesus' choice of twelve men as apostles in the following discussion and throughout this volume.
28. Osborne, "Women in Jesus' Ministry," 280.
29. Tucker, *Women in the Maze*, 89.
30. Ibid.

20:20–28; Mark 9:35–37 and the parallel Matt. 18:3–4; John 13:15). She implies that any role distinction between men and women with regard to ministry is therefore moot. But this is based on a false dichotomy between servanthood and the exercise of authority. As the following discussion will show, servant leadership and the proper exercise of authority can go hand in hand, and church offices do entail the exercise of authority, without violating the principle of servanthood.

### R. T. France

In his 1995 work *Women in the Church's Ministry*, R. T. France includes a brief section on women in the ministry of Jesus, which incorporates a brief discussion of attitudes toward women in ancient Judaism. Helpfully, France acknowledges that the picture was not uniform, and that examples of a "more enlightened attitude" toward women can be found.[31]

According to France, Jesus viewed women in this way:

> [Women were not] mere possessions of men, or even second-class citizens; still less were they primarily of sexual interest. He related to women and valued them as real people of independent worth and personality, and they played a significant role in the movement which arose out of his public ministry.[32]

France sees the fact that no woman was included among the Twelve as a "historical provision of limited duration, not an ideological statement about the permanent values of the kingdom of God."[33] He also contends, based on his reading of Luke 8:1–3, that Jesus' "inner circle was not very sharply distinguished in practice" from the wider group of Jesus' followers "among whom women were prominent."[34]

| Egalitarian Profile 12 |
| --- |
| **Proponent:** R. T. France |
| **Title:** *Women in the Church's Ministry* (1995) |
| **Contribution:** Jesus launched reversal from patriarchalism toward women's liberation |
| **View of Jesus:** Jesus' approach to women contains the seeds of liberation |

France concludes that while the Gospels do not, perhaps, record a total reversal of Jewish prejudice against women and of their exclusion from

31. R. T. France, *Women in the Church's Ministry: A Test Case for Biblical Interpretation* (Grand Rapids, MI: Eerdmans, 1995), 76. This contrasts favorably with Evans's monolithic portrayal of first-century Judaism.
32. Ibid., 77.
33. Ibid., 78.
34. Ibid.

roles of leadership, they "do contain the seeds from which such a reversal was bound to grow."[35] While the church has been slow to respond, "in the ministry of Jesus we see an irreversible turning of the wheel which set the Jesus movement on a new course with regard to the respective roles of men and women."[36]

Overall, France's view is similar to Osborne's. Like Osborne, France claims that Jesus' approach to women contains the seeds of women's liberation. As in Osborne, too, one detects exaggeration, as when France says that the reversal of Jewish attitudes toward women affected through Jesus' ministry "was bound to grow." The fact that Jesus treated women positively and that this stood in marked contrast to much of Jewish patriarchal society does not mean that there was going to be a major movement of reversal toward women's liberation from patriarchalism.

An instance of special pleading is France's insistence that Jesus' inner circle was not sharply distinguished from the wider group of Jesus' followers, among whom women were prominent.

### Stanley Grenz

Stanley Grenz devotes only about six pages in his book *Women in the Church* to a discussion of women in Jesus' ministry.[37] He speaks of "the attitude of our Lord coupled with his liberating message" as forming the foundation for women's roles in the early church.[38] Grenz is convinced that the "gospel's liberation of women comes into full relief only when we view the ministry of Jesus . . . in light of the strictures against women prevalent in the ancient Near East."[39]

Grenz observes that Jesus treated all people, male or female, as persons and that he regularly showed compassion to the needy, including women. Grenz also points out that Jesus, in contrast to other rabbis, frequently included incidents from women's lives in his teaching. While acknowledging that Jesus did not include any women among the Twelve, Grenz contends that this fact should not "blind us to the importance of their presence among Jesus' followers."[40]

35. Ibid.
36. Ibid., 79.
37. S. J. Grenz with D. M. Kjesbo, *Women in the Church: A Biblical Theology of Women in Ministry* (Downers Grove, IL: InterVarsity, 1995), 71–77.
38. Ibid., 71.
39. Ibid., 72.
40. Ibid., 75.

| Egalitarian Profile 13 |
|---|
| **Proponent:** Stanley Grenz |
| **Title:** *Women in the Church* (1995) |
| **Contribution:** speaks of "God's egalitarian intention from the beginning"; says "elevation of women to a ministerial role" is "a sign of the inbreaking kingdom" |
| **View of Jesus:** his "liberating message" laid "foundation for women's roles in the early church" |

Grenz contends that the "new creation vision consists of the renewal and completion of creation" and that the "call for full participation of men and women in the church is the fulfillment of God's egalitarian intention from the beginning."[41]

However, Grenz's explanation as to why Jesus chose only men as apostles is also inadequate. First, his point about the "new creation vision" and his call for full participation of both men and women in the church as the fulfillment of God's egalitarian intention fails to recognize several important pieces of scriptural evidence. Concerning "full participation," Grenz takes a different approach from that of Longenecker, who acknowledges that God's creation entails male headship and female submission but argues that redemption in Christ trumps creation. Grenz, by contrast, claims God's intention was "egalitarian . . . from the beginning," so that redemption does not supersede creation but rather renews and completes it.

Grenz also avers that the notion of the priesthood of all believers, in contrast to Old Testament times when only men could serve as priests, demands that women be allowed to serve as pastors and church leaders. In keeping with this, Grenz maintains that the ultimate point of appeal must be the gifts distributed by God. But his argument fails to convince, as do his contentions that gifting must be the sole determinant of the exercise of spiritual gifts and that a hierarchical view of church leadership must be replaced with an egalitarian one.

In the end, Grenz calls for nothing less than a complete reassessment of the conventional view of leadership and authority. True servant leadership is that of a shepherd who cares for his sheep, not that of a ruler who lords it over his people. Mutual submission must replace a dominance-submission model in the church. Quoting extensively from recent leadership theorists, Grenz makes a case that shared leadership and leadership teams are more effective than the single-leader model. For this reason also, "Because men

---

41. Ibid., 179; this was already argued by Bilezikian, albeit in a much less sophisticated fashion.

and women view the world in different ways, the church leadership team is enhanced by the presence of both."[42]

Grenz also notes that Jesus instructed women and involved them in theological discussion. Also, he notes, the fact that Jesus' first appearance after his resurrection was to women indicates that in God's new economy, men *and* women are credible witnesses and capable messengers of the risen Lord; in the postresurrection community, women and men share in the proclamation of the good news. "This new role for women," Grenz claims, "forms a fitting climax to what developed throughout Jesus' life,"[43] as if to imply that all role distinctions between men and women in the church have now been eliminated.

Grenz largely depends on the exegetical work of others and seeks to tease out the larger theological implications. Another factor to note is that several of Grenz's statements are characterized by a certain ambiguity if not exaggeration, such as when he says that "in the post-resurrection community, women and men share in the proclamation of the good news," as if to imply that all role distinctions between men and women in the church have now been eliminated. However, this conclusion does not follow from the evidence Grenz adduces.

## Evaluation

"The Maturing Movement" maintains a good bit of continuity with arguments advanced during the early years of the evangelical feminist movement. At the same time, we see a certain amount of refinement and maturation of hermeneutical procedure and the introduction of several new lines of argumentation. In terms of continuity, we notice again a fairly straight line drawn from Jesus' "revolutionary" treatment of women to the notion of "the egalitarian Jesus" without considering the possibility that certain boundaries may be drawn in Scripture regarding the role of women in ministry. Many of the writers in this period evidence use of "equal" language that follows from the presupposition of an egalitarian worldview. At the same time, it can be noted that evangelical feminists of this period tend to be a bit more restrained in their use of liberation language than the proponents of egalitarianism in the early years.

Additionally, evangelical feminist writers in this period continue to wrestle with the question of why Jesus did not include women among the Twelve. Compared with the earlier period, evangelical feminist writers here display a greater degree of sophistication in the way in which they deal with Jesus' choice of twelve men as apostles.

42. Ibid., 230.
43. Ibid., 77.

As in the previous period, we also find a pattern of frequent exaggeration or claims that are not adequately supported by the evidence. Several of the writers from this period appeal to the New Testament conception of servant leadership as leveling all role distinctions between men and women. Servanthood and the exercise of authority are presented in dichotomous terms, and the former is elevated above the latter. As argued, however, this dichotomy is false, and both servant leadership and a proper exercise of authority by church leaders are taught in Scripture.

A proposal that is somewhat similar and yet also different from Longenecker's "developmental hermeneutic" is that of R. T. France. France claims that Jesus' treatment of women contains in seed form a full-fledged egalitarianism.[44] However, this extrapolation does not necessarily follow. Similar to France's argument is Osborne's attempt to show coherence between Jesus' practice and Paul's teaching with regard to women's roles. This effort is evidence for the maturing of evangelical feminism as a movement, for it is clearly inadequate to interpret Jesus' treatment of women in the Gospels in isolation from passages in Paul. At the same time, the preponderance of the evidence suggests that both Jesus and Paul did not practice or teach an unfettered form of egalitarianism.

Even bolder is the argument, advanced by Grenz, that God's intentions are "egalitarian from the beginning" and his appeal to the priesthood of believers and the gifts distributed by God in arguing for an egalitarian approach to gender roles. However, it does not logically follow that God's distribution of a particular gift to a woman, such as teaching or administration, precludes setting up certain parameters for the exercise of the particular gift.

---

44. See Bilezikian, *Beyond Sex Roles*, 118, who speaks of Jesus' unleashing of "an *irrepressible ferment* that would change men and women and empower them with the effervescent dynamic of the Spirit."

# 13

# RECENT CONTRIBUTIONS: CREATIVITY AND CONSOLIDATION

*Nowhere does Jesus ever say—or even imply in anything he says—that only men can be leaders in the church.*

—Aida Besançon Spencer, *Discovering Biblical Equality* (2004)[1]

*The third* and final period of evangelical feminist writings that we will examine spans from 2000 to the present. This period features a mixture of creative new proposals and consolidation of previously made arguments. The works considered here include those by evangelical feminists Linda Belleville, William Webb, Douglas Groothuis, John Phelan, and Aida Besançon Spencer.

Table 13.1: Evangelical Feminism: Recent Contributions (2000–Present)

| Proponent | Major Work (Date) |
|---|---|
| Linda Belleville | *Women Leaders and the Church* (2000); *Two Views on Women in Ministry* (2001) |
| William Webb | *Slaves, Women and Homosexuals* (2001) |
| Douglas Groothuis | "What Jesus Thought about Women" (2002) |
| John Phelan | "Women and the Aims of Jesus" (2004) |
| Aida Besançon Spencer | Essay in *Discovering Biblical Equality* (2004) |

1. A. B. Spencer, "Jesus' Treatment of Women in the Gospels," in *Discovering Biblical Equality: Complementarity without Hierarchy*, ed. R. W. Pierce and R. M. Groothuis (Downers Grove, IL: InterVarsity, 2004), 134.

## Recent Contributions (2000–Present)

### Linda Belleville

Linda Belleville is primarily a Pauline scholar, and her contribution to our topic—Jesus and women—is therefore limited. However, there are places in her work where she does address Jesus' stance toward women.

Belleville's work *Women Leaders and the Church* (2000) is part of a series called Three Crucial Questions. The first of these questions is, "In which ministries can women be involved?" In providing an answer Belleville mentions that in light of the Egyptian Isis cult, in which women were equal participants with men, "Jesus is not quite the liberator of women as he is sometimes pictured."[2] Women were not as religiously oppressed in the first century as is sometimes argued. Women in the Isis cult knew equality and liberty, at least in the religious realm. It is unclear, however, why Belleville adduces the Isis cult as a relevant piece of background information in dealing with Jesus' stance toward women, since the evidence that the Isis cult was practiced in Palestine is weak.[3]

Belleville contends that "although Jesus is often hailed as the liberator of women . . . Jesus . . . in fact, did not affirm any roles for women that weren't already a possibility in Roman society."[4] According to Belleville, the difference lies not in roles but in attitudes. Unlike his contemporaries, Jesus encouraged women to learn, was at ease with women in public, and treated women with dignity. The question again arises as to why Belleville compares Jesus to the Greco-Roman world, since his realm of operation was in Jewish Palestine. In any case, it is unclear how women could be liberated with regard to roles but not attitudes in the Greco-Roman world. Normally, these would be related. Belleville neither identifies specific roles in Greco-Roman society nor explains how it is possible for roles and attitudes to be at odds.

Belleville affirms that "there is no lack of women leaders in the pages of the New Testament."[5] She cites Mary the mother of Jesus and the women among the 120 mentioned in Acts (1:8, 14–15; 2:1–4). While there were many male leaders as well, "virtually every ministry role that named a man also named a woman."[6] Belleville acknowledges that "the only roles lacking female names are *overseer* and *elder*, but then specific men are not singled out

---

2. L. L. Belleville, *Women Leaders and the Church: Three Crucial Questions* (Grand Rapids, MI: Baker, 2000), 37.
3. See "Egyptian Deities: Isis, Osiris, and Sarapis," in E. Ferguson, *Backgrounds of Early Christianity*, 2nd ed. (Grand Rapids, MI: Eerdmans, 1993), 249–61.
4. Ibid., 47.
5. Ibid., 49.
6. Ibid., 50.

in these capacities either."[7] She discusses the women mentioned in Luke 8:1–3 under the rubric of ancient patronage and cites the women who served as the first witnesses of the resurrection; Junia is called a "female apostle."[8]

Belleville concludes that "the work of ministry depends on the empowerment of the Holy Spirit, not on the holding of an office. Gift precedes function."[9] She adds that the role of leaders is not to govern or exercise authority but to equip others for ministry.

In dealing with her second question, "What roles can women play in society?" Belleville includes a brief discussion of Jesus' teaching.[10] She claims that Jesus' language was that of mutuality and equality. She does not comment on subordination in marriage. Concerning Jesus' reference to God's creation of male and female (Matt. 19:4), Belleville contends that "the creation order knows nothing of male priority or prerogatives. God created two sexually distinct beings on equal footing."[11]

Belleville observes that Jesus' call to discipleship extended equally to men and women (citing Mark 10:29–31) and considers this particularly significant since the "household (*oikos*) was the domain of the woman, and the bearing and raising of children was her primary responsibility."[12] Jesus treated women as social equals, she says.[13] Yet it should be noted that while all women as well as all men are called to Christian discipleship, there are no necessary implications with regard to women's equal roles in church leadership. Belleville's use of the term "social equals" is potentially ambiguous; while it implies equality of worth and dignity it does not necessarily imply equality of role.

---

### Egalitarian Profile 14

**Proponent:** Linda Belleville

**Titles:** *Women Leaders and the Church* (2000); essay in *Two Views on Women in Ministry* (2001)

**Contribution:** distinguishes between gift and office, service and exercise of authority

**View of Jesus:** Jesus not only "liberator of women" in ancient world; says Jesus' "language was that of mutuality and equality"; treated women as "social equals"

---

In her essay in *Two Views on Women in Ministry*, Belleville makes the argument from Matthew 10:1 that the authority conferred upon the apostles by Jesus was given only to drive out demons and to heal the sick, not to

7. Ibid., 187, n. 34.
8. Ibid., 55–56.
9. Ibid., 69.
10. Ibid., 109–11.
11. Ibid., 109.
12. Ibid., 111.
13. Ibid.

preach and teach. She does acknowledge that the Twelve were sent out to preach the gospel (Mark 3:14) but contends that authority is not mentioned in this context.[14] Belleville adds the by-now conventional rebuttal that Jesus chose not only twelve *men* but twelve *Jewish* men, but no one argues that he intended to restrict church leadership to Jewish men. Be that as it may, Belleville believes it is only the church that possesses authority, not church leaders, whether male or female.[15]

Why would Jesus send out the Twelve to preach the gospel without giving them authority as they do so? Whether or not authority is specifically mentioned, it seems intrinsic to the act of sending and the task to be accomplished.

### William Webb

However one might assess the merits of Webb's book *Slaves, Women and Homosexuals*, he exhibits a considerable degree of creativity in his argument. The overall burden of Webb's work is to argue for a "redemptive-movement hermeneutic" that acknowledges the progressive nature of biblical revelation with regard to ethics and human relationships. He applies this hermeneutic to three topics—slaves, women, and homosexuals—and makes the following case:

1) Slavery is accepted in the Old Testament but the New Testament contains seeds for its being overturned (e.g., Philemon); therefore, the "redemptive movement" is toward the abolition of slavery.

2) Women were subordinate to men in Old Testament times as part of the system of patriarchy, while the New Testament shows signs of women's equal participation in church leadership (e.g., Gal. 3:28); thus, as in slavery, the biblical "redemptive movement" with regard to women is toward equality and liberation.

3) As to homosexuals, there is no progression. It is equally condemned in the Old and New Testaments; therefore, the church today should still not condone homosexuality.

| **Egalitarian Profile 15** |
| --- |
| **Proponent:** William Webb |
| **Title:** *Slaves, Women and Homosexuals* (2001) |
| **Contribution:** redemptive-movement hermeneutic |
| **View of Jesus:** Jesus had female disciples; does not feature prominently in overall scheme |

---

14. L. Belleville, "Women in Ministry," in *Two Views on Women in Ministry*, ed. J. R. Beck and C. L. Blomberg (Grand Rapids, MI: Zondervan, 2001), 107.
15. Ibid., 110.

To arrive at these conclusions, Webb cites almost exclusively texts from the Old Testament and the New Testament Epistles.[16] The only Gospel evidence adduced is the fact that Jesus had female disciples and that women initiated divorce in one of Jesus' sayings (Mark 10:12). It appears, therefore, that Gospel evidence does not feature prominently in Webb's hermeneutical scheme.

His reference to women disciples of Jesus and to women initiating divorce is insufficient evidence to establish progressive movement in redemptive history and does not suffice to establish an evangelical feminist view of gender roles in the church. The issue is considerably more complex. Even if a certain movement in this direction could be discerned, it still does not logically follow that the desired end is complete egalitarianism. An alternative outcome is women's greater participation in worship and ministry that falls short of women's equal participation with men in church leadership. This would seem more likely in light of New Testament passages regarding women's roles in the church.

### Douglas Groothuis

At the outset of his brief article, "What Jesus Thought about Women," the author, professor at Denver Seminary, notes the difference between Jesus and first-century Judaism. He points out that in his parables Jesus "shows no gender favoritism."[17] Citing the example of Mary of Bethany, Groothuis observes that Jesus affirmed women as students. He also highlights Jesus' willingness to interact without condescension with women, using the Samaritan woman in John 4 as an example.

| Egalitarian Profile 16 |
| --- |
| **Proponent:** Douglas Groothuis |
| **Title:** "What Jesus Thought about Women" (2002) |
| **Contribution:** brief survey of Jesus and women |
| **View of Jesus:** "showed no gender favoritism" |

Groothuis also addresses the question as to why no women were among the Twelve. He observes that although women were among Jesus' close followers, "given the highly patriarchal setting of Jesus' ministry, it would have been unlikely if not culturally impossible for him to have ministered effectively with women in his innermost circle."[18] He also points to evidence that women served in leadership during the New Testament period. Groothuis's work here offers nothing groundbreaking.

---

16. W. Webb, *Slaves, Women and Homosexuals* (2001), 46–47.
17. D. Groothuis, "What Jesus Thought about Women," *Priscilla Papers* 16/3 (2002): 18.
18. Ibid., 19.

## John Phelan

John Phelan's short paper "Women and the Aims of Jesus" was originally delivered in 2003 at the international conference of Christians for Biblical Equality (CBE). Phelan cites several Old Testament prophetic passages to support his argument that the purpose of Jesus' mission was "to declare that access to God was possible for all."[19] Thus today, in Christ, all of God's people are priests, have the Holy Spirit, are holy, and have received spiritual gifts. Phelan concludes that for these reasons "any restriction on any of God's people, male or female, is contrary to the kingdom ideal and a violation of the express intent of Jesus." "Hard passages," i.e., passages that seem to restrict women serving in leadership positions, "must be read in light of the intentions of Jesus and the presence of the kingdom of God in the church."[20]

---

**Egalitarian Profile 17**

**Proponent:** John Phelan
**Title:** "Women and the Aims of Jesus" (2003)
**Contribution:** the aims of Jesus are egalitarian; sets aside "problem text" 1 Tim. 2:12
**View of Jesus:** Jesus' kingdom is egalitarian

---

According to Phelan, nothing can contradict "the clear expectation of Jesus" that all barriers be removed and all God's people have the Spirit. Whatever restrictions may be implied in Paul's writings must be seen within the context of his teaching on spiritual gifts and his mention of several women as leaders of house churches, which is "roughly equivalent to pastors today."[21] He maintains that the only "problem text" is 1 Timothy 2:12, which is not applicable today; it was directed only "against the abuse of freedom in a particular setting."[22] Why, Phelan asks, alluding to Paul's argument in Galatians, "go back to the old pattern of restriction and barrier, of slavery and fear?" So, he claims, those who believe Scripture teaches role distinctions between men and women are modern-day "Judaizers" seeking to rob women of their freedom in Christ.

Phelan's thesis can be summarized this way: (1) according to the Old Testament prophets, the Spirit would be given to all, (2) so the purpose of Jesus' mission was to provide access to God for all, and (3) thus no one should erect any barriers to women in leadership. There are several difficulties with this logic, however. Most importantly, there is a difference between what Phelan calls "equal access" and "equal opportunity to serve

19. J. E. Phelan, "Women and the Aims of Jesus," *Priscilla Papers* 18/1 (2004): 10.
20. Ibid., 11.
21. Ibid.
22. Ibid.

in positions of church leadership." Scripture is clear that in Christ, believers, whether male or female, have "equal access" to certain things, such as salvation (Gal. 3:28). But this does not necessarily mean that this equal access extends to all ministerial roles.

### Aida Besançon Spencer

Aida Besançon Spencer, who authored an earlier book, *Beyond the Curse*, in 1985, provides a fifteen-page discussion of Jesus' treatment of women in the Gospels as part of *Discovering Biblical Equality* (2004), a monograph written in response to the highly influential *Recovering Biblical Manhood and Womanhood* (1991). At the outset of her article, Spencer notes that there is common agreement that Jesus affirmed women and treated them with dignity and respect. Jesus' esteem for women is evidenced in his conversations and his teachings. Women formed an important part of Jesus' ministry.

Spencer goes on to say that claiming a woman's place is in the home is purely a cultural viewpoint. She writes, "This emphasis on women's remaining in the household as much as economically possible does not flow from any clear teaching in the Old Testament."[23] She argues that Jesus "does not treat women primarily as homemakers."[24] Yet two of the examples she gives to support her claim—the woman calling Jesus' mother blessed in Luke 11:27–28 and Mary sitting at Jesus' feet in Luke 10:38–42—do not deny that women may have a central role in the home. Jesus' response in Luke 11 is not designed to keep women out of the home or place them in positions of leadership, but rather to emphasize discipleship as more important even than motherhood. This is not a discussion of egalitarian issues or leadership.

According to Spencer, obeying and learning from God are a high priority for men as well as women (see Luke 10:38–42), and rearing children is a significant ministry for both (citing 1 Tim. 3:4–5, 12). Mary's sitting at Jesus' feet likewise shows the importance of Christian discipleship for women as well as men, without reference to female roles or any intention whatsoever of addressing the importance of motherhood. Spencer's point that childrearing is important for men as well as women fails to address women's function of giving birth to children, which is explicitly stated in a passage she cites, 1 Timothy 2:15. It is a biological fact that men cannot give birth to children, and Scripture suggests that there are certain implications for women's role from this fact.

23. Spencer, "Jesus' Treatment of Women in the Gospels," 131.
24. Ibid., 132, citing Luke 11:27–28.

Spencer also contends that in Jesus, obeying and learning from God have a higher priority for both men and women, and rearing children likewise is a significant ministry for both genders, not just women.

In the fourth-century *Constitutions of the Holy Apostles* the argument is made that women ought not to teach in the church because Jesus never commissioned women to preach. According to Spencer, this teaching makes gender the abiding principle and illegitimately assumes that whatever the biblical model does not explicitly establish is therefore forbidden. However, Spencer's argument here unduly reverses logic: she is critiquing a fourth-century document, implying that it is representative of recent argumentation for restricting women's roles in church leadership. Yet contemporary arguments for distinctive male-female roles in the church are considerably more nuanced in considering a variety of passages.

Spencer affirms that while it is true that Jesus appointed only men as his apostles, "nowhere does Jesus ever say—or even imply in anything he says—that only men can be leaders in the church."[25] According to Spencer, this is an argument from silence that represents a limited view of the text, that is, the all-male composition of the Twelve, as supporting male-only leadership in the church. Also, Jesus "does not teach that we will advance God's reign by maintaining male-female distinctions in leadership."[26] Here, again, according to Spencer, is an argument from silence.

---

**Egalitarian Profile 18**

**Proponent:** Aida Besançon Spencer
**Title:** Essay in *Discovering Biblical Equality* (2004)
**Contribution:** Jesus' appointment of twelve men as apostles not paradigmatic
**View of Jesus:** "Nowhere does Jesus ever say—or even imply in anything he says— that only men can be leaders in the church"

---

Spencer argues, like Belleville before her, that the authority given to the apostles by Jesus is not over people but over demons and unclean spirits. Here she leaves behind the issue of male-female roles and moves on to a discussion of the nature of authority. Spencer implies that not even Jesus' apostles were given authority over people; thus apostleship does not involve the exercise of authority over others. Therefore authority in itself is irrelevant as a paradigm for leadership; "leadership no longer is a question of power but rather of service."[27] This argument is not new; it is employed by previous evangelical feminist writers such as Bilezikian, Tucker, and Grenz, among others.

25. Ibid., 134.
26. Ibid.
27. Ibid., 135.

Spencer claims that "apostleship is not synonymous with church leadership";[28] there is no direct link between apostle and elder or overseer. Her purpose here seems to be to argue that even though Jesus did choose only men as apostles, that has nothing to do with church leadership being restricted to men, since apostles cannot be seen as the same as church leaders. However, even if these two roles are not "synonymous," there is a clear link between leadership in Jesus' new messianic community (the apostles) and leadership in the apostolic church (elders, overseers).

While the roles are not strictly synonymous, we should not rule out the obvious equivalency. Doing so would be an instance of a "disjunctive fallacy" or a "fallacy of the excluded middle" by which two extremes are posited (synonymous or irrelevant) and the middle (equivalent) is illegitimately excluded. A logical way to construe the relationship between Jesus' and Paul's pattern of leadership is to see them in essential continuity and agreement.[29]

Spencer argues that the Twelve represented the twelve tribal heads of Israel and thus had to be twelve free males, not women or slaves; therefore the Twelve should not serve as a precedent for leadership. Yet, while Spencer may be correct in seeing a connection between male headship in Old Testament Israel and male headship reflected in Jesus' choice of men among the Twelve, to turn this into an argument for the inclusion of women in church leadership is a logical non sequitur. It is unclear why a connection of the apostles to Israel's tribal heads should serve as a warrant to disqualify the aspect of leadership.

Additionally, few award paradigmatic status to Jesus' appointment of twelve men as apostles. There are not many who would argue that there should be only twelve church leaders today; few, if any, would argue that only Jews should serve in this capacity. Yet while the number and ethnic makeup of the Twelve have a salvation-historical tie-in—the twelve tribes of Israel—which accounts for their composition, the maleness of the group's members is not indicated to be culturally relative.

Also, there is a difference between male and female leadership, and Jewish and Gentile leadership, in the church. The New Testament makes clear that the church unites both Jews and Gentiles and nowhere bars the latter from leadership. With regard to male and female, however, while both are united in the church, there is clear indication in the New Testament writings subsequent to the Gospels that the all-male pattern of leadership, which

28. Ibid.
29. Note that relating Paul's teaching to Jesus is also the burden of the evangelical feminist scholar Grant Osborne, though his argument is different.

spans from the Old Testament to Jesus and beyond, ought to be preserved because it is rooted in God's created order.

Nevertheless, Spencer makes a case that apostles included women. According to Spencer, subsequent to Jesus' resurrection the notion of *apostle* was broadened to include all disciples who were to bear apostolic witness to the resurrection: "In the new covenant era the apostolic witness includes both women and men."[30]

Even though Spencer has just argued that apostles are not synonymous with New Testament church leaders and thus do not provide a suitable paradigm, she goes on to make a case that apostles included women: "They certainly were part of an inner circle that was trained in all ways as the twelve men were."[31] Yet even if it were true that the concept of apostleship in the early church included women as well as men, it remains true that the original set of apostles was unique and distinctive from the rest of the apostles; only the Twelve were with Jesus from the beginning (John 15:27; Acts 1:21–22).

In the end, Spencer states that "women functioned as witnesses or 'apostles' who had been with Jesus, were eyewitnesses of the resurrection and were sent by Jesus to proclaim the good news."[32] "As apostles sent by God, the twelve Jewish men looked back to the old covenant, where the multi-numbered [sic] women and men looked forward, beyond the resurrection to the new covenant."[33]

Spencer's conclusions can be summarized this way: (1) Jesus' appointment of twelve Jewish men as his apostles should not be awarded paradigmatic status for church leadership today, because both the number *twelve* and the ethnicity of those men are culturally relative. (2) Women, such as Junia, functioned as apostles, so women should be able to serve as church leaders today. (3) The ranks of the Twelve were not replenished, with the exception of Judas's replacement, after their deaths, so how can the Twelve serve as precedent for church leadership if their particular ministry was not perpetuated? For these reasons, Spencer argues, we should "emphasize what Jesus emphasized in his teachings: humble mutual service, not male-female distinctions in leadership."[34] Her point is well taken, except that there is no necessary dichotomy between humble servanthood and male leadership.

30. Ibid., 137.
31. Ibid., 138.
32. Ibid., 140.
33. Ibid.
34. Ibid.

## Evaluation

Our critique of recent evangelical feminist contributions illustrates that egalitarian interpretation *in practice* often falls short of the hermeneutical ideal expressed *in theory*. Two essays on the topic of evangelical feminist hermeneutical theory, one each by Roger Nicole and Gordon Fee, which appear in the same volume as Spencer's essay, set forth the theory of this hermeneutic in the following ways:

- the divine authorship and inspiration of Scripture;
- Scripture as a source of intrinsic authority external to the interpreter;
- the primacy of authorial intent over against reader-response criticism and postmodernism;
- the significant role of presuppositions;
- the dual authorship of Scripture (divine and human), meaning that God gave us his Word in a specific historical context and in the form of particular literary genres;
- the importance of distinguishing between literal and figurative meaning; prescriptive or descriptive texts; individual, collective, and universal references; peripheral versus central doctrines; fragmentary versus canonical interpretations; and the situation of those being addressed or represented; and
- the diversity of Scripture within an essential unity.

In principle, all of these tenets are to be commended if properly applied and executed when determining the author's intended meaning. As we have shown, however, evangelical feminist exegesis frequently does not attain to these ideals in its hermeneutical practice.

While the problems with radical and reformist feminism concern broad hermeneutical issues, in evangelical feminism, the problem lies with the exegetical execution of the evangelical feminist hermeneutic.

We have examined the development of the evangelical feminist interpretation of biblical passages relating to Jesus' approach to women in three consecutive periods: (1) the early years of emancipation (1966–1986), (2) the increasing complexity of the maturing movement (1987–1999), and (3) the creativity and consolidation of recent contributions (2000–present). All we have reviewed displays a pattern of consistent and by now familiar argument while at the same time evidencing an increasing hermeneutical complexity.

The early years were largely taken up with an articulation of the evangelical feminist viewpoint over against radical feminism and the historic position of the church. In keeping with this fundamental tenet, early evangelical feminists developed interpretations of key passages on gender roles that, in many cases, differed from the conventional readings but were in keeping with their overall evangelical feminist presuppositions. The early evangelical feminists, on the whole, affirmed a high view of Scripture. Yet, because their vested interpretive interests in egalitarian exegetical outcomes created a conflict between their hermeneutical ideals and the practical exegetical implementation, they developed a faulty system for biblical interpretation. Their system allowed them to read Scripture from an egalitarian viewpoint, but one not always derived from a natural reading of the biblical texts.

The work of evangelical feminist writers from the next period, the maturing movement of 1987 to 1999, issued in the development of a system of evangelical feminist interpretation that, on the whole, was considerably more complex than the efforts of their predecessors. Having moved beyond the interpretation of individual passages in an egalitarian sense, interpreters of this period sought to develop a biblical theology of gender roles relating Jesus to Paul and other parts of the canon. The interpretation of Gospel passages during this period thus served the purpose of using "the egalitarian Jesus" as the foundation and of showing how Paul's teaching was consistent with Jesus' practice with regard to gender roles. Interpreters did not deny that certain Pauline passages seem to restrict women's service in roles of ecclesiastical authority. However, they set these passages aside as irrelevant for the contemporary church.

The final period, from 2000 to the present, provides examples of both creativity and consolidation. Increasingly, evangelical feminists have been found to engage in a fundamental critique of the actual nature of authority and leadership in the church. They claim that authority in Scripture is limited to *service* and that leadership is but a benign inclination to promote the welfare of others. Therefore, they claim, men and women ought to relate to one another, both in the home and in the church, by practicing mutual submission. Their egalitarian outlook has resulted in the erosion of any meaningful notion of authority in the church, whether exercised by men or women.

Unlike radical feminists, who reject Scripture entirely, and reformist feminists, who adopt a hermeneutics of suspicion based on a perceived patriarchal bias in Scripture, evangelical feminists on the whole claim to consider Scripture as authoritative, inspired, and inerrant. For this reason they cannot simply dismiss scriptural passages that do not conform to their egalitarian commitment, nor can they expand the Christian canon or say Paul or other writers of Scripture were in error. Their major interpretive option is therefore to find ways to interpret biblical passages along egalitarian lines, and, where this proves difficult, to postulate a "center of Scripture" with regard to gender roles that allows them to set aside as culturally relative or otherwise inapplicable passages that do not support evangelical feminism.

The result is at times strained exegesis, and at other times unlikely interpretations that seem to be driven more by egalitarian presuppositions than by an inductive study of the text. While it is therefore hard to fault evangelical feminists for their professed view of Scripture or hermeneutical theory, their exegetical practice is frequently vulnerable to criticism.

# PART 5

# JESUS AND THE GOSPELS: AN EVANGELICAL NON-FEMINIST READING

*Redemption in Christ aims at removing the distortions introduced by the curse. In the family, husbands should forsake harsh or selfish leadership and grow in love and care for their wives; wives should forsake resistance to their husbands' authority and grow in willing, joyful submission to their husbands' leadership (Eph. 5:21–33; Col. 3:18–19; Tit. 2:3-5; 1 Pet. 3:1–7). In the church, redemption in Christ gives men and women an equal share in the blessings of salvation; nevertheless, some governing and teaching roles within the church are restricted to men (Gal. 3:28; 1 Cor. 11:2–16; 1 Tim. 2:11–15).*

—Council on Biblical Manhood and Womanhood, "The Danvers Statement" (1988)[1]

Now that we have traversed a considerable amount of territory by considering the various radical, reformist, and evangelical feminist interpretations of Jesus with regard to women, a constructive alternative is in order. It has become clear that the radical feminist rejection of Scripture and its witness to Jesus is unfounded. In fact, radical feminists inexorably abandon Christianity altogether and thus are no longer Christians at all in any sense of the word.

---

1. Council on Biblical Manhood and Womanhood, "The Danvers Statement" (Wheaton, IL, 1988), http://www.cbmw.org.

Reformist feminism's "hermeneutic of suspicion" and its arbitrary and highly selective use of Scripture used to support its feminist outlook likewise fail to do justice to the interpretive task. As we have seen, even many feminists have criticized and abandoned the classic reformist-feminist paradigm, Elisabeth Schüssler Fiorenza's proposal of a "discipleship of equals" supposedly established by Jesus; there is no other commonly agreed-upon paradigm taking its place to date. In fact, if there is any consensus among non-evangelical feminist scholarship at all, it is that the notion of the "feminist Jesus" must be abandoned, because it is not borne out by the biblical data.

Evangelical feminists are placed in a difficult position, because this is also exactly what they are arguing: Jesus was a prototype of Galatians 3:28, a "neither-male-nor-female" type of man, who propagated a gender-blind vision of God's people in the church with no distinctions in role or leadership. Feminists today are essentially "a house divided"; yet, as Jesus rightly said, and as Abraham Lincoln famously echoed, "A house divided against itself cannot stand."

Not everyone reads the biblical data regarding Jesus and women with a feminist perspective, however. Traditionally, it has been understood that the Old Testament consistently demonstrated male leadership in Israel's religion, such as an all-male priesthood. Traditional also has been the understanding that Jesus appointed twelve men as apostles in order to continue the pattern of male leadership. Paul, likewise, spoke of elders as faithful husbands (1 Tim. 3:2) and did not permit women to teach or have authority over men (1 Tim. 2:12). While initial challenges were mounted in the nineteenth and early twentieth centuries—the First and Second Waves of Feminism—only in recent decades has it been *necessary* for the proponents of this traditional view to organize a response to the emerging feminist reading of the scriptural data with regard to women as it influenced the church.

It was in the 1980s and 1990s that evangelical feminism and complementarianism developed as opposing movements within the evangelical world. Both claimed an inerrantist, high view of the Bible and were committed to the authority of Scripture and its application to Christians' lives. Evangelical feminism holds that equality in all things, including gender roles, is the pervasive principle that emerges in the New Testament and that ought to define male-female relationships in the church today. Complementarianism, a non-feminist evangelical approach, contends that male-female equality in personhood and value must be placed within the larger framework of male-female distinctions in role.

Essentially, complementarians look to New Testament passages that teach that male headship and female submission are grounded in the created order. When Paul, for example, states that he does not permit women to teach or have authority over men in the church, he cites as warrant and scriptural support not merely the corruption of the created order in the fall of humanity (1 Tim. 2:14), but the created order itself (1 Tim. 2:13). The apostle, for his part, takes the woman's creation from the man and for the man (1 Cor. 11:8–9) as indication of God's purposes for male-female roles in the church as well as in the home, involving, respectively, male headship and female submission.

A second plank in the complementarian hermeneutic is the scriptural teaching on the husband's being the head of the household and men's authority over the church as God's household (e.g., 1 Tim. 3:15; see also 3:2). Essentially, Paul's teaching on men's authority in the church is seen as the logical extension of the Old Testament teaching on the divinely instituted pattern for marriage and the home. Thus, gender role distinctions, with implications for male authority and leadership, are found not just in a few isolated passages but are actually grounded in the created order and the subsequent sweep of biblical history and teaching.

Complementarians, then, understand Scripture to teach genuine gender equality in terms of personal worth and dignity before God in Christ and desire to see male-female partnership and mutuality in marriage and the church. Nevertheless, they hold that while "there is no longer male or female" as far as salvation in Christ is concerned—all are saved by grace through faith regardless of gender—the created order is not superseded by redemption in Christ. The New Testament writers still command even believers to observe the pattern of wifely submission and male authority, and distinctions in role are maintained in the home (e.g., Eph. 5:21–33; Col. 3:18–19; 1 Pet. 3:1–7) and in the church (e.g., 1 Tim. 2:11–15; 3:1–7).

# 14

# "WHO DO YOU SAY THAT I AM?" A LOOK AT THE GOSPELS

*The twelve were with him, and also some women who had been healed of evil spirits and infirmities: Mary, called Magdalene, from whom seven demons had gone out, and Joanna, the wife of Chuza, Herod's household manager, and Susanna, and many others, who provided for them out of their means.*

—Luke 8:1c–3

***The Gospel*** accounts present four versions of the life of Jesus, in which we see his approach to women. You, the reader of this book, can observe for yourself and draw your own conclusions about Jesus' views and practice related to women. What did Jesus do and what did he say regarding women? What do his encounters with women reveal about his stance toward women? If we do not start out with presupposed notions, we can allow a more nuanced and true picture to emerge—one that reconciles women's full dignity, worth, and salvation—with distinctions made between men and women as to their unique place in God's economy and church.

In order to arrive at this more nuanced and true picture, the interpreter must be careful to follow proper procedures for the interpretation of the relevant passages on Jesus and women. Before embarking on a study of these passages, it will therefore be important to consider briefly the following sound principles for biblical interpretation. For a more thorough presentation, see Appendix 2.

## The Hermeneutical Framework

Our goal is to determine what God's message to us is through the author who wrote each Gospel. Ask yourself the relevant hermeneutical questions in order to answer the question, who was Jesus as far as his views on women are concerned? Was Jesus a feminist?

| Table 14.1: Basic Hermeneutical Tasks for Studying Scripture |
| --- |
| 1. Understand the genre of the document in which the passage is found. |
| 2. Make sure to consider any relevant historical or cultural background information that has a bearing on the meaning of the passage. |
| 3. Interpret a given passage in its immediate and larger literary contexts. |

In addition to the basic hermeneutical tasks listed in Table 14.1, you should also be mindful of these general principles: (1) Remember the need to engage in a "listening hermeneutic"; that is, aim to perceive what the text is actually saying rather than impose your own views onto the passage. (2) Be careful to focus first on understanding what the passage meant in its original context before trying to apply it to your personal life. (3) Exercise proper restraint in not claiming from the passage support for your own viewpoint if it does not clearly follow from what the text actually says.

## A Study of Jesus and Women in the Gospels

In keeping with these principles, it is now possible to conduct a basic study of the relevant passages regarding Jesus' approach to women in the Gospels. This will involve a brief survey of the genre of the Gospels, a study of the first-century historical-cultural background of Jesus, and an initial contextual study of the relevant passages, both in harmony format and Gospel by Gospel.[1]

## The Genre of the Gospels

Gospels are essentially biographies focusing on the life and ministry of Jesus. This means that Jesus' identity as the Messiah and the Son of God and his sacrificial cross-death and resurrection are at the heart of all four Gospels, not his treatment of women or men; though, of course, it was his love for all humans that was an important motivation in his coming and dying in the first place.

Also, as far as the Christian canon is concerned, the Gospels *continue the story of God's dealings with Israel in the Old Testament* by showing that Jesus is the fulfillment of God's covenants with Israel and the promised

---

1. In light of the fact that the primary subject of this volume is a critique of feminist approaches, this study is designed only as a sketch of a constructive alternative to feminist readings and would need to be supplemented by a more in-depth study of each of the relevant pericopes.

Messiah. This means that at the center of biblical revelation is God's provision of salvation through Jesus the Messiah, the son of Abraham, and the son of David (see Matt. 1:1–17). This puts Jesus' interaction with men and women in proper perspective, because it shows that Jesus' agenda was not primarily political, economic, or social, but spiritual, and that redemption from sin was the primary purpose for his coming.

### Historical-cultural Background

We can better understand the way Jesus related to women by taking a look at the first-century milieu in which Jesus lived.[2] Was Jesus patriarchal like his surrounding culture or was he revolutionary in his approach to women? Did he exceed contemporary mores by treating women with respect and dignity, allowing them to learn from him? Our study thus far has shown that Jesus exemplified unusual freedom in his dealings with women, showed great brotherly love toward them, and was signally interested in their spiritual condition.[3] Yet all these things could be said about Jesus' dealings with men as well.

A critical point, then, is this: judging by documented attitudes of first-century Jewish rabbis, Jesus could well have exceeded these first-century views and still not have been a feminist or egalitarian. We do well to remember, however, when speaking of first-century Jewish attitudes, that virtually all the available evidence comes from later documents, such as the Mishnah and the Talmuds, and that Judaism prior to A.D. 70 was variegated; that is, it represented various viewpoints and practices toward women,[4] a fact that is not sufficiently appreciated by those who strenuously argue that Jesus was egalitarian, at least in part because he exceeded the approach of his surrounding culture. In fact, the Gospel evidence shows Jesus' regard for women *and* his retention of ultimate leadership roles for men.

It is true that Jesus' cultural context has featured significantly in the discussion. Some, such as Fiorenza, contended that the Gospels show Jesus standing in judgment over the kind of marginalization of women that is practiced today. Thus, female subordination was not part of the original gospel but resulted from Christianity's accommodation to Greco-Roman culture.

---

2. See S. B. Clark, *Man and Woman in Christ* (Ann Arbor, MI: Servant Books, 1980), 168–76, for a discussion of Jesus and first-century Judaism.

3. See ibid., 172 and 175, who notes that Jesus felt freer to speak and deal with women than other rabbis or scribes of his time did, but that women also felt freer to approach him. Clark also notes that the separation between men and women in Jesus' day (especially in Galilee) was probably not as rigid and formalized as later on in the mishnaic period.

4. See ibid., 170–72, who notes differences with regard to attitudes toward women not only between different Jewish sects but also between the wealthy and the poor and between urban and rural areas.

Recent years of historical Jesus research have shown a pendulum swing from a rural, Galilean context to the Greco-Roman influence in Galilee, especially in light of excavations in Sepphoris, a Galilean city near Nazareth, Jesus' hometown.[5]

While Greco-Roman influence in the Galilee of Jesus' day is rightly noted, the area was not as pervaded by Greco-Roman culture as some have maintained. The inhabitants of Galilee in Jesus' day were mostly Jewish, though a few were Gentiles. Archeological evidence concurs entirely with the portrait of Jesus in the Gospels. As Mark Chancey writes, after careful examination of the evidence, "In short, we can conclude that Galilee was predominantly Jewish during Jesus' lifetime."[6]

If, then, the Galilee of Jesus' day was predominantly Jewish, and Jewish culture, in keeping with the teaching of the Hebrew Scriptures, adhered to a patricentric model where the father was the center of the Jewish household and men formed the leadership structures of the Jewish community, one can assume that this Jewish framework formed the backdrop of Jesus' own activity during his earthly ministry. Just as Jesus accommodated himself to his Jewish surroundings by adopting the role of a Jewish rabbi, he affirmed traditional Jewish teaching with regard to marriage and the family and chose twelve men as his apostles. He showed deep concern for women and healed many of them, but he did not revision gender roles the way some feminists—especially the reformist and evangelical feminists—contend.[7]

### Study of Passages on Jesus and Women in Literary Context

It is now possible to take a look at the various passages on Jesus and women in the Gospels. First, the relevant passages will be reviewed in harmony format, following Jesus' ministry in approximate chronological order with all four accounts represented where available. This will be followed by a presentation of the treatment of women within each of the four canonical Gospels—Matthew, Mark, Luke, and John—and a summary of some of the most pertinent conclusions that can be drawn from the survey of the biblical information in this chapter.

5. R. A. Batey, *Jesus and the Forgotten City: New Light on Sepphoris and the Urban World of Jesus* (Grand Rapids, MI: Baker, 1992).

6. M. A. Chancey, "How Jewish Was Jesus' Galilee?" *Biblical Archaeology Review* 33, no. 4 (July/August 2007): 76. The entire article is found on pp. 42–50 and 76.

7. See Clark, *Man and Woman in Christ*, 171, who contends that Jesus was not a revolutionary in his treatment of women but that he did accord them a higher spiritual status than contemporary Jewish rabbis. Clark also points out that Jesus was not a mere rabbi but acted as a prophet and popular preacher who proclaimed the kingdom of God (p. 172). He also notes that Jesus, in contrast to most rabbis and scribes of his day, did not marry (p. 173).

Table 14.2: Passages on Jesus and Women in the Gospels*

| Jesus and Women | Scripture Reference |
| --- | --- |
| Jesus and his mother at Cana wedding | John 2:1–12 |
| Jesus talks with Samaritan woman | John 4:1–42 |
| Jesus' teaching on adultery and divorce | Matt. 5:28–32; 19:1–12; Mark 10:1–12; Luke 16:18 |
| Jesus heals Peter's mother-in-law | Matt. 8:14–15; Mark 1:30–31; Luke 4:38–39 |
| Jesus raises widow's son at Nain | Luke 7:11–15 |
| Mary and family come to take Jesus home | Matt. 12:46–50; Mark 3:20–21, 31–35; Luke 8:19–21 |
| Jesus raises Jairus's daughter, heals woman with blood flow | Matt. 9:18–26; Mark 5:22–43; Luke 8:40–56 |
| Daughter set against mother, etc. | Matt. 10:35; Luke 12:53 |
| Jesus anointed by sinful woman | Luke 7:36–50 |
| Group of women supports Jesus and the Twelve | Luke 8:2–3 |
| Jesus exorcises demon from girl | Matt. 15:21–28; Mark 7:24–30 |
| Jesus teaches Martha an object lesson | Luke 10:38–42 |
| Woman calls Jesus' mother blessed | Luke 11:27–28 |
| Jesus commends queen of the South | Matt. 12:42; Luke 11:31 |
| Jesus heals crippled woman on Sabbath | Luke 13:10–17 |
| The woman baking | Matt. 13:33; Luke 13:20–21 |
| The woman who lost a coin | Luke 15:8–10 |
| The persistent widow | Luke 18:1–8 |
| Request of mother of sons of Zebedee | Matt. 20:20–28; see Mark 10:35–45 |
| Jesus on marriage in the resurrection | Matt. 22:23–33; Mark 12:18–27; Luke 20:27–40 |
| Teaching on widows and the widow's mite | Mark 12:40–44; Luke 20:47–21:4 |
| Pregnant, nursing mothers in tribulation | Matt. 24:19–21; Mark 13:17–19 |
| Two women grinding at a mill | Matt. 24:41; Luke 17:35 |
| The parable of the ten virgins | Matt. 25:1–13 |
| Mary and Martha grieve for Lazarus | John 11:1–44 |
| Mary anoints Jesus | Matt. 26:6–13; Mark 14:3–9; John 12:1–8 |
| The wailing Jerusalem women | Luke 23:27–31 |
| The women near the cross | Matt. 27:55–56; Mark 15:40–41; Luke 23:49; John 19:25–27 |
| Mary Magdalene and others at Jesus' burial; on third day set out to anoint Jesus' body | Matt. 27:61; 28:1–11; Mark 15:47–16:8; Luke 23:55–24:12; John 20:1–18 |

*Not included are references to women in the Gospels unrelated to Jesus, such as the servant girl challenging Peter as to his association with Jesus, or references to women related to Jesus that are not relevant for assessing Jesus' approach to women, such as the references to Mary in the infancy narratives.

## Jesus' Relationship with His Mother at the Wedding at Cana (John 2:1–12)

> On the third day there was a wedding at Cana in Galilee, and the mother of Jesus was there. Jesus also was invited to the wedding with his disciples. When the wine ran out, the mother of Jesus said to him, "They have no wine." And Jesus said to her, "Woman, what does this have to do with me? My hour has not yet come." His mother said to the servants, "Do whatever he tells you."
> . . . After this he went down to Capernaum, with his mother and his brothers and his disciples, and they stayed there for a few days. (John 2:1–5, 12)

This is the first recorded instance of Jesus relating to a woman, his mother, during his public ministry. During the course of the wedding, Jesus' mother makes him aware that the wedding party has run out of wine. His response suggests that he understands his mother to be asking him to provide additional wine for the wedding guests, perhaps by miraculous means. Jesus reluctantly complies, though not before pointing out that it is not yet time for him to show the world who he is—the Messiah.

Some might consider Jesus' address of his mother, "Woman," and his question, "What does this have to do with me?" as disrespectful if not chauvinistic. As the ensuing course of events shows, however, Jesus does respect his mother and acts on her desire for him to remedy the situation.[8] At the same time, Jesus makes clear that performing a public miracle would be inappropriate at this juncture of his ministry.

Perhaps he chose to perform this miracle in a private manner—not all the members of the wedding party knew where the wine came from—in order not to jettison his public ministry and training of his disciples. As the previous chapter (John 1) indicates, Jesus had just called his disciples to follow him. If his provision of wine had been highly public, this would have drawn major attention to him and might have hastened the Jewish opposition.

## Jesus Talks with the Samaritan Woman (John 4:1–42)

> A woman from Samaria came to draw water. Jesus said to her, "Give me a drink." . . . The Samaritan woman said to him, "How is it that you, a Jew, ask for a drink from me, a woman of Samaria?" . . . Jesus answered her, "If you knew the gift of God, and who it is that is saying to you, 'Give me a drink,' you would have asked him, and he would have given you living water." . . . So the woman left her water jar and went away into town and said to the people,

---

8. D. A. Carson, *The Gospel according to John*, PNTC (Grand Rapids, MI: Eerdmans, 1991), 170–72; A. J. Köstenberger, *John*, BECNT (Grand Rapids, MI: Baker, 2004), 94–95.

"Come, see a man who told me all that I ever did. Can this be the Christ?" They went out of the town and were coming to him. . . . Many Samaritans from that town believed in him because of the woman's testimony, "He told me all that I ever did." (John 4:7–39)

In spite of the full knowledge that Jesus has of her unclean status and her position in society, he goes ahead and asks the Samaritan woman for a drink. Jesus did not have to ask her for a drink, yet he does so in order to initiate their conversation. Jesus gradually helps the woman to realize who he is and who she is in relation to him—a sinner in need of salvation. At the climax of the narrative, the woman informs Jesus that when the Messiah comes "he will tell us all things" (v. 25). In response, Jesus declares that he is the one of whom she speaks (v. 26).

Upon the disciples' return, they are surprised to find Jesus "talking with a woman" (v. 27). Since no reference is made to the woman's ethnic identity, the disciples' comment likely reflects the cultural stereotype: men looked down on other men who engaged in conversation with women.[9] At the very least, Jesus' talking to the Samaritan reflects his openness toward women.

In spite of the confrontational nature of the conversation, Jesus speaks kindly and sensitively to the woman so that she is able to receive him and his words. Jesus shows his love and kindness to help her to come to know who he truly is. His goal is to lead her to receive eternal life, and he does so by drawing her into conversation in an engaging manner. The interchange is quite long and includes a lot of back-and-forth. Given that she left her water jar when she departed (v. 28), the conversation appears to have distracted her if not had a significant effect on her. Jesus' request for a drink may have gone unheeded.

In what follows, the woman turns into an evangelist.[10] She goes and brings the better part of her village to Jesus. Many of them believe that Jesus is the Savior of the world (v. 42). The genuine relationship Jesus has with this woman results in many other Samaritans' putting their trust in him. As Cottrell points out, the woman's ministry of evangelism is regularly interpreted by feminists as Jesus having "commissioned this woman as his

9. Köstenberger, *John*, 158–59; C. S. Keener, *The Gospel of John*, 2 vols. (Peabody, MA: Hendrickson, 2003), 620–21; J. B. Hurley, *Man and Woman in Biblical Perspective* (Grand Rapids, MI: Zondervan, 1981), 84–85; and J. A. Borland, "Women in the Life and Teachings of Jesus," in *Recovering Biblical Manhood and Womanhood: A Response to Evangelical Feminism*, ed. J. Piper and W. Grudem (Wheaton, IL: Crossway, 1991), 114, who discusses this section under the heading "Christ Placed a High Value on Women."

10. See R. G. Maccini, *Her Testimony Is True: Women as Witnesses according to John*, JSNT-Sup 125 (Sheffield: Sheffield Academic Press, 1996), chap. 5.

special messenger."[11] However, it is going beyond the contextual meaning of the passage to elevate the woman as a prototype of modern women preachers if, for no other reason, than that this passage is located in the narrative genre of Scripture.[12]

### Jesus' Teaching on Adultery and Divorce (Matt. 5:28–32; 19:1–12; Mark 10:1–12; Luke 16:18)

> "But I say to you that everyone who looks at a woman with lustful intent has already committed adultery with her in his heart.". . . And Pharisees came up to him and tested him by asking, "Is it lawful to divorce one's wife for any cause?" He answered, . . . "Whoever divorces his wife, except for sexual immorality, and marries another, commits adultery." (Matt. 5:28; 19:3–6, 9)

Jesus' Sermon on the Mount touches on women in his teaching on adultery and divorce. Regarding adultery, Jesus raised the bar considerably when he included in his definition of it a man's lustful glance at a woman not his wife. This reflects the value Jesus placed on women and warned men against treating them as sexual objects. He defined adultery not merely as a sexual act with a woman not one's spouse but also as a mental offense. Remarkably, Jesus "called upon his disciples to discipline their thoughts rather than to avoid women."[13]

Regarding divorce, Jesus in Matthew 5:31–32, as well as in the later, related passage in Matthew 19:1–12, declares that anyone who divorces his wife, "except for sexual immorality" (Matt. 19:9), causes her to become an adulteress and that anyone who marries the divorced woman commits adultery. Again, this protected women from arbitrary divorce in a male-centered society.[14] It also shows that Jesus did not regard women as property but as persons.[15] Notably, the "exception clause" found in both Matthew 5:32 and Matthew 19:9 is absent from the parallels in Mark and Luke.[16]

---

11. See J. Cottrell, *Gender Roles and the Bible: Creation, the Fall, and Redemption* (Joplin, MO: College Press, 1994), 172.

12. See ibid., 184.

13. Hurley, *Man and Woman in Biblical Perspective*, 109, cited in Borland, "Women in the Life and Teachings of Jesus," 115.

14. R. T. France, *The Gospel of Mark*, NIGTC (Grand Rapids, MI: Eerdmans, 2002), 387–89; A. J. Köstenberger, *God, Marriage, and Family: Rebuilding the Biblical Foundation* (Wheaton, IL: Crossway, 2004), chap. 11 (with extensive discussion and additional bibliographic references).

15. Borland, "Women in the Life and Teachings of Jesus," 115.

16. See, e.g., D. A. Hagner, *Matthew*, WBC 33; 2 vols. (Dallas: Word, 1993, 1995), 124–25.

## Jesus Heals Peter's Mother-in-law (Matt. 8:14–15; Mark 1:30–31; Luke 4:38–39)

> And when Jesus entered Peter's house, he saw his mother-in-law lying sick with a fever. He touched her hand, and the fever left her, and she rose and began to serve him. (Matt. 8:14–15)

After leaving the synagogue in Capernaum, Jesus and the disciples, including James and John, depart for the house of Simon Peter and his brother Andrew. Peter's mother-in-law is in bed with a high fever, and they tell Jesus about her and ask him to help her. Jesus bends over her and heals her of her fever. She gets up at once and begins to wait on those in the house.[17] Peter's mother-in-law was not the only one healed that day; Jesus "healed all who were sick," brought to him later that evening (Matt. 8:16). Here is one woman, albeit a relative of one of Jesus' foremost disciples, on whom Jesus has compassion and heals the moment he is asked. Here and thereafter, Jesus seems to heal all kinds of people without discrimination as to their gender. The fact that the woman immediately serves the people in the house indicates the completeness of the healing, as well as perhaps even her gratitude.

## Jesus Raises the Widow's Son at Nain from the Dead (Luke 7:11–15)

> Soon afterward he went to a town called Nain, and his disciples and a great crowd went with him. As he drew near to the gate of the town, behold, a man who had died was being carried out, the only son of his mother, and she was a widow, and a considerable crowd from the town was with her. And when the Lord saw her, he had compassion on her and said to her, "Do not weep." Then he came up and touched the bier, and the bearers stood still. And he said, "Young man, I say to you, arise." And the dead man sat up and began to speak, and Jesus gave him to his mother. (Luke 7:11–15)

As Jesus is approaching the town gate of Nain, he comes upon a funeral procession of a young man, "the only son of his mother" (Luke 7:12), a widow, and a large crowd with her.[18] When Jesus sees the woman crying, his heart goes out to her. He goes up and touches the coffin and tells the dead man to get up; he does and begins to talk. Luke emphasizes that Jesus gave the widow's son back to his mother. This underscores that Jesus had

---

17. For a good discussion see R. A. Guelich, *Mark 1–8:26*, WBC 34A (Dallas: Word, 1989), 62–63.
18. An excellent treatment is found in D. L. Bock, *Luke*, BECNT; 2 vols. (Grand Rapids, MI: Baker, 1994), 649–53.

compassion on a woman in need, a mother who had lost her only son and had previously lost her husband.[19]

### Jesus' Concerned Family Comes to Take Him Home (Matt. 12:46–50; Mark 3:20–21, 31–35; Luke 8:19–21)

> While he was still speaking to the people, behold, his mother and his brothers stood outside, asking to speak to him. But he replied to the man who told him, "Who is my mother, and who are my brothers?" And stretching out his hand toward his disciples, he said, "Here are my mother and my brothers! For whoever does the will of my Father in heaven is my brother and sister and mother." (Matt. 12:46–50)

Early on in Jesus' ministry, his concerned family, including Mary, comes to take him home. The demands on Jesus are so heavy and the crowds so large that Jesus and his disciples are not able even to eat (Mark 3:20). His family fears Jesus "is out of his mind" (Mark 3:21). When Jesus hears of this, however, rather than allow his natural family to rein him in, he tells the crowd that his mother, brothers, and sisters are, in fact, those who do the will of God.[20] He includes in the sphere of his true family anyone—male or female—who is prepared to do God's will. Discipleship has priority over natural relations, whether a person is male or female. Jesus' statement should not be interpreted as affirming an egalitarian model of relationships or doing away with the scriptural roles of husband and wife or father, mother, and children in the home.

### Jesus Raises Jairus's Daughter from the Dead and Heals the Woman with Blood Flow (Matt. 9:18–26; Mark 5:22–43; Luke 8:40–56)

> A ruler came in and knelt before him, saying, "My daughter has just died, but come and lay your hand on her, and she will live." And Jesus rose and followed him, with his disciples. And behold, a woman who had suffered from a discharge of blood for twelve years came up behind him and touched the fringe of his garment, for she said to herself, "If I only touch his garment, I will be made well." Jesus turned, and seeing her he said, "Take heart, daughter; your faith has made you well." And instantly the woman was made well. And when Jesus came to the ruler's house and saw the flute players and the crowd making a commotion, he said, "Go away, for the girl is not dead but sleeping." . . . He went in and took her by the hand, and the girl arose. (Matt. 9:18–25)

19. J. Nolland, *Luke*, 3 vols., WBC 35 (Dallas: Word, 1989, 1993), 323.
20. J. Nolland, *The Gospel of Matthew*, NIGTC (Grand Rapids: Eerdmans, 2005), 518.

In Jesus' incidental encounter with the woman with blood flow, the woman, who was in some desperation owing to a health issue, believes that if she were to touch Jesus' cloak, she would be healed.[21] When Jesus sees her, he acknowledges and encourages her by saying, "Take heart." He refers to her kindly as "daughter" and proceeds to heal her. Even though Jesus is in the midst of responding to another desperate call for help, he stops and treats the woman with kindness and compassion. Hurley points out that in touching this woman, Jesus incurred ceremonial uncleanness, though he did not let this stop him from helping the woman.[22]

In raising the twelve-year-old daughter of Jairus (the synagogue ruler) from the dead, Jesus takes the child's parents, both mother and father, inside with him, as well as three of his disciples. He then takes the dead girl's hand and tells her to get up, which she does, and she starts to walk about. Jesus instructs the bystanders to give the girl something to eat and orders them not to tell anyone what has happened. In this incident, Jesus brings in the mother with only a few others to observe the healing of her daughter. This is a family scene with no probable implications for the subject at hand, other than that Jesus' compassion here extends to a young girl.

### Jesus Teaches That Daughter Will Be Set against Mother, and Daughter-in-law against Mother-in-law, through His Ministry (Matt. 10:35; Luke 12:53)

> "For I have come to set a man against his father, and a daughter against her mother, and a daughter-in-law against her mother-in-law." (Matt. 10:35)

As part of his instructions at the occasion of sending out the Twelve on a mission, Jesus teaches that a man's enemies will be the members of his own household.[23] Specifically, both men and women in a given family will be set in opposition to one another, so that Jesus' ministry will result not in peace but in division. Women are part of the spiritual conflict that will occur in the context of individual families.

### Jesus Is Anointed by a Sinful Woman (Luke 7:36–50)

> Behold, a woman of the city, who was a sinner, when she learned that he was reclining at table in the Pharisee's house, brought an alabaster flask of ointment, and standing behind him at his feet, weeping, she began to wet his feet with her tears and wiped them with the hair of her head and kissed his feet

21. See France, *Gospel of Mark*, 236–37.
22. Hurley, *Man and Woman in Biblical Perspective*, 87.
23. Bock, *Luke*, 1195–96.

and anointed them with the ointment. . . . And [Jesus] said to her, "Your sins are forgiven." Then those who were at table with him began to say among themselves, "Who is this, who even forgives sins?" And he said to the woman, "Your faith has saved you; go in peace." (Luke 7:37–50)

While Jesus is having dinner with a particular Pharisee, Simon, a woman who has lived a sinful life comes with an alabaster jar of perfume and weeps. Her tears wet his feet, and she wipes them with her hair, kisses them, and pours perfume on them. Jesus allows this, but the Pharisee he dines with is indignant. In explanation, Jesus tells Simon a parable about creditors and debtors in order to show that the person who owes more when relieved of his debt is much more grateful than the person who owes less.

Thus the woman is upheld as an example of one who has been forgiven much and as a result loves much. Before all of the guests, Jesus tells her that her sins are forgiven and that her faith has saved her and to go in peace. Jesus' response to the woman is compassionate, kind, and supportive in front of a critical group. He does not condemn the woman for her sinful past and instead forgives her and commends her for her faith.[24]

This strikes the chord of a reversal of expectations that is characteristic of Jesus' kingdom. As Hurley notes, "The faith of the sinful woman led her to acts of public love and gratitude. It is she, not the Pharisee, who exemplifies godly faith in action. Once again we have an example of Jesus dealing with persons as individuals and without reference to their sex."[25]

## A Group of Women Supports Jesus and the Twelve (Luke 8:2–3)

And also some women who had been healed of evil spirits and infirmities: Mary called Magdalene, from whom seven demons had gone out, and Joanna, the wife of Chuza, Herod's household manager, and Susanna, and many others, who provided for them out of their means. (Luke 8:2–3)

While Jesus is traveling from one town and village to another proclaiming the good news of the kingdom of God, some women who have been cured of evil spirits and diseases are with him, along with the Twelve. These women help to support the ministry out of their own means. Jesus, after graciously and mercifully healing them, has allowed them to be with him and accepts their financial support. Jesus was not too proud to include these women in the larger scope of his mission. At the same time, as Hurley notes, "there

24. See ibid., 705.
25. Hurley, *Man and Woman in Biblical Perspective*, 86.

is no evidence that these women had any 'official' function as 'apostles' or alongside the twelve who would *later* become apostles."[26]

### Jesus Exorcises a Demon from the Syrophoenician Woman's Daughter (Matt. 15:21–28; Mark 7:24–30)

> A Canaanite woman from that region came out and was crying, "Have mercy on me, O Lord, Son of David; my daughter is severely oppressed by a demon." But he did not answer her a word. And his disciples came and begged him, saying, "Send her away, for she is crying out after us." He answered, "I was sent only to the lost sheep of the house of Israel." But she came and knelt before him, saying, "Lord, help me." And he answered, "It is not right to take the children's bread and throw it to the dogs." She said, "Yes, Lord, yet even the dogs eat the crumbs that fall from their masters' table." Then Jesus answered her, "O woman, great is your faith! Be it done for you as you desire." And her daughter was healed instantly. (Matt. 15:22–28)

As he withdraws to the region of Tyre, Jesus encounters a Gentile woman whose little daughter is possessed by an evil spirit. This is the first time Matthew shows a woman addressing Jesus.[27] The woman begs Jesus to drive out the demon. Jesus' response at first is to deny her request, saying that his mission is focused on Israel. When the woman persists, Jesus, amazed at her great faith, states that the demon has left her daughter. Returning home, the woman finds her child lying on the bed with the demon gone. Here Jesus frankly acknowledges that his mission is not focused on the Gentiles. The woman humbly accepts her position as a Gentile and begs at least to be allowed to benefit from the leftovers. Jesus sees this as great faith and honors it. As Hurley notes, Jesus "shows respect for the faith of this woman and for her argument. He took women seriously."[28]

### Jesus Teaches Martha an Object Lesson (Luke 10:38–42)

> Jesus entered a village. And a woman named Martha welcomed him into her house. And she had a sister called Mary, who sat at the Lord's feet and listened to his teaching. But Martha was distracted with much serving. And she went up to him and said, "Lord, do you not care that my sister has left me to serve alone? Tell her then to help me." But the Lord answered her, "Martha, Martha, you are anxious and troubled about many things, but one thing is necessary. Mary has chosen the good portion, which will not be taken away from her." (Luke 10:38–42)

26. Ibid., 92.
27. Nolland, *Matthew*, 632.
28. Hurley, *Man and Woman in Biblical Perspective*, 85.

Jesus and his disciples are continuing in their ministry and come to the village where Martha lives. She opens her home to Jesus. Mary, her sister, sits at Jesus' feet, listening to what he says, but Martha is distracted by the preparations. When she approaches Jesus about getting help from Mary, Jesus says to her that Mary has chosen what is better.[29] Jesus is open to going into the home of these women and enjoys their company. He takes the opportunity to teach Martha a lesson about priorities and the need to put discipleship above taking care of material things. As with the women mentioned in Luke 8:2–3, Martha and Mary support Jesus and have a part in his mission.

Evangelical feminists claim that by allowing Mary to sit at his feet and learn from him, Jesus here "overturned the cultural priorities for women" and "completely reversed the priorities and the consequences of those priorities in Jewish life."[30] Rather than prioritizing women's household duties, Jesus encouraged women to learn from him and become his followers. However, we must be careful not to take an instance from the Gospel narrative and invest it simplistically with normative significance. All that is said here is that Jesus rejected Martha's complaint that Mary did not help with household duties. It hardly follows that Jesus was a feminist who rejected women's managing their households and called on them to serve as pastors or elders.[31]

## A Woman in the Crowd Calls Jesus' Mother Blessed (Luke 11:27–28)

> As he said these things, a woman in the crowd raised her voice and said to him, "Blessed is the womb that bore you, and the breasts at which you nursed!" But he said, "Blessed rather are those who hear the word of God and keep it!" (Luke 11:27–28)

Here Jesus challenges a woman who inappropriately focuses on Jesus' mother rather than on Jesus himself. He directs her and the surrounding crowd to hear the word of God and obey it. Jesus' words here indicate that even being the mother of Jesus did not substitute for believing in God's Word and obeying it.

29. See the discussion in Bock, *Luke*, 1040.
30. The quotes are from S. J. Grenz, *Women in the Church* (Downers Grove, IL: InterVarsity, 1995), 75; and A. B. Spencer, *Beyond the Curse: Women Called to Ministry* (Nashville: Thomas Nelson, 1985), 60–61. See also the discussion and references in Cottrell, *Gender Roles and the Bible*, 171–72.
31. See the helpful treatment by W. Grudem, *Evangelical Feminism and Biblical Truth* (Sisters, OR: Multnomah, 2004), 161–64. See also S. B. Clark, *Man and Woman in Christ* (Ann Arbor, MI: Servant Books, 1980), 173, who points out that no woman is called a "disciple" of Jesus in the Gospels, though Mary in Luke 10:39 is shown to adopt the posture of a disciple.

Feminists such as Mollenkott interpret Jesus' statement as one that rejects the notion that "Mary is reduced to one womb and two breasts," nothing but a biological creature: "Jesus will have none of it. He immediately redefines blessedness in a way which transcends either male or female biology."[32] Swidler concurs, claiming that "although it was even uttered by a woman, Jesus clearly felt it necessary to reject this 'baby-machine' image of women and insist again on the personhood, the intellectual and moral faculties, being primary for all."[33] But as Cottrell aptly notes, the focus of the present passage is that even Mary should not be singled out for special veneration just because she was Jesus' mother.[34] Mary was indeed uniquely favored by God, but she still required salvation (cf. Luke 1:47).

## Jesus Commends the "Queen of the South" Who Came to Listen to Solomon (Matt. 12:42; Luke 11:31)

> "The queen of the South will rise up at the judgment with this generation and condemn it, for she came from the ends of the earth to hear the wisdom of Solomon, and behold, something greater than Solomon is here." (Matt. 12:42)

Jesus here uses the example of a woman who will stand in judgment over the people in Jesus' day who reject him. The Queen of Sheba (1 Kings 10:1–13; 2 Chron. 9:1–12; Josephus, *Ant.* 8.6.5–6 §§165–75) is the second such person mentioned after the people of Nineveh who repented at Jonah's preaching.[35] In the present instance, Jesus balances a general example, Nineveh, with that of a woman.

## Jesus Heals a Crippled Woman on the Sabbath (Luke 13:10–13)

> Now he was teaching in one of the synagogues on the Sabbath. And there was a woman who had had a disabling spirit for eighteen years. She was bent over and could not fully straighten herself. When Jesus saw her, he called her over and said to her, "Woman, you are freed from your disability." And he laid his hands on her, and immediately she was made straight, and she glorified God. (Luke 13:10–13)

In response to a challenge issued by an indignant synagogue ruler, Jesus calls him and those like him hypocrites for not allowing a woman such

32. Mollenkott, *Women, Men, and the Bible*, rev. ed. (New York: Crossroad, 1988), 8.
33. L. Swidler, "Jesus Was a Feminist," *Catholic World* 212 (1971): 182.
34. Cottrell, *Gender Roles and the Bible*, 200; see also his discussion on pp. 190–91, which includes the quotes by Mollenkott and Swidler cited in the previous notes.
35. Bock, *Luke*, 1098.

as this, a "daughter of Abraham," to be set free from her predicament on the Sabbath while they, on a Sabbath, would untie their oxen or donkeys and lead them out to give them water. By calling the woman "a daughter of Abraham," Jesus includes her as a member of Israel as the chosen people of God.[36] By choosing to heal the woman, even more in light of the fact that it was a Sabbath, Jesus showed that he valued her enough to heal her.

### The Woman Baking (Matt. 13:33; Luke 13:20–21)

> He told them another parable. "The kingdom of heaven is like leaven that a woman took and hid in three measures of flour, till it was all leavened." (Matt. 13:33)

In another one of his parables on the kingdom, Jesus makes reference to a woman baking. It is interesting to note that the woman is here shown in her domestic sphere. It appears that it is part of Jesus' express purpose to use a woman as part of his teaching in order to ensure that women in his audience would comprehend his message about the kingdom. Jesus' inclusion of a female example in his teaching here underscores the value he places on women understanding spiritual truth, though it is also the case that since Jesus wished to emphasize leaven, this context would have been the most natural and obvious.

### The Woman Who Lost a Coin (Luke 15:8–10)

> "Or what woman, having ten silver coins, if she loses one coin, does not light a lamp and sweep the house and seek diligently until she finds it? And when she has found it, she calls together her friends and neighbors, saying, 'Rejoice with me, for I have found the coin that I had lost.' Just so, I tell you, there is joy before the angels of God over one sinner who repents." (Luke 15:8–10)

In this, the middle of three parables on lost things, Jesus features a woman who had lost a coin. The woman does not rest—lighting a lamp, sweeping the house, and searching carefully—until she finds the coin and then rejoices with friends and neighbors. This is compared with the rejoicing in the presence of the angels of God over one sinner who repents. Here again Jesus uses a woman as a character in one of his parables.

36. See Clark, *Man and Woman in Christ*, 242.

### The Persistent Widow (Luke 18:1–8)

> "Though I neither fear God nor respect man, yet because this widow keeps bothering me, I will give her justice, so that she will not beat me down by her continual coming." And the Lord said, "Hear what the unrighteous judge says. And will not God give justice to his elect, who cry to him day and night? Will he delay long over them? I tell you, he will give justice to them speedily. Nevertheless, when the Son of Man comes, will he find faith on earth?" (Luke 18:4–8)

Jesus again uses a woman in a parable, this time to show his disciples that they should always pray and not give up. The parable is about a widow who is persistent in coming to an ungodly judge, pleading with him to grant her justice, and though he refuses at first, he finally gives in because of the widow's insistent requests. This is compared to God's response to the plea to bring justice to those chosen ones who cry out to him day and night. The use of a woman in this parable again shows Jesus' openness toward women and possibly his desire to have them relate to the spiritual truths he is trying to teach.

### The Request of the Mother of the Sons of Zebedee (Matt. 20:20–28; see also Mark 10:35–45)

> Then the mother of the sons of Zebedee came up to him with her sons, and kneeling before him she asked him for something. And he said to her, "What do you want?" She said to him, "Say that these two sons of mine are to sit, one at your right hand and one at your left, in your kingdom." (Matt. 20:20–21)

According to Matthew's Gospel, the mother of the sons of Zebedee asks Jesus to grant that one of her two sons may sit at his right and the other at his left in his kingdom. (In Mark, it is the sons of Zebedee themselves who pose the question.)[37] Jesus responds that it is not his prerogative to grant these places; they belong to those for whom the Father has prepared them. In the present scene, Jesus speaks openly, honestly, and directly, without condemning the persons making the request but by putting them in their place and instructing them concerning the true nature of leadership in God's kingdom. Here Jesus is not afraid to confront another inappropriate request or statement by a woman, this time a request by a mother for her sons to be given special favor.

37. Nolland, *Matthew*, 819.

## Jesus' Teaching on Marriage in the Resurrection (Matt. 22:23–33; Mark 12:18–27; Luke 20:27–40)

> But Jesus answered them, "You are wrong, because you know neither the Scriptures nor the power of God. For in the resurrection they neither marry nor are given in marriage, but are like angels in heaven. And as for the resurrection of the dead, have you not read what was said to you by God: 'I am the God of Abraham, and the God of Isaac, and the God of Jacob'? He is not God of the dead, but of the living." (Matt. 22:29–32)

In response to an insincere question by the Sadducees who raise a hypothetical scenario about a woman who was successively married to seven different brothers, Jesus clarifies that there will be no marriage in heaven but that people will be like angels in heaven. In so doing, he puts men and women on a level playing field with regard to life in the eternal state and removes the necessity for levirate marriage (see the book of Ruth).[38]

## Teaching on Widows and the Widow's Mite (Mark 12:41–44; Luke 20:47–21:4)

> [Jesus] sat down opposite the treasury and watched the people putting money into the offering box. Many rich people put in large sums. And a poor widow came and put in two small copper coins, which make a penny. And he called his disciples to him and said to them, "Truly, I say to you, this poor widow has put in more than all those who are contributing to the offering box. For they all contributed out of their abundance, but she out of her poverty has put in everything she had, all she had to live on." (Mark 12:41–44)

In a few statements regarding the teachers of the law, Jesus tells his followers to be careful concerning them. Though they appear important in the synagogues and at banquets and in the way they dress, they act unrighteously, taking financial advantage of widows and for a show make lengthy prayers.[39] Jesus states that such men will be punished most severely. Though it is not obvious in this lifetime, Jesus gives us a foretaste of the coming judgment, thus expressing his care for these widows and his contempt for the way they are being treated. These women are truly valued by Jesus.

Immediately after this, Jesus observes the crowd putting their money into the temple treasury. He notices that many rich people throw in large

38. A helpful treatment is found in Bock, *Luke*, 1622–24.
39. On the vulnerability of widows in Jesus' day see France, *Gospel of Mark*, 491–92.

amounts, but a poor widow comes and puts in two very small copper coins. Calling his disciples to himself, he tells them that the widow has put more into the treasury than all the others, because she gave all that she had to live on, while they gave out of their wealth. This shows that Jesus appreciates the heart of this woman and the sacrifice that she made. This is the kind of woman Jesus commends in private to his disciples.

### The Fate of Pregnant Women and Nursing Mothers during the Tribulation (Matt. 24:19–21; Mark 13:17–19)

> "And alas for women who are pregnant and for those who are nursing infants in those days! Pray that your flight may not be in winter or on a Sabbath. For then there will be great tribulation, such as has not been from the beginning of the world until now, no, and never will be." (Matt. 24:19–21)

In the Olivet Discourse, where Jesus discusses signs of the end of the age, he states how dreadful it will be for pregnant women and nursing mothers. He tells his listeners to pray that the end will not come in the winter or on the Sabbath, because there will be great distress never to be equaled again in the world. The fact that he mentions pregnant women and nursing mothers indicates Jesus' sensitivity, even when talking about most momentous end-time events, toward the needs of women during these challenging and particularly vulnerable stages in their lives.[40]

### Two Women Grinding at a Mill (Matt. 24:41; Luke 17:35)

> "Two women will be grinding at the mill; one will be taken and one left." (Matt. 24:41)

Further on in the Olivet Discourse, Jesus mentions that at his return (Matt. 24:3, 36, 39; Luke 17:35) two women will be grinding with a hand mill, and one will be taken and the other left. He also mentions that two men will be in the field, and one will be taken and the other left. This is another instance of the characteristic pairing of male and female examples in Jesus' teaching. Here it is seen that both men and women face the same judgment and the same responsibility for keeping watch.

### The Parable of the Ten Virgins (Matt. 25:1–13)

> "Then the kingdom of heaven will be like ten virgins who took their lamps and went to meet the bridegroom. Five of them were foolish, and five were

40. Nolland, *Matthew*, 973.

wise. For when the foolish took their lamps, they took no oil with them, but the wise took flasks of oil with their lamps." (Matt. 25:1–4)

The setting for the parable of the ten virgins is that of a Jewish wedding party where the bridegroom is delayed, and only half of the bridesmaids are ready for the bridegroom's coming, which could be at any time. The ones who are not prepared miss the bridegroom's coming and are shut out of the wedding banquet. Again, Jesus juxtaposes parables featuring female characters with male or general ones in order to impart a particular lesson—here, the need for both men and women to be prepared for Jesus' return (see also the parable of the talents in Matt. 25:14–30).[41]

## Mary and Martha Grieve for Lazarus (John 11:1–44)

> Now a certain man was ill, Lazarus of Bethany, the village of Mary and her sister Martha. It was Mary who anointed the Lord with ointment and wiped his feet with her hair, whose brother Lazarus was ill. . . . Now Jesus loved Martha and her sister and Lazarus. (John 11:1–5)

At Lazarus's tomb, when Jesus tells people to move the stone, Martha challenges him, saying there would be a bad odor, for Lazarus had been dead four days. Jesus responds, "Did I not tell you that if you believed you would see the glory of God?" (v. 40). After a brief prayer, Jesus raises Lazarus from the dead.

Jesus' relationship with Mary and Martha is clearly very close; their interaction is straightforward and honest. Jesus relates to these women openly and compassionately and treats them with love, taking seriously their comments and requests. Yet he still acts with authority, instructing the women and challenging their faith.[42] As Cottrell notes, feminists point to this account "as another example of Jesus' great respect for women's intellectual and spiritual abilities, and how he thus 'conversed with them on theological topics.'"[43]

Indeed, Martha's confession of Jesus is remarkable and anticipates John's purpose statement at the end of the Gospel (John 20:30–31), and, clearly, Jesus reveals himself to Mary and Martha as the Messiah, allowing them to respond to him in faith. This does not mean, however, that Jesus was a feminist or pursued an egalitarian agenda.

---

41. Ibid., 1010.
42. See the discussion in Köstenberger, *John*, 336–38.
43. Cottrell, *Gender Roles and the Bible*, 173, with reference to S. E. McClelland, "The New Reality in Christ: Perspectives from Biblical Studies," in *Gender Matters: Women's Studies for the Christian Community*, ed. J. S. Hagen (Grand Rapids, MI: Zondervan, 1990), 62. Cottrell also cites G. Bilezikian, *Beyond Sex Roles*, 2nd ed. (Grand Rapids: Baker, 1985), 101, and L. Swidler, "Jesus Was A Feminist," 181.

## Mary Anoints Jesus (Matt. 26:6–13; Mark 14:3–9; John 12:1–8)

A woman came up to him with an alabaster flask of very expensive ointment, and she poured it on his head as he reclined at table. And when the disciples saw it, they were indignant, saying, "Why this waste? For this could have been sold for a large sum and given to the poor." But Jesus, aware of this, said to them, "Why do you trouble the woman? . . . Truly, I say to you, wherever this gospel is proclaimed in the whole world, what she has done will also be told in memory of her." (Matt. 26:7–13)

In recounting the story, Matthew, Mark, and John most likely refer to the same incident.[44] Jesus supports and defends Mary's actions against Judas's challenge. Mary performs an act of unusual, sacrificial devotion and honors Jesus without any concern about the negative reactions of others. This is acknowledged by Jesus, who states that wherever the gospel is preached, Mary's act will also be told in memory of her.[45] This passage, of course, provided Elisabeth Schüssler Fiorenza with the title of her influential book *In Memory of Her*. Clearly, Mary's act was one of unusual devotion, yet it does not prove that Jesus came to establish a "discipleship of equals," as Fiorenza contended.

## The Wailing Jerusalem Women (Luke 23:27–29)

And there followed him a great multitude of the people and of women who were mourning and lamenting for him. But turning to them Jesus said, "Daughters of Jerusalem, do not weep for me, but weep for yourselves and for your children. For behold, the days are coming when they will say, 'Blessed are the barren and the wombs that never bore and the breasts that never nursed!'" (Luke 23:27–29)

On this occasion, Jesus is on the way to his crucifixion and observes the large number of people following him, including women who mourn and wail. He tells them not to weep for him but instead to be concerned for themselves and their children. This hints at the future judgment that would befall Jerusalem owing to Jesus' rejection by the Jewish nation (see Luke 21:20–23).

In this instance, these women may not realize who Jesus truly is. The weeping and wailing may be because they see the horrors of crucifixion. Even so, Jesus challenges the validity of their sorrow, pointing out the horrors they themselves will face in the near future. Here Jesus, under significant duress himself, takes time to address these women and to speak the truth to them.

---

44. See the comparative study by A. J. Köstenberger, *Studies in John and Gender* (New York: Peter Lang, 2001), 49–63.
45. On the Markan version, see France, *Gospel of Mark*, 555.

## The Women near the Cross (Matt. 27:55–56; Mark 15:40–41;
## Luke 23:49; John 19:25–27)

> There were also many women there, looking on from a distance, who had
> followed Jesus from Galilee, ministering to him, among whom were Mary
> Magdalene and Mary the mother of James and Joseph and the mother of the
> sons of Zebedee. (Matt. 27:55–56)

A large group of women—Mary Magdalene, Mary the mother of James and
of Joseph (i.e., Jesus' mother; see Matt. 13:55; Mark 6:3), Salome (perhaps
his mother's sister), Mary the wife of Clopas, and the mother of the sons of
Zebedee—watch the crucifixion from a distance. They have followed Jesus
from Galilee to care for his needs (see Luke 8:2–3).[46] John also recounts
how Jesus entrusts care for his mother to the "disciple whom he loved"
(probably John the son of Zebedee).

This is a very moving scene, particularly Jesus' parting words to his mother.
Jesus' care for his mother is seen in his deliberate placing of her in a new
family, assigning her care to someone he trusts more than the members of his
earthly family.[47] Once again, Jesus shows sensitivity to the needs of a woman
(here, his mother). The fact that a large group of women had followed Jesus
all the way from Galilee is an indication of how devoted they were to him.

### Mary Magdalene and Others Are Present at Jesus' Burial
### and on the Third Day Set Out to Anoint Jesus' Body (Matt. 27:61;
### 28:1–11; Mark 15:47–16:8; Luke 23:55–24:12; John 20:1–18)

> Now after the Sabbath, toward the dawn of the first day of the week, Mary
> Magdalene and the other Mary went to see the tomb. . . . The angel said to the
> women, "Do not be afraid, for I know that you seek Jesus who was crucified.
> He is not here, for he has risen, as he said." . . . So they departed quickly from
> the tomb with fear and great joy, and ran to tell his disciples. (Matt. 28:1–8)

Matthew and Mark record that Mary Magdalene and Mary the mother of
Jesus saw where Jesus was buried (Matt. 27:61; Mark 15:47; see also Luke
23:55). Luke also notes that the women went home and prepared spices and
perfumes but rested on the Sabbath as commanded (Luke 23:56).

In John's Gospel, Mary Magdalene is the first to go to the tomb and
see the stone removed. She runs to tell Peter and the "disciple whom Jesus

---

46. See Bock, *Luke*, 1866, who also notes in n. 35 that the present participle "those who
are following" implies that these women are still following Jesus. See also the reference to
Bauckham's work below.
47. See the discussion in Köstenberger, *John*, 548–49.

loved." They head for the tomb with Mary. After they leave, Mary stands outside the tomb crying, and bending over to look into the tomb, sees two angels where Jesus' body had lain. After a brief interchange, Mary turns and sees Jesus. Thinking he is the gardener, she urges him to tell her where he has put Jesus' body so she can get it. In response, Jesus calls her by name: "Mary," and, in a moving recognition scene, she turns toward him and cries out, "Rabboni!" ("Teacher" in Aramaic). Jesus tells her not to cling to him but to go and relay a message to the disciples, which she does.[48]

Several of the women who had closely followed Jesus during his earthly ministry are the first to see him after the resurrection. In keeping with Jewish custom, these women are faithful to wait for the Sabbath to pass and then set out to care for Jesus' body, which is why they are the first to see the empty tomb, encounter the angels, see the risen Lord, and report what they have seen to the disciples. Mary Magdalene apparently had great devotion to Jesus, and her encounter with the risen Lord is particularly stirring.[49]

Evangelical feminists have argued that the fact that women were chosen as the first witnesses to Jesus' resurrection implies that "he wanted these women whom he had taught to go on to take authoritative leadership positions themselves."[50] It is certainly a wonderful privilege for women to have been the first witnesses to Jesus' resurrection, but it does not follow from this privilege that Jesus was a feminist or that he wanted women to serve as pastors or elders.[51]

### Jesus' Approach to Women according to the Four Gospels

How do each of the four evangelists, as early witnesses to Jesus and the events of his life and ministry, conceive of Jesus' approach to women? Do the Gospel evidence as a whole and the theology of the respective Gospel writers support a certain view of women?

### Women in the Gospel of Matthew

Matthew's most distinctive references to women are found in the very first chapter of his Gospel. Matthew shows that the apparent scandal attached to Mary's virgin conception was not unprecedented in Israel's history; there were several reputedly scandalous women included by God in the line of promise in the past. Matthew mentions Tamar, who was raped by her half-brother; Rahab, a prostitute; Ruth, who lay down beside Boaz overnight;

---

48. Köstenberger (ibid., 570, with reference to Maccini, *Her Testimony Is True*) notes that "Jesus' entrusting Mary with this important message surely is significant."
49. Nolland, *Matthew*, 1251–54.
50. Spencer, *Beyond the Curse*, 62. See also the discussion and additional references to feminist literature in Cottrell, *Gender Roles and the Bible*, 174–75.
51. So rightly Grudem, *Evangelical Feminism and Biblical Truth*, 164–65.

and Bathsheba, with whom King David committed adultery (Matt. 1:3, 5, 6, 16).[52] Matthew also includes several references to Jesus' mother, Mary, in the opening chapters of his Gospel (Matt. 1:18–25; 2:11, 13–14, 20–21).

Apart from references to women that are found in several of Jesus' parables: a woman baking (Matt. 13:33), two women grinding at a mill (Matt. 24:41), and ten virgins at a wedding (Matt. 25:1–13), there is little that is distinctive in Matthew's presentation of Jesus in relation to women, in comparison with the other Synoptic Gospels, Mark and Luke. Table 14.3 provides a list of the women featured in Matthew's Gospel.

Table 14.3: Jesus and Women in the Gospel of Matthew*

| Matthew | Woman character(s) | Description |
|---|---|---|
| 1:3, 5, 6, 16 | Tamar, Rahab, Ruth, Bathsheba, Mary | Jesus' genealogy |
| 1:18–25 | Mary (Joseph's perspective) | **Jesus' birth** |
| 2:11 | Mary | **Visit of magi** |
| 2:13–14, 20–21 | Mary | **To Egypt, return to Nazareth** |
| 8:14–15 | Simon Peter's mother-in-law | Fever healed |
| 9:18–19, 23–26 | Ruler's daughter | Raised from the dead |
| 9:20–22 | Woman with blood flow | Healed |
| 10:35 | **Daughter vs. mother, etc.** | **No peace but division** |
| 12:42 | **Queen of Sheba** | **Came to Solomon** |
| 12:46–50 | Jesus' family (including Mary) | Wanting to talk to Jesus |
| 13:33 | **A woman baking** | **Kingdom parable** |
| 13:53–57 | Mary and Jesus' sisters | People in Jesus' hometown |
| 14:3–12 | Herodias and her daughter | Plot to have John beheaded |
| 15:21–28 | Syrophoenician woman and daughter | Demon exorcised, faith |
| 20:20–21 | Mother of sons of Zebedee | Request on behalf of her sons |
| 24:19 | Pregnant women, nursing mothers | Tribulation |
| 24:41 | Two women grinding at a mill | Coming of Son of Man |
| 25:1–13 | Ten virgins | Parable on watchfulness |
| 26:6–13 | Woman at Bethany | Anointing Jesus |
| 26:69–72 | Servant girl, another girl | Presses Peter |
| 27:55–56 | Mary Magdalene; Mary mother of James and Joseph; mother of sons of Zebedee | Watching from a distance; had followed Jesus in Galilee |
| 28:1–11 | Mary Magdalene, other Mary | Set out to anoint Jesus' body |

*Material distinct from what is found in Mark and Luke is in bold font.

52. See, e.g., E. D. Freed, "The Women in Matthew's Genealogy," *Journal for the Study of the New Testament* 29 (1987): 3–19 and J. Nolland, "The Four (Five) Women and Other Annotations in Matthew's Genealogy," *New Testament Studies* 43 (1997): 527–39.

On the whole, Jesus' encounters with women that are narrated in Matthew's Gospel show women in familiar roles as mothers and women working in the domestic realm. There is no particular emphasis on women, and certainly no indication that women are to be included on par with men in leadership in the church.

### Women in the Gospel of Mark

The women characters featured in Mark's Gospel are an integral part of the story of Jesus.[53] In several cases, they approach Jesus to ask for healing, whether for themselves or a loved one. One such example is the Syrophoenician woman, who is commended for her faith. Other women show noteworthy devotion, such as the woman at Bethany who anoints Jesus, the women at the cross, or the women who set out to anoint Jesus' body at the end of the Gospel.

There is really no material unique to Mark's Gospel, which may mean that, assuming Mark was the first canonical Gospel to be written, all of Mark's material on women was subsequently incorporated into the other Synoptic Gospels, Matthew and Luke. Alternatively, if Matthew was written first, Mark just took from that, not adding any material of his own. In either case, the lack of unique material in Mark's Gospel indicates that Mark did not show a particular interest in women in his Gospel. References to women in Mark's Gospel appear in Table 14.4.

Table 14.4: Jesus and Women in the Gospel of Mark

| Mark | Woman character(s) | Description |
| --- | --- | --- |
| 1:30–31 | Simon Peter's mother-in-law | Fever healed |
| 3:20–21, 31–35 | Mary | Family concerned for Jesus |
| 5:22–23, 35–43 | Jairus's daughter (12 years old) | Raised from the dead |
| 5:25–34 | Woman with blood flow | Healed |
| 6:17–29 | Herodias and her daughter | Plot to kill John the Baptist |
| 7:24–30 | Syrophoenician woman and daughter | Demon exorcised, faith |
| 12:41–44 | Poor widow | Commended for giving |
| 13:17 | Pregnant women, nursing mothers | Tribulation |
| 14:3–9 | Woman at Bethany | Anointing Jesus |
| 14:66–70 | Servant girl of the high priest | Presses Peter |
| 15:40–41 | Mary Magdalene; Mary mother of James and Joseph; Salome; other women | Looking on from a distance at the cross |
| 16:1–8 | Mary Magdalene; Mary mother of James; Salome | Set out to anoint Jesus' body |

53. Studies of women in Mark include W. M. Swartley, "The Role of Women in Mark's Gospel: A Narrative Analysis," *Biblical Theological Bulletin* 27 (1997): 16–22; J. Kopas, "Jesus and Women in Mark's Gospel," *Religious Studies Review* 44 (1985): 912–20; and W. Munro, "Women Disciples in Mark," *Catholic Biblical Quarterly* 44 (1982): 225–241.

As in the case of Matthew's Gospel, there is nothing pertaining to women in Mark's accounts that strikes us as out of the ordinary. Women are shown in their customary roles as concerned, loving—and in at least one case, scheming—mothers, and devoted followers. Jesus heals the woman with blood flow and the daughters of Jairus and the Syrophoenician woman and commends the poor widow. The familiar group of women is found at the cross and at the empty tomb.[54] Again, however, Jesus is not shown to demonstrate any new approach to women in leadership.

## Women in the Gospel of Luke

The Gospel of Luke stands out in giving significant attention to women, which is in keeping with Luke's concern for those of low status in society, including the poor, children, Gentiles, the disabled or sick, tax-collectors, and women.[55] The birth narratives of John the Baptist and of Jesus are told from a female perspective, possibly on the basis of accounts by Elizabeth and Mary. The group of women following Jesus from Galilee all the way to the cross serves as a significant source of eyewitness testimony (note the "inclusio of eyewitness testimony" in Luke 8:2–3 and 23:49).[56]

Thus Luke stands apart from Matthew and Mark in his significantly more pronounced interest in women and their part in the story of Jesus. Table 14.5 provides a complete list of female characters in Luke's Gospel.[57]

In addition, we observe a consistent, most likely deliberate, pattern of significant pairing of female and male characters in material, most of which is unique to Luke's Gospel.[58] While not necessarily indicating male-female

54. See the studies by C. E. B. Cranfield, "St. Mark 16.1–8," *Scottish Journal of Theology* 5 (1952): 282–98 and 398–414; and P. Danove, "The Characterization and Narrative Function of the Women at the Tomb (Mark 15, 40–41, 47; 16, 1–8," *Biblica* 77 (1996): 375–97.

55. Luke's treatment of women has attracted significant attention among scholars, and the literature on this topic is extensive, especially studies on the sinful woman anointing Jesus (7:36–50), the women followers of Jesus (8:1–3), Mary and Martha (10:38–42), and the women at the cross and at the empty tomb (24:1–11).

56. See R. Bauckham, *Jesus and the Eyewitnesses: The Gospels as Eyewitness Testimony* (Grand Rapids, MI: Eerdmans, 2006), 130–31.

57. Since the topic of this book is Jesus, we will not include a chart on women in the book of Acts. It should be noted, however, that the latter continues the pattern of Luke's Gospel of giving significant coverage to women, such as noting that both men and women suffered persecution (Acts 8:3; 9:2; 22:4) or mentioning significant women in the early church, including Lydia (Acts 16:14–15) or Priscilla (Acts 18:2–3, 18–19, 26). For a treatment of many of these women see A. J. Köstenberger, "Women in the Pauline Mission," in *Gospel of the Nations*, ed. P. G. Bolt and M. D. Thompson (Leicester: Inter-Varsity, 2000), 221–47; reprinted in *Studies on John and Gender*, 323–52.

58. As is acknowledged widely in the scholarly literature, this is part of a larger pattern of presenting things in doublets and parallels (or lists of three) in Luke and other ancient literature (see, e.g., chap. 2 in T. K. Seim, *The Double Message: Patterns of Gender in Luke–Acts* [Edinburgh: T and T Clark; Nashville: Abingdon, 1994]). The pattern even

Table 14.5: Jesus and Women in the Gospel of Luke*

| Luke | Woman character(s) | Description |
| --- | --- | --- |
| 1:5–25 | Elizabeth | Birth announcement |
| 1:26–38 | Mary | Birth announcement |
| 1:39–56 | Mary and Elizabeth | Visit, Mary's song |
| 1:57–58 | Elizabeth | Birth of John the Baptist |
| 2:1–20 | Mary | Birth of Jesus |
| 2:21–35 | Mary | Presentation in the temple |
| 2:36–38 | Anna the prophetess | Prophesies regarding Jesus |
| 2:39–52 | Mary | 12-year-old Jesus at temple |
| 4:38–39 | Simon Peter's mother-in-law | Fever healed |
| 7:11–15 | Widow at Nain | Son raised from the dead |
| 7:36–50 | Woman who had led sinful life | Earlier anointing of Jesus |
| 8:2–3 | Mary Magdalene; Joanna, wife of Chuza; Susanna; and many others | Supporting Jesus and the Twelve from their own means |
| 8:19–21 | Mary (and family) | Wanting to talk to Jesus |
| 8:40–42a, 49–56 | Jairus's daughter | Raised from the dead |
| 10:38–42 | Mary and Martha (sisters) | Listening vs. serving |
| 11:27–28 | Woman in the crowd | Blessed is Jesus' mother |
| 12:53 | Mother vs. daughter, etc. | Not peace, but division |
| 13:10–13 | Woman crippled for 18 years | Healed |
| 15:8–10 | Woman who lost a coin | Figure in parable |
| 18:1–8 | Persistent widow | Figure in parable |
| 21:1–4 | Poor widow | Commended for giving |
| 21:23 | Pregnant women, nursing mothers | Tribulation |
| 22:56–57 | Servant girl | Presses Peter |
| 23:27–31 | Wailing Jerusalem women | Mourn for your children |
| 23:49 | Women who had followed from Galilee | Watching from a distance |
| 23:55–24:11 | Mary Magdalene; Joanna; Mary mother of James; and others | Set out to anoint Jesus' body |

*Material unique to Luke's Gospel appears in bold.

equality in positions of leadership among Jesus' followers or the early church, this pattern does seem to indicate, similar to Paul's emphasis on "neither male nor female" in Galatians 3:28, that with regard to salvation in Jesus

---

obtains in Luke's production of a two-volume work, Luke–Acts. The same device can be found in the book of Acts (e.g., Ananias and Sapphira; Aeneas and Tabitha; Lydia and the Philippian jailer; Dionysius and Damaris, etc.). Acts is not covered here in detail owing to the emphasis on Jesus.

there is no distinction between women and men. These male-female pairs in Luke, then, may include but are not necessarily limited to those shown in Table 14.6.

Table 14.6: Male-Female Pairs in the Gospel of Luke

| Luke | Male characters | Luke | Female characters |
|------|------------------|------|--------------------|
| 1:5–23 | Zechariah | 1:26–56 | Mary |
| 2:25–35 | Simeon | 2:36–38 | Anna |
| 4:27 | Naaman | 4:26 | Widow of Zarephath |
| 4:31–37 | Demon-possessed man | 4:38–39 | Peter's mother-in-law |
| 6:12–16 | Group of male disciples | 8:2–3 | Group of female disciples |
| 7:11–17 | Widow's son raised | 8:40–56 | Jairus's daughter raised |
| 10:25–37 | Teacher of the law | 10:38–42 | Martha and Mary |
| 11:5–13 | Persistent friend | 18:1–8 | Persistent widow |
| 11:32 | Men of Nineveh | 11:31 | Queen of Sheba |
| 13:19 | Man sowing | 13:21 | Woman baking |
| 14:1–6 | Man healed on Sabbath | 13:10–17 | Woman healed on Sabbath |
| 15:3–7 | Man with lost sheep | 15:8–10 | Woman with lost coin |
| 17:34 | Two men at Jesus' return | 17:35 | Two women at Jesus' return |
| 19:9 | Son of Abraham | 13:16 | Daughter of Abraham |
| 24:13–35 | Jesus appears to Emmaus disciples | 24:1–11 | Jesus appears to women |

In his Gospel, Luke puts his reader in closer touch with women by showing us their perspective, such as that of Mary or Elizabeth in being the mothers of Jesus and John the Baptist, respectively. He also provides us with memorable female characters, which we see featured in Jesus' parables, such as the woman who lost a coin or the persistent widow. Perhaps more than the other Synoptic Gospels, Luke features Jesus' devoted female followers as disciples, most notably the group of women from Galilee[59] as well as Mary and Martha. Nevertheless, Jesus is not shown to overturn the pattern of the man as the head of the household or in leadership of the community.

### Women in the Gospel of John
In keeping with his principle of selecting just a few significant episodes in Jesus' ministry and recounting these in considerable detail, John features

---

59. See the brief discussion in L. H. Cohick, "Why Women Followed Jesus: A Discussion of Female Piety," *Scottish Bulletin of Evangelical Theology* 25/2 (2007): 178–79, with further references. Cohick provides much helpful information, but she does not adequately support her assertion that the "Jesus movement . . . had a visible presence of women participating in significant ways, *including leadership responsibilities*, within the group" (ibid., 192; emphasis added).

several accounts that include women. Salient examples are Jesus' mother at the Cana wedding, the Samaritan woman, and Mary and Martha at the raising of Lazarus. A list of female characters in John appears in Table 14.7.

Table 14.7: Jesus and Women in the Gospel of John*

| John | Woman character(s) | Description |
|------|--------------------|-------------|
| 2:1–11 | **Jesus' mother** | **Wedding at Cana** |
| 2:12 | **Jesus' mother** | **Jesus' family in Capernaum** |
| 4:1–42 | **Samaritan woman** | **Believes in Jesus, witnesses** |
| 11:1–37 | **Mary and Martha** | **Raising of Lazarus** |
| 12:1–8 | Mary and Martha | Dinner, Mary anoints Jesus |
| 18:16–17 | Servant girl of the high priest | Presses Peter |
| 19:25–27 | Jesus' mother; mother's sister; Mary, wife of Clopas; Mary Magdalene | Near the cross; Jesus ensures care of his mother |
| 20:1–18 | Mary Magdalene | Recognition scene |

*Material unique to John's Gospel appears in bold.

Some scholarly works have highlighted the significance of women in John's Gospel.[60] On the whole, however, it is important not to overstate the case. The Samaritan woman is shown as an important witness to Jesus, and Mary Magdalene significantly is the first witness of the resurrection in the Gospel. This clearly affirms the value of women as witnesses to the gospel story and of their calling to share their faith with others. It does not necessarily indicate that they served on par with men in roles of leadership among the circle of Jesus' followers, however.

## Observations

The most pertinent observations from the presentation of women in the four Gospels are as follows.[61] First, *Jesus treated women consistently with respect, dignity, compassion, and kindness.* This is characteristic of his dealings with the numerous women who approached him for help, be it on their own behalf or on behalf of a loved one. James Borland puts this well: "Jesus showed how highly he valued women by ministering to them and

60. E.g., T. Okure, *The Johannine Approach to Mission*, WUNT 2/31 (Tübingen: Mohr-Siebeck, 1987); Maccini, *Her Testimony is True*; C. M. Conway, *Men and Women in the Fourth Gospel: Gender and Johannine Characterization*, SBL Dissertation Series 167 (Atlanta: Scholars Press, 1999).

61. For a similar survey along *topical* lines, see Borland, "Women in the Life and Teachings of Jesus," 113–23, who organizes the material under the following headings: I. Christ Placed a High Value on Women; A. Jesus Demonstrated the High Value He Placed on Women by Recognizing Their Intrinsic Value as Persons; B. Jesus Demonstrated the High Value He Placed on Women by Ministering to Women; C. Jesus Demonstrated the High Value He Placed on Women by According Them Dignity in His Ministry; II. Jesus Recognized Role Distinctions of Men and Women.

meeting their needs. . . . He healed them, dialogued with them, and showed women the same care and concern He showed to men."[62]

Second, at the same time it is clear that *Jesus dealt with women firmly, honestly, and straightforwardly*, and resisted any attempts to be manipulated or otherwise unduly swayed from truth. This is seen in Jesus' dealings with his own mother, his interaction with the Samaritan woman, the Syrophoenician woman, Martha, a woman in a crowd who called Jesus' mother blessed, and the mother of the sons of Zebedee. It should be noted, however, that Jesus did the same with men, treating men and women equally as sinful and in need of correction.

Third, in his teaching, *Jesus often used women alongside men as illustrations*, especially in his parables. This indicates Jesus' desire that his message resonate with women as well as with men and that women can identify with his teaching on the kingdom.

Fourth, there were times when *Jesus showed special sensitivity to women's concerns*, such as when he commented on the fate of pregnant women and nursing mothers at the coming tribulation and his remark to the wailing Jerusalem women on his way to the cross.

Fifth, *women followed Jesus and supported him financially*. Women were thus an important part of Jesus' mission.

Sixth, *women served as witnesses to Jesus*. Examples of this are the Samaritan woman and, after Jesus' resurrection, Mary Magdalene, who was told to pass on the news to his disciples. This contrasts with the generally negative Jewish attitude toward women witnesses, such as that seen in Josephus: "But let not the testimony of women be admitted, on account of the levity and boldness of their sex" (*Antiquities* iv.8.15).[63]

The important insight for our present purposes is that none of these first six summary observations of Jesus' approach to women establishes that Jesus was a feminist or adopted an egalitarian approach to gender roles. While Jesus did affirm that both men and women were made in God's image (Matt. 19:4), while he was open and receptive to women's requests for help, and while he showed great brotherly love toward women and was genuinely interested in their spiritual welfare,[64] none of this makes him a feminist, that is, one who elevated women to positions of leadership on par with men.

This is further supported by the seventh and crucial observation that *none of the passages we have studied gives any indication that Jesus envisioned a community where men and women would be equal in positions of leadership*.

---

62. Ibid., 117.
63. Ibid., 119.
64. This is rightly noted by Clark, *Man and Woman in Christ*, 175, especially with regard to the Gospels of Luke and John.

Jesus chose twelve men as his apostles (Matt. 10:2–4; Mark 3:13–19). As James Borland sums up, this fact is significant for the following reasons:

1) the apostles were to be with Christ to learn from him and to be trained by him firsthand (Mark 3:14–15);
2) the apostles were the official leaders of the early church (Acts 2:14; 5:12, 18, 40, 42; 6:2–4; 9:29; 15:2; Gal. 1:17);
3) the apostles were given special rulership (Matt. 19:28; Luke 22:30);
4) Jesus promised the apostles the teaching ministry of the Holy Spirit and special revelation (John 14:26; 16:13–15); and
5) as a testimony to the permanence of male leadership in the church, the names of the twelve apostles are inscribed on the foundation of the New Jerusalem (Rev. 21:14; cf. Eph. 2:20).[65]

Also, as Borland points out, when a need arose to replace Judas as twelfth apostle after Jesus' ascension, one of the requirements was that his replacement be male (Acts 1:21–22): "So one of the *men* [Gk. *andrōn*] who have accompanied us during all the time that the Lord Jesus went in and out among us . . . one of these *men* must become with us a witness to his resurrection."[66] Despite advancing various explanations, feminists have not been able to account satisfactorily for the fact that Jesus appointed twelve men as apostles.[67]

Stephen Clark sums up well the New Testament evidence with regard to Jesus and women when he writes:

Jesus related to women with love and respect. He spoke to them, taught them, healed them. He never spoke of them in a contemptuous or downgrading manner and never treated them as if they were unimportant. In his eyes, they had the same spiritual status as men. At the same time, the evidence is that he accepted a role difference for men and women and that he even respected the normal Jewish customs in the area. . . . Jesus was not revolutionary with regard to the roles of men and women. His revolution lay rather in the area of what constituted true righteousness and of the spiritual relationship of men and women alike to God and to Israel.[68]

65. See also Grudem, *Evangelical Feminism and Biblical Truth*, with reference to Matt. 19:28 and Rev. 21:14.
66. Borland, "Women in the Life and Teachings of Jesus," 122. See also Grudem, *Evangelical Feminism and Biblical Truth*, 161, 165.
67. In addition to the interaction with various feminist authors on this issue in the present volume, see Grudem, *Evangelical Feminism and Biblical Truth*, 170–74, who deals with the objections that Jesus' choice of twelve men as apostles was merely a function of culture and that no special authority attached to the role of the Twelve. See also Cottrell, *Gender Roles and the Bible*, 208–11.
68. Clark, *Man and Woman in Christ*, 175–76.

## Was Jesus a Feminist?

Was Jesus a feminist? Ironically, this is a question on which feminists cannot agree. As we have seen, some feminists, in particular the radical variety, believe that Christianity is an irredeemably patriarchal religion and that Jesus, too, was steeped in patriarchalism. Others, especially evangelical feminists, claim that Jesus, in contrast to his patriarchal Jewish contemporary culture, paved the way for full male-female equality in the church. How are we to resolve these contradictory feminist assessments?

Evangelical feminists and others rightly observe how Jesus broke with male chauvinism and a derogatory, discriminatory treatment of women. This observation must be given full weight. What they have overlooked, however, is that this does not necessarily mean that Jesus obliterated gender-related distinctions in the church altogether, especially with regard to leadership roles. This is the critical balance Jesus found, and believers would do well to strike the same balance in the church today. Jesus was not a chauvinist, but he also was not a feminist; to claim that these are the only two options is akin to saying that men are either weak and passive or harsh dictators, and women are either doormats or feminists.

The implication from what has been said is that a Christlike approach toward women does not necessarily mean that biblical parameters concerning the appropriate ministry of men and women no longer apply. To the contrary, it is precisely by upholding and adhering to God's will and order in this area that God will be glorified, and men and women will please God and experience fulfillment and deeper meaning in their lives and relationships.

At the same time, all Christian men, and the Christian church in general, ought to award women the honor and dignity that are rightly theirs by virtue of being created in God's image (Gen. 1:27) and of being redeemed by Christ (Gal. 3:28). In this day and until Christ returns, God still invites both men and women to a more loving way of living together as heirs together of the grace of life (1 Pet. 3:7).

# CONCLUSION

*He said to them, "But who do you say that I am?" Simon Peter replied, "You are the Christ, the Son of the living God."*

—Matthew 16:15–16

**The feminist** revolution has swept over the general culture and left its indelible mark. Feminism has also had a tremendous impact on the study of Scripture and, in particular, on the reading of the Gospels' portrait of Jesus and his approach to women. This is true of radical as well as reformist feminism. It is also true of feminism's evangelical counterpart—egalitarianism or evangelical feminism. Yet, as we have seen, there is considerable disagreement about the proper interpretation of Scripture in general and concerning Jesus' treatment of women in particular.

As women struggle to determine their place in both the religious academy and in church ministry, how one interprets the relevant passages of Scripture is of critical importance. Jesus and his approach to women have been a major focus of attention, as Jesus' stance is an important indication of how Christian women should view themselves and function within the church.

If anything has been learned from our study, it is that there is no such thing as a uniform feminist or egalitarian hermeneutic. We can speak of such a hermeneutic only in a general sense on the basis of certain traits that most practitioners of feminism or egalitarianism share.

In general, feminist hermeneutics is united in its commitment to feminism and its critique of Scripture as patriarchal and androcentric. Scripture is not awarded an authoritative status that is external to the interpreter but, rather, is subjected to critique on the basis of the interpreter's feminist outlook. This runs counter to the conventional notion of valid interpretation.

### Comparison of Feminist Approaches to Jesus and Women

Overall, there is a considerable spectrum within feminist interpretation. On the one extreme lies *radical feminism* that rejects Scripture in its entirety as irredeemably patriarchal and turns to other sources of validation. In a sense, radical feminism is more consistent than reformist feminism. It carries through with its critique of Scripture and does not seek to salvage usable elements through revisionist exegesis; rather, it defines itself in direct antithesis to Scripture.

We saw this with all three representative radical feminists studied in this volume: Mary Daly, Virginia Mollenkott, and Daphne Hampson. Nevertheless, from the standpoint of a conservative evangelical viewpoint, radical feminism's substitution of women's experience for scriptural authority does not adequately consider Scripture's own claim of being divine self-revelation. As a result, Christianity is replaced by a pagan or even occult form of religious expression and experience.[1]

Closer to the middle is *reformist feminism*, which is characterized by a certain degree of ambivalence toward Scripture. Tradition and other reasons cause interpreters in this feminist category to retain the idea of Scripture as a useful source for theological formulation. Large portions of Scripture are questioned through the use of a hermeneutic of suspicion. On the one hand Scripture is mined as a source, while on the other it is rejected as unacceptable in light of feminist presuppositions. As we have seen, many reformist feminist interpreters are well aware of this tension, and they describe it as paradoxical since they struggle with its legitimacy.

There are a large number of reformist feminists who view Jesus as a feminist. Letty Russell, for example, says Jesus was a feminist "in the sense that he considered men and women equal."[2] Fiorenza, likewise, famously sought to make a case for Jesus' establishment of an egalitarian circle of followers.[3] Ruether repeatedly speaks of "the feminism of Jesus."[4] According to these reformist feminists, the problem lies with the church's suppression of these earlier egalitarian impulses and with its reversion to a patriarchal, male-dominated model. Here Scripture and the church must be liberated from their patriarchal captivity.

---

1. See J. Cottrell, *Feminism and the Bible: An Introduction to Feminism for Christians* (Joplin, MO: College Press, 1992), chaps. 3 and 4.
2. L. M. Russell, *Human Liberation in a Feminist Perspective: A Theology* (Philadelphia: Westminster, 1974), 138.
3. See chaps. 8 and 9 above.
4. R. R. Ruether, *New Woman, New Earth: Sexist Ideologies and Human Liberation* (New York: Seabury, 1975), 63–64.

Still closer to the middle are representatives of *the new feminism*, a group of feminist scholars that eschews labels such as "reformist" or "liberationist," engaging in a variety of literary approaches to biblical interpretation.[5] While this group of writers, likewise, is characterized by a considerable amount of variety, they are united in a methodology that may be described as more textually oriented and literary in nature. Unlike Elisabeth Schüssler Fiorenza and others, whose efforts aim primarily at a historical reconstruction of early Christianity behind the text, these writers seek to find answers in the text itself.

On the other side of the spectrum lies *evangelical feminism*, which professes a belief in Scripture as authoritative, inspired, and inerrant. Evangelical feminists, similar to many reformist feminists, are virtually united in their belief that Jesus practiced egalitarianism, despite the fact that all members of the Twelve were men and Jesus affirmed traditional marriage. Some argue that redemption in Christ supersedes the patriarchalism characteristic of the Old Testament, allowing them to go beyond what the Scripture actually teaches to what they think the Scripture might have been pointing to.[6] Others contend that God's intentions were egalitarian from the beginning.[7]

It may be observed that these egalitarian writers sustain an interesting relationship with radical and reformist feminists as well as the practitioners of the new feminist school. On the one hand, they share with these groups the conviction that feminism is a given, a nonnegotiable. On the other hand, they differ in their claims regarding the nature and authority of Scripture. Rather than adopting an attitude of rebellion, like that of the radical feminists, or suspicion, like that of the reformist feminists, they profess to affirm the absolute trustworthiness of Scripture in the canonical configuration of the Protestant Bible. Yet they are still faced with the challenge of justifying a scriptural feminist viewpoint.

Overall, each of these feminist interpreters differs sharply as to the method used to arrive at the teaching of Scripture, whether Scripture itself is understood to teach feminism or egalitarianism. Both radical and reformist feminists, albeit to a differing degree, contend that Scripture is characterized by a patriarchal bias and must therefore be subjected to a rigorous critique in light of feminist tenets. Evangelical feminists, conversely, believe that Scripture, rightly interpreted, teaches egalitarianism, the notion of complete gender

---

5. See chap. 10.

6. R. N. Longenecker, "Authority, Hierarchy and Leadership Patterns in the Bible," in *Women, Authority and the Bible*, ed. A. Mickelsen (Downers Grove, IL: InterVarsity, 1986), 66–85; W. J. Webb, *Slaves, Women and Homosexuals: Exploring the Hermeneutics of Cultural Analysis* (Downers Grove, IL: InterVarsity, 2001).

7. S. J. Grenz with D. M. Kjesbo, *Women in the Church: A Biblical Theology of Women in Ministry* (Downers Grove, IL: InterVarsity, 1995), 179.

equality in personhood, worth, and role. It must be concluded that both cannot be right. Either Scripture teaches egalitarianism, or it does not.

### Toward a Proper Understanding of Jesus' Approach to Women

Clearly, the feminist/egalitarian presupposition of radical gender equality tends to influence the interpretive outcome of scriptural texts, which is especially problematic where these texts do not easily lend themselves to a feminist reading. Additionally, evangelical feminism is allowed to preempt full-fledged exegesis. This stands in contradiction to proper hermeneutics; interpretation must be concerned with determining the author's intended meaning expressed in the text rather than with validating one's own presuppositions.

All in all, what we have is a cumulative case built on a weak textual foundation. Evangelical feminist interpreters are in a difficult position, for unlike other feminist interpreters they cannot charge Scripture with "patriarchal bias" and substitute their own preferred paradigm. Evangelical feminists have a hard time claiming genuine openness with regard to the interpretive outcome, since by virtue of their dual commitment to gender equality and scriptural authority they must of necessity arrive at an interpretation of Scripture that is consistent with their egalitarian viewpoint.

### Final Insights

Our study of feminist scholarship on Jesus' approach to women has yielded several important insights. First, the literature on the subject has revealed a considerable amount of diversity. An important example of divergent views among *feminist* writers is found in the serious reservations expressed in recent years about Elisabeth Schüssler Fiorenza's paradigm of a "community of equals."[8] An example of *egalitarian* diversity is the varying viewpoints about whether God's purposes were originally egalitarian.

Second, the fact that Fiorenza's "community of equals" has been seriously challenged, even by feminist scholars, brings into question the original feminist contention that feminism is rooted in the practice of Jesus and the early church. It also brings into question the central tenet of egalitarianism, that Jesus treated women as equals, not only in terms of personhood but also with regard to ecclesiastical role. Here a greater problem is posed for evangelical feminists than for radical or reformist feminists, for while the latter are able to reject Scripture as patriarchal and to substitute other sources, this option is not available for evangelical feminists, who are committed to a high view of Scripture.

Third, there are many concerns about the hermeneutic of suspicion employed by many feminists. To begin with, the location of authority in the

8. See chap. 9.

experience of the interpreter leads to subjectivism and renders interpretation without a sufficient standard for validity. Also, it is potentially inconsistent for an interpreter to use as a source the very document she considers inadequate. Feminist writers, such as Mary Ann Tolbert, acknowledge that the feminist stance toward Scripture is at the root "paradoxical" in that Scripture is at the same time critiqued as patriarchal yet continues to be used as a useful source for feminist theology.[9]

Fourth, evangelical feminism is generally sound in hermeneutical theory but at times inconsistent in exegesis of specific biblical passages. The evangelical feminist reading of Scripture in light of their feminist viewpoint, such as that of Scanzoni and Hardesty, Bilezikian, Belleville, and Spencer, has resulted in interpretations that go beyond the evidence given in particular biblical texts.[10]

Fifth, in general terms, there are certain affinities between the exegetical practice of reformist feminists and evangelical feminists, which include: (1) an effort to identify and magnify the contributions of women in Scripture; (2) the reinterpretation of biblical passages dealing with women in keeping with feminist or egalitarian presuppositions; (3) the use of a "canon within a canon" approach, by which certain biblical passages are elevated to normative status while others are marginalized; and (4) the characterization of authority as intrinsically negative and the substitution of an authority-less servanthood model for leadership.[11] This may suggest that reformist feminism exercised a certain degree of influence on evangelical feminist scholarship, especially in the area of exegetical practice and argumentation.

It has become clear that radical and reformist scholarship has largely concluded that Jesus was not a feminist and that he did not pursue a radically egalitarian agenda. It has also become clear that evangelical feminists must come to terms with this conclusion, which contradicts their argument that Scripture presents Jesus as egalitarian. From a hermeneutical standpoint, their approach to biblical interpretation is problematic because it vitiates a "listening hermeneutic" that is essential for determining the meaning intended by the original authors of Scripture.

In the end, differences in one's understanding of Jesus' stance toward women may remain, but there must be no question regarding the proper answer to Jesus' question: "Who do you say that I am?" With Peter, we must affirm unequivocally, "You are the Christ, the Son of the living God" (Matt. 16:16). As Jesus said, Peter was blessed not because he arrived at

9. See chap. 10.
10. See chaps. 11–13.
11. See the helpful response by W. Grudem, *Evangelical Feminism and Biblical Truth* (Sisters, OR: Multnomah, 2004), 167–68.

this insight through his own inductive reasoning but because he had been receptive to divine revelation: "Blessed are you, Simon Bar-Jonah! For flesh and blood has not revealed this to you, but my Father who is in heaven" (v. 17). In fact, this acknowledgment of Jesus as Messiah and Son of God, who must "be killed, and on the third day be raised" (v. 21), is indispensable for anyone who would be part of Christ's messianic community. This acknowledgment also calls for humility as we together, in Christ, attempt to get closer to the truth as God intended us to understand it on any issue.

If Scripture—including the Gospels—is, then, the inspired account of God's revelation, centered on his provision of salvation in Jesus, "We must pay much closer attention to what we have heard, lest we drift away from it" (Heb. 2:1). We must be careful not to subvert the message of Scripture regarding Jesus but treat God's Word with utmost respect as attentive listeners rather than ideological critics. We must take our place in a stance of submission to God's Word, putting ourselves beneath it rather than sitting in critical judgment over it. Women as well as men must draw near to God's Word "to listen" rather than "to offer the sacrifice of fools" (Eccl. 5:1). If that means self-sacrifice and self-denial of the world's promises of independence and human rights and liberties, so be it; for the true follower of Christ has forsaken such false promises, knowing Christ's words to be trustworthy:

> If anyone would come after me, let him deny himself and take up his cross and follow me. For whoever would save his life will lose it, but whoever loses his life for my sake will find it. For what will it profit a man if he gains the whole world and forfeits his soul? Or what shall a man give in return for his soul? For the Son of Man is going to come with his angels in the glory of his Father, and then he will repay each person according to what he has done. (Matt. 16:24–27)

Table A1.1: Feminist Scholarship on Jesus: Who Do They Say That He Is?

| Name | Title of Major Work(s) | Type of Feminist | View of Jesus |
|---|---|---|---|
| Mary Daly | *The Church and the Second Sex* (1968); *Beyond God the Father* (1973) | Radical | Worship of Jesus is idolatry; must overcome Christian fixation on Jesus |
| Virginia Mollenkott | *The Divine Feminine* (1983); *Godding* (1987); *Sensuous Spirituality* (1992); *Omnigender* (2001) | Radical | Jesus is our Elder Brother; humanity is corporately "Christed" into God-consciousness; erase gender boundaries |
| Daphne Hampson | *Theology and Feminism* (1990); *After Christianity* (1996) | Radical | Jesus is not God; Jesus did not die for our sins; Christianity is a myth |
| Letty Russell | *Human Liberation in a Feminist Perspective* (1974); *Becoming Human* (1982); *Feminist Interpretation of the Bible* (1985) | Reformist | Jesus is a unique revelation of true personhood; is a feminist who considered men and women to be equal |
| Rosemary Radford Ruether | *Sexism and God-Talk* (1983); *Womanguides* (1985) | Reformist/ Radical | Jesus is a mere man, a religious seeker inspired by a vision; this-worldly vision of the kingdom; speaks of feminism of Jesus; Jesus is paradigmatic liberator, yet asks, "How can a male savior save women?" |

*Continued on next page*

**Table A1.1** (*continued*)

| Name | Title of Major Work(s) | Type of Feminist | View of Jesus |
|---|---|---|---|
| Elisabeth Schüssler Fiorenza | *In Memory of Her* (1983); *Jesus: Miriam's Child, Sophia's Prophet* (1995); *Jesus and the Politics of Interpretation* (2001) | Reformist/ Radical | Sophia's prophet; Jesus launched renewal movement within Judaism, established discipleship of equals; decenter Jesus, focus on movement |
| Kathleen Corley | *Women & the Historical Jesus* (2002) | Jesus Seminar (Historical) | Notion that Jesus established discipleship of equals is itself a feminist myth of Christian origins; Jesus reaffirmed traditional marriage |
| Amy-Jill Levine | Editor, *The Feminist Companion* (2003–2004) | New feminism (Literary) | Judaism is more diverse, Jesus movement less egalitarian than alleged by Fiorenza; feminism has priority to Scripture; critical stance toward Scripture; variety of literary methods |
| Aida Spencer | *Beyond the Curse* (1985); essay in *Discovering Biblical Equality* (2004) | Evangelical (egalitarian) | Jesus was an egalitarian who taught humble mutual service, not male-female distinctions in leadership |
| Ruth Tucker | *Daughters of the Church* (1987); *Women in the Maze* (1992) | Evangelical (egalitarian) | Jesus' approach to women was revolutionary; taught ministry entails servanthood, not exercising authority |
| Linda Belleville | *Women Leaders and the Church* (2000); essay in *Two Views on Women in Ministry* (2001) | Evangelical (egalitarian) | Jesus was not quite the liberator of women he is sometimes supposed to be; Jesus treated women as social equals; called men *and* women as his disciples |

# THE NATURE OF BIBLICAL INTERPRETATION

*There are* vital questions that need to be answered in determining the meaning of Jesus' words and actions: How does one actually determine the meaning of a given text? What are the proper criteria for valid interpretation? Are texts to be understood as autonomous, meaning that they should be interpreted without reference to any historical-cultural factors? What influence does the reader or interpreter of the text have in discerning its meaning? What about the author? What is the role of one's "interpretive community," that is, the presuppositions and traditions shared by your particular affinity group (moderate Southern Baptists, conservative evangelicals, and so on)?

What, then, is the nature of biblical interpretation, properly conceived?[1] If *exegesis* is the task of explaining the biblical text, *hermeneutics* is the theory behind explaining the meaning of the biblical text, that is, the principles used to understand what a given passage means.[2] All of us engage in this task in ordinary, everyday communication when we communicate with words orally, in written form, electronically, or through other mediums. We

---

1. Summarized in W. W. Klein, "Evangelical Hermeneutics," in *Initiation into Theology*, ed. S. Maimela and A. König (Pretoria: J L van Schaik, 1998), 319–35.
2. Ibid., 319.

interpret the meaning that a person intended to communicate to us based on the words he or she used. Often we misunderstand because we incorrectly interpret their words.

The difficulty confronting the interpreter of Scripture's words, however, is bound up with the distance between the time when the Bible was originally written and today when the world is so different. Therefore, methods are needed to help us bridge this distance, methods that are not merely arbitrary and suit our own preferences but that fit the subject to be studied and are universally valid and result in determining the truth of Scripture.[3]

### The Foundation of Hermeneutics: View of Scripture

In keeping with Scripture's testimony regarding itself,[4] it is eminently fitting and appropriate to start an interpretive journey of Scripture with an affirmation of its inerrancy, inspiration, and final authority.[5] According to the testimony of the Bible, Scripture is both a divine and a human word; that is, God so inspired the writing of the biblical documents that the human authors remained free to express themselves in the words used at that time and in the cultural context, the customs of the time (1 Tim. 3:16; 2 Pet. 1:21; see Luke 1:1–4). This is a phenomenon described by B. B. Warfield as "concursive operation."[6]

While it is beyond the scope of this volume to provide a full-fledged defense of the inerrancy and inspiration of Scripture,[7] it is indisputable that an interpreter's view of Scripture forms one of the most important presuppositions he or she brings to the interpretation of the biblical text.

---

3. It may be helpful to note at this point that this approach to hermeneutics cannot be fit into a postmodern classification in the sense that it does not see itself as one of a group of legitimate hermeneutical options (e.g., charismatic hermeneutic, ecological hermeneutic). Rather, the approach taken here is to determine meaning in a way that is not contingent on the life situation of the interpreter. Therefore it would be erroneous to give this hermeneutic the title "patriarchal hermeneutic," since the interpreter, including this author who did not originally come to the text with this presupposition, does not enter into the hermeneutical process with the expectation to find patriarchy validated in the exegetical outcome.

4. W. Grudem, "Scripture's Self-Attestation and the Problem of Formulating a Doctrine of Scripture," in *Scripture and Truth*, ed. D. A. Carson and J. D. Woodbridge (Grand Rapids, MI: Zondervan, 1983), 19–59.

5. N. L. Geisler, *Inerrancy* (Grand Rapids, MI: Zondervan, 1980); D. S. Dockery, *Christian Scripture: An Evangelical Perspective on Inspiration, Authority and Interpretation* (Nashville: Broadman, 1995).

6. B. B. Warfield, "Revelation," in *The International Standard Bible Encyclopedia*, ed. J. Orr (Chicago: Howard-Severance, 1915), 4:2580a.

7. See the classic treatment by B. B. Warfield, *The Inspiration and Authority of Scripture*, rev. ed. (Philadelphia: Presbyterian & Reformed, 1948). See also Geisler, *Inerrancy*, esp. P. Feinberg, "The Meaning of Inerrancy," in ibid., 267–304; Dockery, *Christian Scripture*; and E. Schnabel, *Inspiration und Offenbarung: Die Lehre vom Ursprung und Wesen der Bibel*, 2nd ed. (Wuppertal: R. Brockhaus, 1997).

Those who take a more critical stance will use other criteria to judge the relevance of the biblical teaching for our world today. Such criteria include the interpreter's experience, reason, or ecclesiastical tradition. Contrarily, those who believe Scripture to be inerrant and inspired will approach it with a willingness to obey its teaching whether it fits with their personal preference or conforms to contemporary criteria of relevance.

### The Goal of Hermeneutics: Understanding Meaning

The objective of hermeneutics is to come as close as possible to the actual meaning of the text, that is, to the meaning intended by the biblical writers.[8] As Hirsch notes, "Validity requires a norm—a meaning that is stable and determinate no matter how broad its range of implication and application. A stable and determinate meaning requires an author's determining will. . . . All valid interpretation of every sort is founded on the re-cognition of what an author meant."[9] Klein likewise equates "*the meaning of the text*" with "*the meaning of the text that the biblical writers or editors intended their readers to understand.*"[10] He explains, "The *meaning of the texts themselves,*" in turn, is "the meaning the people at the time of the texts' composition would have been most likely to accept."[11]

To be sure, recent interpreters have severely criticized this approach to Scripture, and the pendulum has swung significantly to the notion that textual meaning is a function of the significance *perceived* by the reader rather than the meaning intended by the author. However, as Kevin Vanhoozer contends, this death of the author is not a liberating but a debilitating hermeneutical event.[12] If the notion of "the author" dies, so does the possibility of speaking truly about texts. Any interpretation will be as good as any other, with no adequate criteria to judge between valid and invalid understandings. If the author dies, so too does the possibility of meaning in texts. The reader has taken the place vacated by the author, and hence the entire notion of meaning has become ultimately meaningless.

---

8. E. D. Hirsch Jr., *Validity in Interpretation* (New Haven; London: Yale University Press, 1967); A. J. Köstenberger, R. D. Patterson, and S. R. Swain, *Invitation to Biblical Interpretation* (Grand Rapids: Kregel, forthcoming); G. R. Osborne, *The Hermeneutical Spiral: A Comprehensive Introduction to Biblical Interpretation*, rev. and exp. ed. (Downers Grove, IL: InterVarsity, 2006); M. J. Erickson, *Evangelical Interpretation: Perspectives on Hermeneutical Issues* (Grand Rapids, MI: Baker, 1993); K. J. Vanhoozer, *Is There a Meaning in This Text? The Bible, the Reader, and the Morality of Literary Knowledge* (Grand Rapids, MI: Zondervan, 1998); for a good summary of the hermeneutic used in the present work see Klein, "Evangelical Hermeneutics," 319–35; and more fully W. W. Klein, C. L. Blomberg, and R. L. Hubbard Jr., *Introduction to Biblical Interpretation*, 2nd ed. (Dallas: Word, 2004).
9. Hirsch, *Validity*, 126.
10. Klein, "Evangelical Hermeneutics," 325 (emphasis original).
11. Ibid. (emphasis original).
12. Vanhoozer, *Is There a Meaning?* 88.

Indeed, it is very difficult, and sometimes as good as impossible, to be certain that one has discovered the meaning intended by the original author, but as the author had something specifically in mind, it is imperative to try to come as close as possible to this meaning. As Klein writes:

> The meaning of a text is: *that which the words and grammatical structures of that text disclose about the probable intention of its author/editor and the probable understanding of the text by its intended readers*. . . . We cannot always perceive a text's meaning accurately or easily. Our modern preunderstandings and prejudices may cloud our ability to see the meaning clearly. But these difficulties do not obscure the goal: the text's meaning. It is God's word that we seek to unpack; only the inspired text possesses authority as God's word. Any other meaning besides the text's meaning is a meaning imposed onto the text. For the Evangelical, this would violate the divine character and purpose of the Scriptures: to reveal God's meaning.[13]

Once this meaning is identified, interpreters can apply it to their lives; i.e., they assess the text's significance for themselves. It is critical, however, that application follow interpretation.[14]

Some may object that the obscure origin and transmission of the biblical text alone testify to the fact that the aim of discovering the original intention of the author is academically naïve and untenable. This is part of the larger concern that it is impossible for us today to recover history "as it really was" by means of historical research. However, modern textual critics have demonstrated that biblical texts, particularly those of the New Testament, can allow for a confident determination of the original readings.[15] Therefore, the notion that the available text provides an adequate basis for seeking to reconstruct authorial intention is an academically defensible position with considerable support in the scientific academic community.[16]

### The Major Tasks of Exegesis

Evangelicals should be open to any method that is helpful in ascertaining the true meaning of a given biblical text on the basis of their belief that the

13. Klein, "Evangelical Hermeneutics," 326 (emphasis original).
14. Ibid.; see also the section "From Interpretation to Application" on pp. 332–34; and chap. 12, "Application," in Klein, Blomberg, and Hubbard, *Introduction.*
15. K. and B. Aland, *The Text of the New Testament*, 2nd rev. ed. (Grand Rapids, MI: Eerdmans, 1995); B. M. Metzger and B. D. Ehrman, *The Text of the New Testament: Its Transmission, Corruption, and Restoration*, 4th ed. (New York; Oxford: Oxford University Press, 2005); J. E. Komoszewski, M. J. Sawyer, and D. B. Wallace, *Reinventing Jesus* (Grand Rapids, MI: Kregel, 2006).
16. For defenses of the hermeneutical enterprise of reconstructing authorial intent, see the sources cited in n. 8 above.

Bible is the revealed and inspired Word of God.[17] In essence, interpretive competency entails skill in studying: (1) literary genre; (2) historical-cultural background; (3) the passage in its literary context.[18]

**Table A2.1: The Three Steps of Contextual Exegesis**

1) Determination of genre
2) Study of relevant historical-cultural background
3) Study of literary passage in context

The first step in proper interpretation is the accurate determination of the genre of a given passage; i.e., what kind of literature is represented by the text?[19] Biblical genres include historical narrative, poetry, wisdom, parable, epistle, prophecy, and apocalyptic. The determination of the genre of a given piece of communication is critical, because each genre has its own rules for interpretation, just as a board game is played by observing certain applicable rules.[20] In the present work, the major genre is gospel, which is itself a subgenre of historical narrative, recounting the teachings and actions of Jesus Christ and other figures with whom he had contact.[21]

The second task of interpretation as conceived by evangelicals is the determination of the historical-cultural background of a particular passage.[22] In the case of Jesus' stance toward women, the major primary sources are the canonical Gospels.[23] The Gospels are the primary sources due to their apostolic origin (or in the case of Mark and Luke, their connection to Peter and Paul, respectively), their early date, and the church's recognition of these writings as authentic, authoritative, and inspired. Once the relevant passages are studied on a case-by-case basis, a composite picture emerges that provides a cumulative understanding of how Jesus treated women.

17. Klein, "Evangelical Hermeneutics," 325.
18. For a helpful concise treatment of each of these tasks see Klein, "Evangelical Hermeneutics," 327–32; for a helpful discussion of the second, third, and fourth tasks see P. Cotterell and M. Turner, *Linguistics and Biblical Interpretation* (Downers Grove, IL: InterVarsity, 1989).
19. See especially Hirsch, *Validity*; G. D. Fee and D. Stuart, *How to Read the Bible for All Its Worth*, 3rd ed. (Grand Rapids, MI: Zondervan, 2003).
20. Hirsch, *Validity*.
21. The seminal work here is R. Burridge, *What Are the Gospels? A Comparison with Graeco-Roman Biography*, 2nd ed. (Grand Rapids, MI: Eerdmans, 2004); see also R. Bauckham, ed., *The Gospels for All Christians: Rethinking the Gospel Audiences* (Grand Rapids, MI: Eerdmans, 1997).
22. Osborne, *Hermeneutical Spiral*, chap. 5.
23. For a helpful treatment of the historical reliability of the Gospels see C. L. Blomberg, *The Historical Reliability of the Gospels*, 2nd ed. (Downers Grove, IL: InterVarsity, 2007).

In reconstructing the historical milieu in which Jesus operated, that is, first-century Palestinian Judaism, extrabiblical sources can be useful as well. The same is true for reconstructing the historical context of the respective evangelists. Caution must be exercised, however, when reconstructing historical background. Presuppositions will invariably affect historical research.[24] In order to avoid circularity, presuppositions must be carefully considered and bias clearly identified before attempting to engage in historical reconstruction.

The third task of interpretation is the study of a passage in its literary context. This entails the proper delimitation of the various literary contexts in the form of widening concentric circles, from immediate context (sentence, paragraph), to larger context (narrative unit, i.e., pericope), to the context of the book as a whole. For example, Jesus' words to Mary of Bethany at the anointing in John 12:5 have as their immediate context the anointing pericope as a whole (John 12:1–8). The larger context is the raising of Lazarus, which is narrated in John 11 (preceding the anointing) and the betrayal of Judas in John 13 (in the subsequent narrative). The whole-book context is the demonstration that Jesus is the Messiah and Son of God (John 20:30–31).

The study of a passage in its literary context involves determining the meaning of the various words that make up a particular text of Scripture.[25] The determination of word meanings is rendered even more critical for evangelicals who believe in the verbal inspiration of Scripture. Word meaning is best discerned by studying a word's usage in context and in parallel usage in other comparable texts. In the case of difficult or rare terms the determination of the meaning of a given word may be uncertain and remain in the realm of probability rather than certainty. The goal of interpretation in this regard, as conceived by evangelicals, is the approximation of the author's meaning as expressed in the text and as it would most likely have been understood by its first hearers or readers.

Also involved in a study of a passage in its literary context is the study of grammatical or syntactical relationships between the individual words of a particular text.[26] This step is called by many evangelicals "historical-grammatical exegesis," that is, interpretation that seeks to understand the meaning of a given biblical passage according to the rules of normal grammar as it was used at the time a given document was written. This means that biblical Hebrew, Aramaic, and Greek each follow certain patterns of expression, including rules for word order, case relations, verb tenses, conjunctions, and

24. See chap. 5, "The Interpreter," in Klein, Blomberg, and Hubbard, *Introduction*.
25. M. Silva, *Biblical Words and Their Meaning* (Grand Rapids, MI: Zondervan, 1983); J. P. Louw and E. A. Nida, *Greek-English Lexicon of the New Testament Based on Semantic Domains*, 2 vols. (New York: United Bible Societies, 1988, 1989).
26. Cotterell and Turner, *Linguistics*.

so on, which must be properly discerned and decoded for accurate interpretation to take place.

## General Hermeneutical Principles

In order to come as close as possible to the actual meaning of the text as intended by the author and to engage in the exegetical task, the following general hermeneutical principles should be kept in mind.

First, there is a need for a *listening hermeneutic*. As the German theologian Adolf Schlatter rightly notes, biblical exegesis ought to be based on the perception of what the texts are actually saying rather than the interpreter's creativity or ingenuity: "It is the historical objective that should govern our conceptual work exclusively and completely, stretching our perceptive faculties to the limit. We turn away decisively from ourselves and our time to what was found in the men through whom the church came into being. Our main interest should be the thought as it was conceived by them and the truth that was valid for them."[27]

Second, there is the need to *distinguish between the "first horizon" and the "second horizon" of biblical interpretation*. This involves understanding biblical language within its own context, which must be done before we start exploring its relevance to our own concerns, and "keeping the essential biblical context in view as a control on the way we apply biblical language to current issues."[28]

Third, there is a need for *interpretive restraint*, particularly where viewpoints tend to be entrenched and presuppositions threaten to skew the interpretive outcome. This means that the interpreter's conclusions should not exceed the evidence and must be stated cautiously. A cumulative case that is built on precarious interpretations of individual biblical passages will not be able to carry the weight of careful examination. This pertains particularly to the way in which interpreters read between the lines and supply information not stated explicitly in the text.

Table A2.2: General Hermeneutical Principles

| Principle | Explanation |
|---|---|
| 1) Listening hermeneutic | Cultivate perceptiveness in interpretation |
| 2) Distinguish between two horizons | First find original meaning, then assess significance |
| 3) Need for interpretive restraint | Recognize own biases; do not exceed the evidence |

27. A. Schlatter, *The History of the Christ: The Foundation of New Testament Theology*, trans. A. J. Köstenberger (Grand Rapids, MI: Baker, 1997 [1923]), 18.
28. Osborne, *Hermeneutical Spiral*, 521, citing R. T. France, "The Church and the Kingdom of God: Some Hermeneutical Issues," in *Biblical Interpretation and the Church: The Problem of Contextualization*, ed. D. A. Carson (Nashville: Thomas Nelson, 1984), 42.

# BIBLIOGRAPHY

Abrahams, L. A. L. "A critical comparison of Elisabeth Schüssler Fiorenza's notion of Christian ministry as a 'Discipleship of Equals' and Mercy Amba Oduyoye's notion as a 'Partnership of both men and women.'" Minithesis, University of Western Cape, 2005.

Ackermann, D. M. "Feminist and Womanist Hermeneutics." In *Initiation into Theology: The Rich Variety of Theology and Hermeneutics*, edited by S. Maimela and A. König, 349–58. Pretoria: J L van Schaik, 1998.

Aland, K. and B. *The Text of the New Testament*. 2nd rev. ed. Grand Rapids, MI: Eerdmans, 1995.

Anderson, J. C. "Matthew: Gender and Reading." *Semeia* 28 (1983): 3–27. Reprinted in *A Feminist Companion to Matthew*, edited by A.-J. Levine, 25–51. Cleveland, OH: Pilgrim, 2004.

Baird, W. *History of New Testament Research*. Vol. 1, *From Deism to Tübingen*. Minneapolis: Augsburg Fortress, 1992.

____. *History of New Testament Research*. Vol. 2, *From Jonathan Edwards to Rudolf Bultmann*. Minneapolis: Augsburg Fortress, 2003.

Barr, J. *Fundamentalism*. 2nd ed. London: SCM, 1981.

Batey, R. A. *Jesus and the Forgotten City: New Light on Sepphoris and the Urban World of Jesus*. Grand Rapids, MI: Baker, 1992.

Bauckham, R., ed. *The Gospels for All Christians: Rethinking the Gospel Audiences*. Grand Rapids, MI: Eerdmans, 1997.

____. *Jesus and the Eyewitnesses: The Gospels as Eyewitness Testimony*. Grand Rapids, MI: Eerdmans, 2006.

Baumgardner, J., and A. Richards. *Manifesta: Young Women, Feminism, and the Future*. New York: Farrar, Straus and Giroux, 2000.

Belleville, L. L. *Women Leaders and the Church: Three Crucial Questions*. Grand Rapids, MI: Baker, 2000.

____. "Women in Ministry." In *Two Views on Women in Ministry*, edited by J. R. Beck and C. L. Blomberg, 75–154. Grand Rapids: Zondervan, 2001.

Bianchi, E. C., and R. R. Ruether. *From Machismo to Mutuality: Essays on Sexism and Woman-Man Liberation*. New York: Paulist, 1976.

Bilezikian, G. *Beyond Sex Roles*. 2nd ed. Grand Rapids, MI: Baker, 1985.

Block, D. I. "Marriage and Family in Ancient Israel." In *Marriage and Family in the Biblical World*, edited by K. M. Campbell, 33–102. Downers Grove, IL: InterVarsity, 2003.

Blomberg, C. L. *The Historical Reliability of the Gospels*. 2nd ed. Downers Grove, IL: InterVarsity, 2007.

Bock, Darrell L. *Luke*. Baker Exegetical Commentary on the New Testament. 2 vols. Grand Rapids, MI: Baker, 1994, 1996.

Bolt, C. *The Women's Movements in the United States and Britain from the 1790s to the 1920s*. Amherst, MA: The University of Massachusetts Press, 1993.

Bolt, P. G., and M. D. Thompson, eds. *Gospel of the Nations*. Leicester: InterVarsity, 2000.

Borland, J. A. "Women in the Life and Teachings of Jesus." In *Recovering Biblical Manhood and Womanhood: A Response to Evangelical Feminism*, edited by J. Piper and W. Grudem, 113–23. Wheaton, IL: Crossway, 1991.

Brooten, B. J. *Women Leaders in the Ancient Synagogue: Inscriptional Evidence and Background Issues*. Brown Judaic Studies 36. Chico, CA: Scholars Press, 1982.

Brown, A. "Exegesis of I Corinthians XIV, 34, 35 and I Timothy II, 11, 12." *Oberlin Quarterly* 4 (1849): 358–73.

Bruce, F. F. *Apostle of the Heart Set Free*. Grand Rapids, MI: Eerdmans, 1977.

____. *The Canon of Scripture*. Downers Grove, IL: InterVarsity, 1988.

Burridge, R. *What Are the Gospels? A Comparison with Graeco-Roman Biography*. 2nd ed. Grand Rapids, MI: Eerdmans, 2004.

Bush, L. R., and T. J. Nettles. *Baptists and the Bible*. Nashville: Broadman, 1980. Rev. and exp. ed. 1999.

Carlston, C. E. "Proverbs, Maxims, and the Historical Jesus." *Journal of Biblical Literature* 99 (1980): 87–105.

Carson, D. A. *Exegetical Fallacies*. 2nd ed. Grand Rapids, MI: Baker, 1996.

____. *The Gagging of God: Christianity Confronts Pluralism*. Grand Rapids, MI: Zondervan, 1996.

____. *The Gospel according to John*. Pillar New Testament Commentary. Grand Rapids, MI: Eerdmans, 1991.

Carson, D. A., and D. J. Moo. *An Introduction to the New Testament*. 2nd ed. Grand Rapids, MI: Zondervan, 2005.

Carson, D. A., and J. D. Woodbridge, eds. *Hermeneutics, Authority, and Canon*. Grand Rapids, MI: Zondervan, 1986.

____. *Scripture and Truth*. Grand Rapids, MI: Zondervan, 1983.

Carter, W. "Getting Martha out of the Kitchen: Luke 10.38–42 Again." In *A Feminist Companion to Luke*, edited by A.-J. Levine, 214–31. Cleveland, OH: Pilgrim, 2004.

Chancey, M. A. "How Jewish Was Jesus' Galilee?" *Biblical Archaeology Review* 33, no. 4 (July/August 2007): 42–50, 76.

Clark, S. B. *Man and Woman in Christ*. Ann Arbor, MI: Servant Books, 1980.

Cochran, P. D. H. *Evangelical Feminism: A History*. New York; London: New York University Press, 2005.

Cohick, L. H. "Why Women Followed Jesus: A Discussion of Female Piety." *Scottish Bulletin of Evangelical Theology* 25 (2007): 172–93.

Collins, A. Y., ed. *Feminist Perspectives on Biblical Scholarship*. Biblical Scholarship in North America 10. Chico, CA: Scholars Press, 1985.

Conway, C. M. "Gender Matters in John." In *A Feminist Companion to John*. Vol. 2, edited by A.-J. Levine, 79–103. Cleveland, OH: Pilgrim, 2003.

____. *Men and Women in the Fourth Gospel: Gender and Johannine Characterization*. SBL Dissertation Series 167. Atlanta: Scholars Press, 1999.

____. "The Production of the Johannine Community: A New Historicist Perspective." *Journal of Biblical Literature* 121 (2002): 479–95.

Corley, K. E. "The Egalitarian Jesus. A Christian Myth of Origins." *Forum* n.s. 1–2 (1998): 291–325.

____. "Slaves, Servants and Prostitutes: Gender and Social Class in Mark." In *A Feminist Companion to Mark*, edited by A.-J. Levine. Cleveland, OH: Pilgrim, 2004, 191–221.

____. *Women and the Historical Jesus: Feminist Myths of Christian Origins*. Santa Rosa, CA: Polebridge, 2002.

Cotterell, P., and M. Turner. *Linguistics and Biblical Interpretation*. Downers Grove, IL: InterVarsity, 1989.

Cottrell, J. *Feminism and the Bible*. Joplin, MO: College Press, 1992.

Cranfield, C. E. B. "St. Mark 16.1–8." *Scottish Journal of Theology* 5 (1952): 282–98; 398–414.

Crossan, J. D. *The Historical Jesus: The Life of a Mediterranean Jewish Peasant*. San Francisco: Harper, 1991.

D'Angelo, M. R. "Theology in Mark and Q: Abba and 'Father' in Context." *Harvard Theological Review* 85 (1992): 149–74.

Daly, M. *Beyond God the Father: Toward a Philosophy of Women's Liberation*. Boston: Beacon, 1973.

____. *The Church and the Second Sex*. Boston: Beacon, 1968.

____. *Gyn/Ecology: The Metaethics of Radical Feminism*. Boston: Beacon, 1978.

____. *Pure Lust: Elemental Feminist Philosophy*. Boston: Beacon, 1984.

Dandamayev, M. A. "Slavery." In *Anchor Bible Dictionary*. Vol. 6, edited by D. N. Freedman, 58–73. Garden City, NY: Doubleday, 1992.

Danove, P. "The Characterization and Narrative Function of the Women at the Tomb (Mark 15, 40–41, 47; 16, 1–8." *Biblica* 77 (1996): 375–97.

Dayton, D. W. *Discovering an Evangelical Heritage*. New York: Harper, 1976.

De Beauvoir, S. *The Second Sex*. New York: Random House, 1952 [1949].

De Boer, E. A. "The Lukan Mary Magdalene and the Other Women Following Jesus." In *A Feminist Companion to Mark*, edited by A.-J. Levine, 106–20. Cleveland, OH: Pilgrim, 2004.

Dewey, J. "The Gospel of Mark." In *Searching the Scriptures*. Vol. 2, *A Feminist Commentary*, edited by E. S. Fiorenza, 470–509. New York: Crossroad, 1994.

Dockery, D. S. *Christian Scripture: An Evangelical Perspective on Inspiration, Authority and Interpretation*. Nashville: Broadman, 1995.

Du Toit, C. "African Hermeneutics." In *Initiation into Theology: The Rich Variety of Theology and Hermeneutics*, edited by S. Maimela and A. König. Pretoria: J L van Schaik, 1998.

Elliott, J. H. "The Jesus Movement Was Not Egalitarian but Family-Oriented." *Biblical Interpretation* 11/2 (2003): 173–210.

____. "Jesus Was Not an Egalitarian. A Critique of an Anachronistic and Idealist Theory." *Biblical Theology Bulletin* 32/3 (2002): 75–91.

Erickson, M. J. *Evangelical Interpretation: Perspectives on Hermeneutical Issues*. Grand Rapids, MI: Baker, 1993.

____. *Truth or Consequences: The Promise and Perils of Postmodernism*. Downers Grove, IL: InterVarsity, 2001.

Evans, M. J. *Woman in the Bible*. Downers Grove, IL: InterVarsity, 1983.

Fander, M. "Historical-Critical Methods." In *Searching the Scriptures*, Vol. 1, *A Feminist Introduction*, edited by E. S. Fiorenza 205–24. New York: Crossroad, 1994.

Farley, M. A. "Feminist Consciousness and the Interpretation of Scripture." In *Feminist Interpretation of the Bible*, edited by L. M. Russell, 41–51. Philadelphia: Westminster, 1985.

Fee, G. D., and D. Stuart. *How to Read the Bible for All It's Worth*. 3rd ed. Grand Rapids, MI: Zondervan, 2003.

Feinberg, P. "The Meaning of Inerrancy." In *Inerrancy*, edited by N. L. Geisler, 267–304. Grand Rapids, MI: Zondervan, 1980.

Felix, P. W., Sr. "The Hermeneutics of Evangelical Feminism." In *Evangelical Hermeneutics: The New Versus the Old*, edited by R. L. Thomas, 373–405. Grand Rapids, MI: Kregel, 2002.

Ferguson, E. "Egyptian Deities: Isis, Osiris, and Sarapis." In *Backgrounds of Early Christianity*, 2nd ed, 249–61. Grand Rapids, MI: Eerdmans, 1993.

Fiorenza, E. S. *Bread Not Stone: The Challenge of Feminist Interpretation*. Boston: Beacon, 1995.

____. *But She Said: Feminist Practices of Biblical Interpretation*. Boston: Beacon, 1993.

____. *Discipleship of Equals*. New York: Herder, 1993.

____. "Emerging Issues in Feminist Biblical Interpretation." In *Christian Feminism: Visions of a New Humanity*, edited by J. L. Weidman, 33–54. San Francisco: Harper, 1984.

____. "A Feminist Critical Interpretation for Liberation: Martha and Mary: Lk. 10:39–42." *Religion & Intellectual Life* 3/2 (1986): 21–36.

____. *In Memory of Her: A Feminist Theological Reconstruction of Christian Origins*. New York: Crossroad, 1983

____. *Jesus and the Politics of Interpretation*. New York: Continuum, 2000.

____. *Jesus: Miriam's Child, Sophia's Prophet: Critical Issues in Feminist Christology*. New York: Continuum, 1994.

____. *The Power of Naming*. Maryknoll, NY: Orbis, 1996.

____. "Remembering the Past in Creating the Future: Historical-Critical Scholarship and Feminist Biblical Interpretation." In *Feminist Perspectives on Biblical Scholarship*, edited by A. Y. Collins, 43–64. Chico, CA: Scholars Press, 1985.

____. *Rhetoric and Ethic: The Politics of Biblical Studies*. Minneapolis: Augsburg Fortress, 1999.

____, ed. *Searching the Scriptures*. 2 vols. New York: Crossroad, 1994.

____. *Sharing Her Word: Feminist Biblical Interpretation in Context*. Boston: Beacon, 1999.

____. "Toward a Feminist Biblical Hermeneutics: Biblical Interpretation and Liberation Theology." In *The Challenge of Liberation Theology: A First World Response*, edited by B. Mahan and L. D. Richesin. Maryknoll, 91–112. New York: Orbis, 1981.

____. "Transgressing Canonical Boundaries." In *Searching the Scriptures*. Vol. 2: *A Feminist Commentary*, edited by E. S. Fiorenza, 1–14. New York: Crossroad, 1994.

____. *Wisdom Ways: Introducing Feminist Biblical Interpretation*. Maryknoll, NY: Orbis, 2001.

Foh, S. T. *Women and the Word of God: A Response to Biblical Feminism*. Phillipsburg, NJ: Presbyterian and Reformed, 1979.

France, R. T. "The Church and the Kingdom of God: Some Hermeneutical Issues." In *Biblical Interpretation and the Church: The Problem of Contextualization*, edited by D. A. Carson, 30–44. Nashville: Nelson, 1984.

____. *The Gospel of Mark*. New International Greek Testament Commentary. Grand Rapids, MI: Eerdmans, 2002.

____. *Women in the Church's Ministry: A Test Case for Biblical Interpretation*. Grand Rapids, MI: Eerdmans, 1995.

Freed, E. D. "The Women in Matthew's Genealogy." *Journal for the Study of the New Testament* 29 (1987): 3–19.

Gadamer, H.-G. *Truth and Method*. Translated by G. Broden and J. Cumming. 2nd ed. New York: Crossroad, 1982 [1965].

Geisler, N. L., ed. *Inerrancy*. Grand Rapids, MI: Zondervan, 1980.

Gifford, C. "American Women and the Bible: The Nature of Woman as a Hermeneutical Issue." In *Feminist Perspectives on Biblical Scholarship*, edited by A. Y. Collins, 11–34. Chico, CA: Scholars Press, 1985.

Grassi, J. A. "The Secret Heroine of Mark's Drama." *Biblical Theology Bulletin* 18 (1988): 10–15.

Greene-McCreight, K. *Feminist Reconstructions of Christian Doctrine: Narrative Analysis and Appraisal*. New York; Oxford: Oxford University Press, 2000.

Grenz, S. J. with D. M. Kjesbo. *Women in the Church: A Biblical Theology of Women in Ministry*. Downers Grove, IL: InterVarsity, 1995.

Grimké, A. *Appeal to Christian Women in the South*. New York, 1836.

Grimké, S. "Letters on the Equality of the Sexes and the Condition of Women." New York, 1837.

Groothuis, D. "What Jesus Thought about Women." *Priscilla Papers* 16, no. 3 (2002): 17–20.

Grudem, W. *Evangelical Feminism and Biblical Truth*. Sisters, OR: Multnomah, 2004.

____. "The Myth of 'Mutual Submission.'" *CBMW News* 1, no. 4 (October 1996): 1, 3–4.

____. "Scripture's Self-Attestation and the Problem of Formulating a Doctrine of Scripture." In *Scripture and Truth*, edited by D. A. Carson and J. D. Woodbridge, 19–59. Grand Rapids, MI: Zondervan, 1983.

Guelich, R. A. *Mark 1–8:26*. Word Biblical Commentary 34A. Dallas: Word, 1989.

Gundry, Stanley N. "Evangelical Theology: Where *Should* We Be Going?" *Journal of the Evangelical Theological Society* 22/1 (1979): 3–13.

Gutierrez, G. *A Theology of Liberation: History, Politics, and Salvation*. Maryknoll, NY: Orbis, 1973 [1972].

Hagner, D. A. *Matthew*. WBC 33. 2 vols. Dallas: Word, 1993, 1995.

Hampson, D. *After Christianity*. Valley Forge, PA: Trinity Press International, 1996.

____. "BISFT Interview with Dr Daphne Hampson." *Feminist Theology* 17 (1998): 39–57.

____. "On Not Remembering Her." *Feminist Theology* 19 (1998): 63–83.

____. "On Power and Gender." *Modern Theology* 4, no. 3 (1988): 234–50.

____, ed. *Swallowing a Fishbone: Feminist Theologians Debate Christianity*. London: SPCK, 1996.

____. *Theology and Feminism*. Oxford: Blackwell, 1990.

Hampson, D., and R. R. Ruether. "Is there a place for feminists in the Christian Church?" *New Blackfriars* 68 (1987): 7–24.

Harris, R. L. *Inspiration and Canonicity of the Scriptures*. Greenville, SC: A Press, 1995.

Hays, R. B. *The Moral Vision of the New Testament*. New York: Harper, 1996.

Hayter, M. *The New Eve in Christ: The Use and Abuse of the Bible in the Debate about Women in the Church*. Grand Rapids, MI: Eerdmans, 1987.

Henry, C. F. H. *God, Revelation and Authority*. 6 vols. Waco, TX: Word, 1976–1983.

Herrstrom, D. S. "The Book of Unknowing: Ranging the Landscape." Unpublished manuscript, 1999.

Heywood, L. L., ed. *The Women's Movement Today: An Encyclopedia of Third-Wave Feminism*. 2 vols. Westport, CT: Greenwood Press, 2005.

Heywood, L., and J. Drake, eds. *Third Wave Agenda: Being Feminist, Doing Feminism*. Minneapolis; London: University of Minnesota Press, 1997.

Hirsch, E. D., Jr. *Validity in Interpretation*. New Haven; London: Yale University Press, 1967.

Hornsby, T. J. "The Woman Is a Sinner/The Sinner Is a Woman." In *A Feminist Companion to Mark*, edited by A.-J. Levine, 121–32. Cleveland, OH: Pilgrim, 2004.

Hove, R. *Equal in Christ? Galatians 3:28 and the Gender Dispute*. Wheaton, IL: Crossway, 1999.

Hughes, P. E. "The Truth of Scripture and the Problem of Historical Relativity." In *Scripture and Truth*, edited by D. A. Carson and J. D. Woodbridge, 173–94. Grand Rapids, MI: Zondervan, 1983.

Humphries-Brooks, S. "The Canaanite Women in Matthew." In *A Feminist Companion to Matthew*, edited by A.-J. Levine, 138–56. Cleveland, OH: Pilgrim, 2004.

Hurley, J. B. *Man and Woman in Biblical Perspective*. Grand Rapids, MI: Zondervan, 1981.

Jeremias, J. *Jerusalem in the Time of Jesus*. Philadelphia: Fortress, 1969.

Jewett, P. K. *Man as Male and Female: A Study of Sexual Relationships from a Theological Point of View*. Grand Rapids, MI: Eerdmans, 1975.

Kassian, M. A. *The Feminist Gospel: The Movement to Unite Feminism with the Church*. Wheaton, IL: Crossway, 1992. Rev. ed.

____. *The Feminist Mistake: The Radical Impact of Feminism on the Church and Culture*. Wheaton, IL: Crossway, 2005.

Keener, C. S. *The Gospel of John*. 2 vols. Peabody, MA: Hendrickson, 2003.

Kelsey, D. H. *The Uses of Scripture in Recent Theology*. Philadelphia: Fortress, 1975.

Kitzberger, I. R. "Transcending Gender Boundaries in John." In *A Feminist Companion to John*, vol. 1, edited by A.-J. Levine, 173–207. Cleveland, OH: Pilgrim, 2003.

Klein, W. W. "Evangelical Hermeneutics." In *Initiation into Theology: The Rich Variety of Theology and Hermeneutics*, edited by S. Maimela and A. König, 319–35. Pretoria: J L van Schaik, 1998.

Klein, W. W., C. L. Blomberg, and R. L. Hubbard, Jr. *Introduction to Biblical Interpretation*. 2nd ed. Dallas: Word, 2004.

Komoszewski, J. E., M. J. Sawyer, and D. B. Wallace. *Reinventing Jesus*. Grand Rapids, MI: Kregel, 2006.

Kopas, J. "Jesus and Women in Mark's Gospel." *Religious Studies Review* 44 (1985): 912–20.

Köstenberger, A. J. "Gender Passages in the NT: Hermeneutical Fallacies Critiqued." *Westminster Theological Journal* 56 (1994): 259–83.

____. *God, Marriage, and Family: Rebuilding the Biblical Foundation*. Wheaton, IL: Crossway, 2004.

____. "Head." In *The New Interpreter's Dictionary of the Bible*. Vol. 2, *D–H*, edited by K. D. Sakenfeld, 754–55. Nashville: Abingdon, 2007.

____. *John*. BECNT. Grand Rapids, MI: Baker, 2004.

____, ed. Quo Vadis, *Evangelicals? Perspectives on the Past, Direction for the Future: Nine Presidential Addresses from the First Fifty Years of the* Journal of the Evangelical Theological Society. Wheaton, IL: Crossway, 2007.

____. *Studies in John and Gender: A Decade of Scholarship*. Studies in Biblical Literature 38. New York: Peter Lang, 2001.

____, ed. *Whatever Happened to Truth?* Wheaton, IL: Crossway, 2005.

____. "Women in the Pauline Mission." In *Studies on John and Gender: A Decade of Scholarship*. Studies in Biblical Literature 38, 323–52. New York: Peter Lang, 2001.

Köstenberger, A. J., T. R. Schreiner, and H. S. Baldwin, eds. *Women in the Church: A Fresh Analysis of 1 Timothy 2:9–15*. Grand Rapids, MI: Baker, 1995. 2nd ed. Köstenberger, A. J. and T. R. Schreiner, eds. *Women in the Church: An Analysis and Application of 1 Timothy 2:9–15*. Grand Rapids, MI: Baker, 2005.

Köstenberger, M. E. "Feminist Biblical Interpretation" and "Feminist Theology." In *Encyclopedia of Christian Civilization*, edited by G. T. Kurian. Oxford: Blackwell, forthcoming.

Krause, D. "Simon Peter's Mother-in-Law—Disciple or Domestic Servant? Feminist Biblical Hermeneutics and the Interpretation of Mark 1.29–31." In *A Feminist Companion to Mark*, edited by A.-J. Levine, 37–53. Cleveland, OH: Pilgrim, 2004.

Lee, D. A. "Abiding in the Fourth Gospel: A Case Study in Feminist Biblical Theology." In *A Feminist Companion to John*. Vol. 2, edited by A.-J. Levine, 64–78. Cleveland, OH: Pilgrim, 2003.

____. "Beyond Suspicion? The Fatherhood of God in the Fourth Gospel." *Pacifica* 8 (1995): 140–54.

____. "Reclaiming the Sacred Text—Christian Feminism and Spirituality." In *Claiming Our Ties: Studies in Religion by Australian Women Scholars*, edited by J. Morny and P. Magee, 80–84. Sydney: Australian Association for the Study of Religion, 1994.

Levine, A.-J., ed. *A Feminist Companion to John*. 2 vols. Cleveland, OH: Pilgrim, 2003.

____, ed. *A Feminist Companion to Luke*. Cleveland, OH: Pilgrim, 2004.

____, ed. *A Feminist Companion to Mark*. Cleveland, OH: Pilgrim, 2004.

____, ed. *A Feminist Companion to Matthew*. Cleveland, OH: Pilgrim, 2004.

____. "Second Temple Judaism, Jesus, and Women: Yeast of Eden." *Biblical Interpretation* 2/1 (1994): 8–33.

Longenecker, R. N. "Authority, Hierarchy & Leadership Patterns in the Bible." In *Women, Authority and the Bible*, edited by A. Mickelsen, 66–85. Downers Grove, IL: InterVarsity, 1986.

____. *New Testament Social Ethics for Today*. Grand Rapids, MI: Eerdmans, 1984.

____. "On the Concept of Development in Pauline Thought." In *Perspectives on Evangelical Theology*, edited by K. S. Kantzer and S. N. Gundry, 195–207. Grand Rapids, MI: Baker, 1979.

Louw, J. P., and E. A. Nida. *Greek-English Lexicon of the New Testament Based on Semantic Domains*. 2 vols. New York: United Bible Societies, 1988, 1989.

Maccini, R. G. *Her Testimony Is True: Women as Witnesses according to John*. JSNTSup 125. Sheffield: Sheffield Academic Press, 1996.

Maimela, S., and A. König, eds. *Initiation into Theology: The Rich Variety of Theology and Hermeneutics*. Pretoria: J L van Schaik, 1998.

Malbon, E. S. "Fallible Followers: Women and Men in the Gospel of Mark." *Semeia* 28 (1983): 29–48.

Malbon, E. S., and J. C. Anderson. "Literary-Critical Methods." In *Searching the Scriptures*. Vol. 1, *A Feminist Introduction*, edited by E. S. Fiorenza, 241–54. New York: Crossroad, 1994.

McClelland, S. E. "The New Reality in Christ: Perspectives from Biblical Studies." In *Gender Matters: Women's Studies for the Christian Community*, edited by J. S. Hagen, 51–78. Grand Rapids, MI: Zondervan, 1990.

McDonald, L. M. "Canon." In *Dictionary of the Later New Testament and Its Developments*, edited by R. Martin and P. H. Davids, 134–44. Downers Grove, IL: InterVarsity, 1997.

Metzger, B. M. *The Canon of the New Testament: Its Origin, Development, and Significance*. Oxford: Clarendon, 1987.

Metzger, B. M., and B. D. Ehrman. *The Text of the New Testament: Its Transmission, Corruption, and Restoration*. 4th ed. New York; Oxford: Oxford University Press, 2005.

Mickelsen, A., ed. *Women, Authority and the Bible*. Downers Grove, IL: InterVarsity, 1986.

Mollenkott, V. R. *The Divine Feminine: The Biblical Imagery of God as Female*. New York: Crossroad, 1983.

____. *Godding: Human Responsibility and the Bible*. New York: Crossroad, 1987.

____. *Omnigender: A Trans-Religious Approach*. Cleveland, OH: Pilgrim Press, 2001.

____. *Sensuous Spirituality: Out from Fundamentalism*. New York: Crossroad, 1992.

____. *Speech, Silence, Action! The Cycle of Faith*. Nashville: Abingdon, 1980.

____. *Women, Men & the Bible*. 2nd ed. Nashville: Abingdon, 1988 [1977].

Moore, S. D. "Are There Impurities in the Living Water That the Johannine Jesus Dispenses?" In *A Feminist Companion to John*. Vol. 1, edited by A.-J. Levine, 78–97. Cleveland, OH: Pilgrim, 2003.

Moreland, J. P. "Truth, Contemporary Philosophy, and the Postmodern Turn." In *Whatever Happened to Truth?* edited by A. J. Köstenberger, 75–92. Wheaton, IL: Crossway, 2005.

Munro, W. "Women Disciples in Mark?" *Catholic Biblical Quarterly* 44 (1982): 225–41.

Neuer, W. *Man and Woman in Christian Perspective*. Wheaton, IL: Crossway, 1991.

Newsom, C. A., and S. H. Ringe, eds. *The Women's Bible Commentary*. Louisville: Westminster, 1992.

Neyrey, J. H. "What's Wrong with This Picture? John 4, Cultural Stereotypes of Women, and Public and Private Space." In *A Feminist Companion to John*. Vol. 1, edited by A.-J. Levine, 98–125. Cleveland, OH: Pilgrim, 2003.

Ng, E. Y. L. *Reconstructing Christian Origins? The Feminist Theology of Elisabeth Schüssler Fiorenza: An Evaluation.* Carlisle: Paternoster, 2002.

Nolland, J. "The Four (Five) Women and Other Annotations in Matthew's Genealogy." *New Testament Studies* 43 (1997): 527–39.

____. *The Gospel of Matthew.* New International Greek Testament Commentary. Grand Rapids, MI: Eerdmans, 2005.

____. *Luke.* 3 vols. Word Biblical Commentary 35. Dallas: Word, 1989, 1993.

Nordling, C. F. "Feminist Biblical Interpretation." In *Dictionary for Theological Interpretation of the Bible,* edited by K. J. Vanhoozer, 228–30. Grand Rapids, MI: Baker, 2005.

O'Day, G. R. "Surprised by Faith: Jesus and the Canaanite Woman." In *A Feminist Companion to Matthew,* edited by A.-J. Levine, 114–25. Cleveland, OH: Pilgrim, 2004.

Oduyoye, M. A. "African Women's Hermeneutics." In *Initiation into Theology: The Rich Variety of Theology and Hermeneutics,* edited by S. Maimela and A. König, 359–71. Pretoria: J L van Schaik, 1998.

Okure, T. *The Johannine Approach to Mission.* WUNT 2/31. Tübingen: Mohr-Siebeck, 1987.

Osborne, G. R. "Women in Jesus' Ministry." *Westminster Theological Journal* 51 (1989): 259–91.

____. *The Hermeneutical Spiral: A Comprehensive Introduction to Biblical Interpretation.* 2nd ed. Downers Grove, IL: InterVarsity, 2006.

Osborne, H., ed. *Whom Do Men Say That I Am? A Collection of the Views of the Most Notable Christian and Non-Christian Modern Authors about Jesus of Nazareth.* London: Faber & Faber, 1932.

Osiek, C. "The Feminist and the Bible: Hermeneutical Alternatives." In *Feminist Perspectives on Biblical Scholarship,* edited by A. Y. Collins, 93–105. SBL Cent. Publ. 10. Chico, CA: Scholars Press, 1985.

Pache, R. *The Inspiration and Authority of Scripture.* Translated by H. I. Needham. Chicago: Moody, 1969.

Pape, D. *In Search of God's Ideal Woman: A Personal Examination of the New Testament.* Downers Grove, IL: InterVarsity, 1978.

Patterson, D. K. "Aspects of a Biblical Theology of Womanhood." Th.D. thesis, University of South Africa, 1997.

Phelan, J. E. "Women and the Aims of Jesus." *Priscilla Papers* 18/1 (2004): 7–11.

Phillips, V. C. "Feminist Interpretation." In *Dictionary of Biblical Interpretation,* edited by J. H. Hayes, 388–98. Nashville: Abingdon, 1999.

Pierce, R. W., and R. M. Groothuis, eds. *Discovering Biblical Equality: Complementarity without Hierarchy.* Downers Grove, IL: InterVarsity, 2004.

Piper, J., and W. Grudem, eds. *Recovering Biblical Manhood and Womanhood.* Wheaton, IL: Crossway, 1991.

Reid, B. E. "'Do You See This Woman?' A Liberative Look at Luke 7:36–50 and Strategies for Reading Other Lukan Stories against the Grain." In *A Feminist Companion to Mark,* edited by A.-J. Levine, 106–20. Cleveland, OH: Pilgrim, 2004.

Reinhartz, A. "The Gospel of John." In *Searching the Scriptures*. Vol. 2, *A Feminist Commentary*, edited by E. S. Fiorenza, 561–600. New York: Crossroad, 1994.

____. "Women in the Johannine Community: An Exercise in Historical Imagination." In *A Feminist Companion to John*. Vol. 2, edited by A.-J. Levine, 14–33. Cleveland, OH: Pilgrim, 2003.

Ringe, S. H. "A Gentile Woman's Story, Revisited: Rereading Mark 7.24–31a." In *A Feminist Companion to Mark*, edited by A.-J. Levine, 79–100. Cleveland, OH: Pilgrim, 2004.

Rogers, J. B., and D. K. McKim. *The Authority and Interpretation of the Bible: An Historical Approach*. New York: Harper, 1979.

Ruether, R. R. *The Church against Itself: An Inquiry into the Conditions of Historical Existence for the Eschatological Community*. New York: Herder, 1967.

____. *Liberation Theology: Human Hope Confronts Christian History and American Power*. New York: Paulist, 1972.

____. *Mary, the Feminine Face of the Church*. Philadelphia: Westminster, 1979 [1977].

____. *New Woman, New Earth: Sexist Ideologies and Human Liberation*. New York: Seabury, 1975.

____. *The Radical Kingdom: The Western Experience of Messianic Hope*. New York: Harper, 1970.

____, ed. *Religion and Sexism: Images of Woman in the Jewish and Christian Traditions*. New York: Simon & Schuster, 1974.

Ruether, R. R., and E. McLaughlin, eds. "Feminist Interpretation: A Method of Correlation." In *Feminist Interpretation of the Bible*, edited by L. M. Russell, 111–24. Philadelphia: Westminster, 1985.

____. *Gaia and God: An Ecofeminist Theology of Earth Healing*. San Francisco: HarperSanFrancisco, 1992.

____. *Introducing Redemption in Christian Feminism*. Sheffield: Sheffield Academic Press, 1998.

____. *Sexism and God-Talk: Toward a Feminist Theology*. Boston: Beacon, 1993 [1983].

____. *To Change the World: Christology and Cultural Criticism*. New York: Crossroad, 1981.

____. *Womanguides: Readings toward a Feminist Theology*. Boston: Beacon, 1985.

____. *Women and Redemption: A Theological History*. Minneapolis: Augsburg Fortress, 1998.

____. *Women of Spirit: Female Leadership in the Jewish and Christian Traditions*. New York: Simon & Schuster, 1979.

____. *Women-Church: Theology and Practice of Feminist Liturgical Communities*. San Francisco: HarperSanFrancisco, 1985.

Russell, L. M. *Becoming Human*. Philadelphia: Westminster, 1982.

____. *Church in the Round: Feminist Interpretation of the Church*. Louisville: Westminster John Knox, 1993.

____, ed. *Feminist Interpretation of the Bible*. Philadelphia: Westminster, 1985.

_____. *Household of Freedom: Authority in Feminist Theology.* Philadelphia: Westminster, 1987.

_____. *Human Liberation in a Feminist Perspective: A Theology.* Philadelphia: Westminster, 1974.

_____, ed. *The Liberating Word: A Guide to Nonsexist Interpretation of the Bible.* Philadelphia: Westminster, 1976.

Sakenfeld, K. D. "Feminist Uses of Biblical Materials." In *Feminist Interpretation of the Bible,* edited by L. M. Russell, 55–64. Philadelphia: Westminster, 1985.

Sanders, E. P. *Judaism: Practice and Belief, 63 BCE–66 CE.* Philadelphia: Trinity Press International, 1992.

Sawicki, M. "Making Bread with Jesus." In *A Feminist Companion to Mark,* edited by A.-J. Levine, 136–70. Cleveland, OH: Pilgrim, 2004.

Scanzoni, L., and N. Hardesty. *All We're Meant to Be: A Biblical Approach to Women's Liberation.* Waco, TX: Word, 1974. 3rd rev. ed., *All We're Meant to Be: Biblical Feminism for Today.* Grand Rapids, MI: Eerdmans, 1992.

Scanzoni, L., and V. R. Mollenkott. *Is the Homosexual My Neighbor? Another Christian View.* San Francisco: HarperSanFrancisco, 1978.

Schlatter, A. *The History of the Christ: The Foundation of New Testament Theology,* translated by A. J. Köstenberger. Grand Rapids, MI: Baker, 1997 [1923].

Schnabel, E. *Inspiration und Offenbarung: Die Lehre vom Ursprung und Wesen der Bibel.* 2nd ed. Wuppertal: R. Brockhaus, 1997.

_____. *Sind Evangelikale Fundamentalisten?* Wuppertal: R. Brockhaus, 1995.

Schneiders, S. M. "Feminist Hermeneutics." In *Hearing the New Testament: Strategies for Interpretation,* edited by J. B. Green, 349–69. Grand Rapids, MI: Eerdmans; Carlisle: Paternoster, 1995.

Schottrott, L., S. Schroer, and M.-T. Wacker, eds. *Feminist Interpretation: The Bible in Women's Perspective.* Minneapolis: Augsburg Fortress, 1998.

Schweitzer, A. *The Quest of the Historical Jesus: A Critical Study of Its Progress from Reimarus to Wrede.* London: A. & C. Black, 1968.

Seim, T. K. *The Double Message: Patterns of Gender in Luke-Acts.* Edinburgh: T&T Clark; Nashville: Abingdon, 1994.

_____. "The Gospel of Luke." In *Searching the Scriptures.* Vol. 2, *A Feminist Commentary,* edited by E. S. Fiorenza, 728–62. New York: Crossroad, 1994.

_____. "The Virgin Mother: Mary and Ascetic Discipleship in Luke." In *A Feminist Companion to Mark,* edited by A.-J. Levine, 89–105. Cleveland, OH: Pilgrim, 2004.

Silva, M. *Biblical Words and Their Meaning.* Grand Rapids, MI: Zondervan, 1983.

_____. "'Can Two Walk Together Unless They Be Agreed?' Evangelical Theology and Biblical Scholarship." In Quo Vadis, *Evangelicalism? Perspectives on the Past, Direction for the Future. Presidential Addresses from the First Fifty Years of the* Journal of the Evangelical Theological Society, edited by A. J. Köstenberger, 111–20. Wheaton, IL: Crossway, 2007.

Smit, D. J. "Biblical Hermeneutics: The First 19 Centuries." In *Initiation into Theology: The Rich Variety of Theology and Hermeneutics*, edited by S. Maimela and A. König, 275–96. Pretoria: J L van Schaik, 1998.

____. "Biblical Hermeneutics: The 20th Century." In *Initiation into Theology: The Rich Variety of Theology and Hermeneutics*, edited by S. Maimela and A. König, 297–317. Pretoria: J L van Schaik, 1998.

Spencer, A. B. *Beyond the Curse: Women Called to Ministry*. Nashville: Thomas Nelson, 1985.

____. "Jesus' Treatment of Women in the Gospels." In *Discovering Biblical Equality: Complementarity without Hierarchy*, edited by R. W. Pierce and R. M. Groothuis, 126–41. Downers Grove: InterVarsity, 2004.

Spencer, F. S. "'You Just Don't Understand' (Or Do You?): Jesus, Women, and Conversation in the Fourth Gospel." In *A Feminist Companion to John*. Vol. 1, edited by A.-J. Levine, 15–47. Cleveland, OH: Pilgrim, 2003.

Spohn, W. *What Are They Saying about Scripture and Ethics?* New York: Paulist, 1995.

Stanton, E. C. *The Woman's Bible*. Repr. New York: Arno, 1972 [1895, 1898].

Stendahl, K. *The Bible and the Role of Women*. Facet Books. Philadelphia: Fortress, 1966.

Strauch, A. *Men & Women: Equal Yet Different*. Littleton, CO: Lewis and Roth, 1999.

Swartley, W. M. "The Role of Women in Mark's Gospel: A Narrative Analysis." *Biblical Theology Bulletin* 27 (1997): 16–22.

Swidler, L. "Jesus Was a Feminist." *Catholic World* 212 (1971): 177–83.

Toensing, H. J. "Divine Intervention or Divine Intrusion? Jesus and the Adulteress in John's Gospel." In *A Feminist Companion to John*. Vol. 1, edited by A.-J. Levine, 159–72. Cleveland, OH: Pilgrim, 2003.

Tolbert, M. A. "Defining the Problem: The Bible and Feminist Hermeneutics." *Semeia* 28 (1983): 113–26.

____. "Social, Sociological, and Anthropological Methods." In *Searching the Scriptures*. Vol. 1, *A Feminist Introduction*, edited by E. S. Fiorenza, 255–71. New York: Crossroad, 1994.

Torjesen, K. J. "Reconstruction of Women's Early Christian History." In *Searching the Scriptures*. Vol. 1, *A Feminist Introduction*, edited by E. S. Fiorenza, 290–310. New York: Crossroad, 1994.

Trible, P. "Eve and Adam: Genesis 2–3 Reread." In *Womanspirit Rising: A Feminist Reader in Religion*, edited by C. P. Christ and J. Plaskow, 74–83. San Francisco: HarperSanFrancisco, 1979 [1973].

____. *God and the Rhetoric of Sexuality*. Philadelphia: Fortress, 1978.

____. "The Pilgrim Bible on a Feminine Journey." *The Auburn News* (1988): 4.

____. *Texts of Terror: Literary-Feminist Readings of Biblical Narratives*. Philadelphia: Fortress, 1984.

Tucker, R. A. *Women in the Maze: Questions & Answers on Biblical Equality*. Downers Grove, IL: InterVarsity, 1992.

Tucker, R. A., and W. L. Liefeld. *Daughters of the Church: Women and Ministry from New Testament Times to the Present.* Grand Rapids, MI: Baker, 1987.

Vanhoozer, K. J. *Is There a Meaning in This Text? The Bible, the Reader, and the Morality of Literary Knowledge.* Grand Rapids, MI: Zondervan, 1998.

Wainwright, E. M. "The Gospel of Matthew." In *Searching the Scriptures.* Vol. 2, *A Feminist Commentary,* edited by E. S. Fiorenza, 635–77. New York: Crossroad, 1994.

Warfield, B. B. *The Inspiration and Authority of Scripture.* Rev. ed. Philadelphia: Presbyterian & Reformed, 1948.

____. "Revelation." In *The International Standard Bible Encyclopedia.* Vol. 4, edited by J. Orr, 2573–82. Chicago: Howard-Severance, 1915.

Webb, W. J. *Slaves, Women & Homosexuals: Exploring the Hermeneutics of Cultural Analysis.* Downers Grove, IL: InterVarsity, 2001.

Westcott, B. F. *A General Survey of the History of the Canon of the New Testament.* 7th ed. London: Macmillan, 1896.

Wimsatt, W. K., and M. C. Beardsley. "The Intentional Fallacy." In *On Literary Intention.* Edited by D. Newton-deMolina, 1–13. Edinburgh: Edinburgh University Press, 1976.

Witherington, B. "Women (NT)." In *Anchor Bible Dictionary.* Vol. 6, edited by D. N. Freedman, 957–61. Garden City, NY: Doubleday, 1992.

____. *Women in the Ministry of Jesus.* SNTSMS 51. Cambridge: Cambridge University Press, 1984.

Woodbridge, J. D. *Biblical Authority: A Critique of the Rogers/McKim Proposal.* Grand Rapids, MI: Zondervan, 1982.

____. "Some Misconceptions of the Impact of the 'Enlightenment' on the Doctrine of Scripture." In *Hermeneutics, Authority, and Canon,* edited by D. A. Carson and J. D. Woodbridge, 237–70. Grand Rapids, MI: Zondervan, 1986.

Yarbrough, R. W. "The Hermeneutics of 1 Timothy 2:9–15." In *Women in the Church: A Fresh Analysis of 1 Timothy 2:9–15,* edited by A. J. Köstenberger, T. R. Schreiner, and H. S. Baldwin, 155–96. Grand Rapids, MI: Baker, 1995. In *Women in the Church: An Analysis and Application of 1 Timothy 2:9–15.* 2nd ed., edited by A. J. Köstenberger and T. R. Schreiner, 121–48. Grand Rapids, MI: Baker, 2005.

# General Index

Abrahams, L. A.-L., 22n17
Adams, Abigail, 17–18
Adams, John, 17–18
Anderson, Janice Capel, 122, 125
Anthony, Susan B., 21
atheism, 58
*authentein* (Greek), 136–37
authority, scriptural paradigm of, 57, 71–72, 73, 119; authority requiring submission, 72

Beauvoir, Simone de, 21–23; *The Second Sex* (1949), 21
Belleville, Linda, 165, 166, 172, 219; "egalitarian profile" of, 167; view of Jesus, 222; "Women in Ministry" (2001), 167–68; *Women Leaders and the Church* (2000), 166–67
Bilezikian, Gilbert, 134, 152, 153, 164n44, 172, 219; *Beyond Sex Roles* (1985), 146–49; "egalitarian profile" of, 146
Block, Daniel, 33
Blomberg, C. L., 227n33
Bock, Darrell, 204n46
Bolt, C., 19nn3, 4
Booth, Catherine, 19, 19n3
Borland, John, 148n71, 211–12, 211n61, 213
Brandon, S. G. F., 79
Brown, Antoinette, 19
Bultmann, Rudolf, 118
Bushnell, Katharine, 19

Carson, D. A., 27n5, 143
Carter, Warren, 123–24, 125

Chancey, Mark, 186
Christians for Biblical Equality (CBE), 22, 23, 132; 1989 statement by, 131
Clark, Stephen, 185nn2–4, 186n7, 196n31, 212n64, 213
Cohick, L. H., 210n59
Collins, Patricia Hill, 96
complementarianism, 180–81
*Constitutions of the Holy Apostles*, 172
Conway, Colleen, 99, 124
Corley, Kathleen, 63, 94, 96, 102, 103, 107, 111; "fact sheet" on, 104; view of Jesus, 222; *Women and the Historical Jesus* (2002), 103–5
Cottrell, J., 37n3, 63n7, 153n84, 189–90, 197, 202
Council on Biblical Motherhood and Womanhood (CBMW), 23; "The Danvers Statement" (1988), 179
Cox, Harvey, 67
creation mandate, 73
Creator-creature distinction, 58
Crossan, John Dominic, 83, 92, 96; *The Historical Jesus* (1993), 83
Cullmann, Oscar, 79

Daly, Mary, 38, 39, 39–40, 216; *Beyond God the Father* (1973), 40–41; *The Church and the Second Sex* (1968), 40; evaluation of, 42; "fact sheet" on, 40; other publications of, 41; progression of her thought, 42; rejection of Jesus and Scripture, 41–42; view of Jesus, 221
D'Angelo, Mary Rose, 107
de Boer, Esther, 123

244

# Scripture Index